KOREA

Traces of a Forgotten War

JAMES N. BUTCHER

HELLGATE PRESS   ASHLAND, OREGON

KOREA: TRACES OF A FORGOTTEN WAR
©2013 JAMES N. BUTCHER

Published by Hellgate Press
(An imprint of L&R Publishing, LLC)

Hellgate Press

PO Box 3531

Ashland, OR 97520

www.hellgatepress.com

Editing: Harley B. Patrick
Cover Design: Richard Butcher, L. Redding

Library of Congress Cataloging-in-Publication Data

Butcher, James Neal, 1933-
Korea : traces of a forgotten war / James N. Butcher. -- First edition.
    pages cm
Includes bibliographical references.
ISBN 978-1-55571-724-7
1. Butcher, James Neal, 1933- 2. Korean War, 1950-1953--Personal nar-
ratives, American. 3. United States. Army. Infantry Regiment, 17th. 4.
Soldiers--United States--Biography. I. Title.
DS921.6.B88 2013
951.904'242092--dc23
[B]
                            2012045184

Printed and bound in the United States of America

First edition 10 9 8 7 6 5 4 3 2

To the memory of all my friends in the 17th Infantry who did not come home. Your sacrifices for the greater good are not forgotten by those who survived.

Also By the Author

Abnormal Psychology and Modern Life (15th edition)
With S. Mineka & J. Hooley (2013)

A Beginner's Guide to the MMPI-2 (3rd Edition, 2011)

A Beginner's Guide to the MMPI-A
With C.L. Williams (2011)

Oxford Handbook of Personality Assessment
J.N. Butcher (Ed) (2009)

Personality Assessment in Treatment Planning
With J.L. Perry (2008)

Assessing Hispanic Clients Using the MMPI-2 and MMPI-A
With J. Cabiya, E.M. Lucio, & M. Garrido (2007)

The MMPI/MMPI-2/MMPI-A in Court (3rd edition)
With K.S. Pope & J. Seelen (2006)

MMPI-2: A Practitioner's Guide
J.N. Butcher (Ed.) (2005)

Table of Contents

Preface & Acknowledgments.........*vii*

Permissions.........*xiii*

The People.........*xv*

Chapter 1   A Search For a Place in Life...1

Chapter 2   Merger of the Human Mind and the Army
              Mind in Basic Training...25

Chapter 3   Arrival in the Land of the Morning Calm...................53

Chapter 4   The Battle of Triangle Ridge: Our Assault
              on Jane Russell Hill...69

Chapter 5   Life in the Trenches..95

Chapter 6   A Tour on Koje-do: A Rest or What?.........................119

Chapter 7   Return to the Frozen Front.......................................139

Chapter 8   Patrols in Korea...165

Chapter 9   Rotation Blues and R&R..185

Chapter 10   From the Softball Field to the Gates of Hell:
              The First Battle of Pork Chop Hill...........................199

Chapter 11   The Spring Rains...221

Chapter 12   Outpost Duty..235

Chapter 13   Armistice: Return of the Morning Calm.....................255

Chapter 14   Questions That Endure...267

Appendix A   Propaganda Leaflet Obtained from Joe's
              Mailbox in the Alligator Jaws.................................281

Appendix B   Strength of the United Nations Ground Forces
              in Korea 285

Cited References.........287

General Readings.........291

About the Author.........295

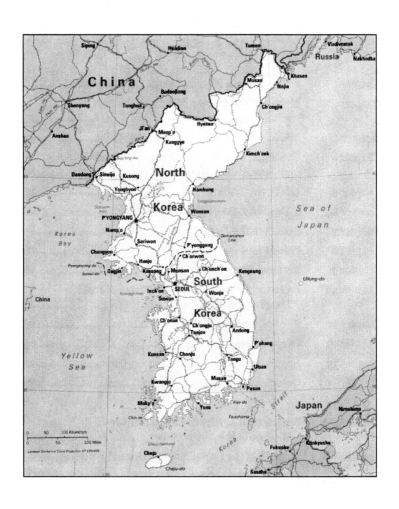

Preface & Acknowledgments

IT HAS TAKEN MANY YEARS FOR ME TO FINALLY DECIDE to put these experiences from the Korean War in a book. Although I began this project in the 1960s, my professional life took over, and limited my attention to it. In addition, I tend to keep the Korea of 1952-1953 to myself, perhaps because my life is so different since the war ended. Many of the people that I have come to know quite well over my professional career have no knowledge of this earlier life and will, in all likelihood, have some difficulty seeing the person that they have known as a professor or colleague as having experienced these events. All that aside, I decided that it is due time to share these wartime experiences. Events in Korea had a powerful impact, not only on me, but on countless others as well, and relatively little first hand accounts are available.

This book is a description of one infantryman's experiences during the final year of that war and, obviously, not an objective history of the Korean War. The experiences recounted here are highly personal and subjective. If one of my buddies had written of these situations they might have taken a different emphasis or focus. On the other hand, my experiences may be representative of what a lot of other soldiers went through during the later months of the Korean War. The events we were caught up in during the war were accompanied by powerful fears and uncertainties that have left indelible marks on those of us who were there—some veterans have tried to forget these things; others have simply set them aside to go on with the rest of life.

For me, and likely other veterans, our wartime experiences remain quite vivid. Not a day has gone by since I left Korea that I have not replayed some of these scenes in my own consciousness—they are always ready for instant replay, and often do so even when I do not actively seek them out. These images are like those wagon trails that you can see while flying over western mountains—trails that were worn into the rock and clay by the early pioneers as they moved West in the middle of the 19th century or like the deep wheel grooves that were cut into the stone pavement of the ancient city Ephesus by countless Roman chariots as they made their way through them thousands of years ago.

For various reasons, the Korean War has become known as the "Forgotten War." Many Americans know nothing of the battles and conditions described here, one of the primary reasons for writing this book. I feel compelled to keep alive the memories of some of the great guys with whom I served during the Korean War, especially those who died so young. Relatively few Korean War vets have written first person accounts. Others have interviewed some of us. Bill McWilliams' excellent 2004 book, *On Hallowed Ground*, includes descriptions of the battles for Pork Chop Hill based on interviews from people who were there, like me. Anthony Sobieski included in his book a description of a two-man patrol that Bill Estes and I conducted to direct artillery fire against Chinese forces in the Yokkokechon Valley in his valuable 2005 account, *Fire For Effect*, about artillery in the Korean War.

I contributed a few brief articles about my experiences in published sources. A special issue of *Stars and Stripes*, commemorating the fiftieth anniversary of the beginning of the Korean War, described the eerie last night of the war on the front (Butcher, 2000). Two articles appeared in the *Buffalo Bugle* describing events in the Battle for Pork Chop Hill (Butcher, 2000) and an ambush patrol action (Butcher, 2001). Finally, some material included in this book appeared in an invited autobiographical article for the *Journal of Personality Assessment* (Butcher, 2003).

Affirmation of my strong positive feelings toward the South Korean people is another powerful motivator. Many Koreans—both civilians and fellow combatants—showed compassion and thoughtfulness in difficult times. Civilians gave me food when I needed it and they had little. One third of our company was Republic of Korea (ROK) soldiers sharing the horrors of the war on dark nights when we were so alone. Even though we did not share a common language, we supported one another and survived together. I appreciated their efforts at the time as I do now.

This book is a departure from my usual professional publications in psychology journals and books. Although there are themes in this book that are explored by clinical psychologists in academic writings—like the influence of severe stress on human memory or the long term consequences of terrifying events on adult development—they are presented here in a personal context, not intended as psychological observations. Furthermore, my experiences in the Army and Korea cannot be lumped together as all traumatic or stressful. There were many good times; perhaps more good times and close bonds with friends than there were horrific ones. Boredom during the quiet times along the front should also be mentioned.

I have a word of caution and apology for some of the language used in this book. It is my first publication that includes offensive language like "fuck" and racial epithets like "Japs," "Gooks," "Chinks," and "Darkies." I would be inaccurately portraying the words used during this era if I cleaned up the language. In the 1940-50s racial epithets were commonly used to describe the enemy, and served the purpose of dehumanizing them. I grew up reading newspapers and listening to the radio about "Japs" and "Krauts." Derogatory terms for African-Americans were less commonly used where I grew up in West Virginia. But, as you will see in Chapter 2, I encountered them once joining the Army. My buddies and I never used such terms, but we heard them all too often in 1950s civilian America.

Well after the Korean War, and in "another life," I have had the occasion to work extensively and collaboratively with many Chinese people. I traveled to China on three occasions for lecture tours and have developed close friendships with several colleagues there. I met a Chinese psychologist who had been in the army at the same time as me—but on the other side. Given the fact that I spent almost an entire year fighting the Chinese Peoples Army I had some initial difficulty managing the visits to China. They turned out to be, in our new spirit of cooperation and peace, wonderful experiences. I hope that my experiences and descriptions included in this book will be taken in the perspective of bygone times and will not be considered offensive by my Chinese colleagues.

Sixty years is a long time in the evolution of social and cultural values. My attitudes towards my time in Japan on R&R have changed dramatically, as you will see in Chapter 9. The events described in that chapter took place when I was nineteen years old and had barely made it through high school. I grew up with a mother whose education was cut short when she married at thirteen. I was not prepared to understand the underlying human rights issues regarding my activities during R&R. The military leadership of the time facilitated those activities. My changed perspective was aided through writings by several other scholars and human rights advocates, as well as many discussions with my wife about her work with refugee women in Asia (Williams, 1991; Williams & Berry, 1991).

All of the things described herein occurred as they remain in my memory, which was aided by notes I began shortly after the war ended. I also had the benefit of notes and dated keepsakes that I had sent home to my sister, Joan, during the war. In addition, I have had the benefit of some valuable memory jogs by several friends from the war or relatives of buddies long departed that I met later. These friends and their relatives encouraged me to document our shared experiences. It has been my pleasure to renew those acquaintances. I would like to thank Ray Daggett (Rhode Island), Don Schoen (Pennsylvania), and Frank "Vito" Field (Virginia) for providing information that was valuable in drafting this book. I would also like to thank the family of Robert Huggins (West Virginia) for talking with me about Bob (who was, at the time, in a nursing home).

I would like to express special appreciation to my West Virginia buddies, Carlos Coleman and the late Bill Estes. Each provided extensive and key information, including photographs, company rosters, and materials captured from the Chinese. I would also like to thank Regina Millsap, the wife of Ray Millsap (Illinois), for sharing information from Ray's letters that were sent to her from Korea. I owe them a great deal for specific information that helped in dating some of the memories of those times long ago. I would like to thank Dale Moss' niece, Kathy Moss, who contacted me by the Internet and sent me pictures that Dale had sent home to Missouri.

I sent copies of a draft of the book to my two brothers, Jerry and Richard (Dickie) Butcher, for comments on the information provided on our early days. Dickie assembled an early manuscript into a book—complete with a cover he designed—to my surprise and delight. His efforts and Jerry's strong encouragement spurred me to finish the book.

My son, Janus (Jay) Dale Butcher (physician and colonel, Air Force Reserves), has also provided strong encouragement to publish this book. Jay was named for two of my closest friends who died on the front, Janus Krumins and Dale Moss. Not only that, both Jay and his son Benjamin Butcher (warrant officer and Army helicopter pilot) served together in Iraq, and his daughter Sarah Butcher was just commissioned a lieutenant in the Air Force Reserve. Both Janus Krumins and Dale Moss would be shocked that their namesake and his offspring outrank us all!

I am equally proud of the rest of my family and wish to acknowledge their love and support: daughters Sherry Butcher Wickstrom and Holly Krista Butcher; daughter-in-law Cindi Butcher; and grandchildren Bryce Thompson, Nicholas Younghans, and Neal Younghans. Holly, with her MA in Journalism, provided valuable editorial suggestions. Although my son Neal Butcher is no longer with us, his memory should also be acknowledged here.

Finally, this book would never have been completed without the extensive assistance of my wife, Carolyn L. Williams. She urged me on a number of occasions to write about my Korean War experiences and even signed me up for a workshop on writing memoirs! Without her encouragement over the years I would not have been able to complete the task. Not only is she a strong advocate for human rights, but also a very thorough researcher. She provided meticulous reviews of several versions of this memoir and our subsequent discussions greatly improved my work. I, of course, take full responsibility for any faults that remain.

Permissions

THE AUTHOR WISHES TO THANK THE FOLLOWING FOR permission to reproduce or adapt material included in this book: The University of Texas at El Paso Library for reproducing materials from S. L. A. Marshall's *Pork Chop Hill* (1986); Taylor & Francis for adapting material from Butcher, J. N. (2003), "Discontinuities, side steps, and finding a proper place: An autobiographical account," *Journal of Personality Assessment*, 80, 223-236; and Tannen Music to cite the lyrics of "Rotation Blues."

The People

Family and Friends

Lionel Glen Butcher: Father (Chapter 1)
Georgia Neal Butcher: Mother (Chapter 1)
Delbert Butcher (Bub): Uncle (Chapter 1)
Jerome Butcher (Jerry): Brother (Chapter 1)
Richard Butcher (Dickie): Brother (Chapter 1)
Gloria Butcher Chandler Brannon: Sister (Chapter 1)
Joan Butcher Hissom: Sister (Chapter 1)
George Hissom (Corky): Brother-in-law (Chapter 1)
Russell Chandler: Brother-in-law (Chapter 1)
Mark Neal: Uncle and guardian (Chapter 1)
Jay Tilley: Uncle (Chapter 1)
Carolyn Williams: Spouse (Chapters 14)
Nicholas Younghans (Nic): Grandson (Chapter 14)
Robert Baker (Bob): High school friend (Chapters 1, 5)
Gordon Bostick: Middle school friend (Chapter 1)
Thomas Hill: High school teacher (Chapters 1, 7)
Fanny Cheung: International colleague (Chapter 4)
Kyunghee Han: Graduate student from Minnesota (Chapter 14)
Jee Young Lim: Graduate student from Minnesota (Chapter 14)

Basic Training

Gary Baker: Buddy from West Virginia (Chapter 2)
Sergeant Scarface*: NCO (Chapter 2,10)

Stateside Duty with 82nd Airborne

James Jude (Jim): Buddy from West Virginia (Chapter 2)
Sergeant Swedish**: First sergeant (Chapter 2)
Sergeant Wolf**: Platoon sergeant (Chapter 2)
Taras Zacharco: Buddy from Ohio (Chapter 2)

FAR EAST COMMAND: MILITARY AND CIVILIANS

Lieutenant Ferdinand Barger: Fox Company Executive Officer (Chapters 6-7)

Kon Do Baull (Moosemaid): ROK buddy, rifleman, KIA (Chapters 5, 10, 14)

Dale Barnhardt (Ziggy): Buddy from Wisconsin, ammunition carrier, KIA (Chapters 5-6, 10, 14)

Sergeant Bill ***: 2nd Division soldier on R & R (Chapter 9)

Corporal Buckley **: Medic on Jane Russell Hill (Chapter 4)

Lieutenant John Brandenberg: Fox Company CO (Chapters 6-7)

Sergeant Henry Casper: Fox Company platoon sergeant (Chapters 3-4)

Carlos Coleman: Buddy from West Virginia, machine gunner (Chapters 4-5, 9)

Raymond Daggett (Ray): Buddy from Rhode Island, radio man (Chapters 4, 8)

William Estes (Bill): Buddy from West Virginia, rifleman (Chapters 6, 8, 10, 12)

Lieutenant Robert Feiner: Fox Company Platoon leader (Chapter 6)

Frank Field (Vito): Buddy from Virginia, point man (Chapters 4-9, 12

Clark Gable*: ROK buddy, rifleman (Chapters 5, 6, 10)

Ronald Grasshold (Ron): Buddy from Wisconsin, radio man, KIA (Chapters 6, 12, 14)

Colonel William Hardick: Commander, 17th Infantry (Chapter 3)

Robert Huggins (Bob): Buddy from West Virginia, truck driver (Chapter 6)

Delbert Kenway (Del): Buddy from Texas, BAR**** man (Chapters 4, 6-8)

Private Kim**: ROK buddy on Jane Russell Hill, rifleman, KIA (Chapter 4)

Captain King**: Fox Company CO on Pork Chop (Chapter 7, 10)

Colonel Dong Koo Lee: ROK officer (Chapter 14)

Janis Krumins: Buddy from Wisconsin, BAR**** man, KIA (Chapter 11, 14)

Private Lee**: ROK buddy from Koje-do, KIA (Chapter 6)

Jerry Manning: Buddy, rifleman (Chapter 12)

Emmett Dale Moss: Buddy from Missouri, machine gunner, KIA (Chapters 5, 6-10, 12, 14)

William Marshall (Billy): Buddy from Virginia, rifleman (Chapters 5, 6,10)

General S. L. A. Marshall: Author, historian who interviewed sol diers and wrote about Pork Chop Hill (Chapter 10)

Raymond Millsap (Ray): Buddy from Missouri, rifleman (Chapters 5-7)

Sepulveda Munoz: Buddy from Puerto Rico, rifleman Chapters 6, 10)

Myon-Hee***: Civilian on Koje-Do (Chapter 6)

Major Noble**: Battalion Executive Officer (Chapter 7)

Charles Otto: Buddy from South Dakota, BAR**** man (Chapter 6)

Lee Rogers: Fox Company platoon sergeant (Chapter 10)

Donald Schoen (Don): Buddy from Pennsylvania, rifleman (Chapters 4, 12)

Stanley Stinson (Stan): Buddy from Florida, platoon sergeant (Chapters 3, 8)
James Sullivan (Sully): Buddy, rifleman, KIA (Chapter 3-4)
Sumiko***: Civilian in Japan (Chapter 9)
Captain Vaughn**: Fox Company CO on Jane Russell Hill (Chapters 3-4, 7)
Michael Yancik (Mike): Buddy, rifleman (Chapters 3-4)
Yoshiko*: Civilian in Japan (Chapter 9)
Donald Zimdahl (Zimmy): Buddy from New York, rifleman, KIA (Chapters 6, 10, 14)

* Pseudonym
** First name unknown
*** Last name unknown
**** Browning Automatic Rifle

1

A Search for a Place in Life

WAR IS THE PROVINCE OF THE YOUNG, FOR IT IS in the youth that nations find the necessary impetuousness and careless abandon to pursue their military goals. At perilous times in the history of most civilizations young men are pressed into military service though they might prefer otherwise. Former President Herbert Hoover, in a speech to the Republican National Convention in Chicago in 1944, observed, "Older men declare war. But it is youth who must fight and die. And it is youth who must inherit the tribulation, the sorrow, and the triumphs that are the aftermath of war." In every era and culture some young men, perhaps buoyed by their youthful feelings of invulnerability, voluntarily reach out for such experiences. This book is a recounting of the events and circumstances of one who voluntarily and actively pursued a dream of hazardous military service.

Why would a young person willingly and knowingly volunteer for such things? Why would anyone actively seek to experience the horrors of war when other options might be available to them? The answers to this question are likely complex and probably reside in the early life experiences of such volunteers. Clauswitz, the noted 19th Century Prussian military strategist, considered war to be "continuation of policy" and thereby provided insight into the reasons nations seek warlike aims. But what of individuals? National policies are made by the elders—the politicians and diplomats—but it is youth who bear the brunt, make the personal sacrifices, and reap the personal tragedies of those policies. It is also quite likely that these circumstances underlying volunteerism, in part, results from the youth of society being shaped to think a particular way, by being formed by society to accept those motives as their own.

My life circumstances that lead me to join the Army and seek combat provide a context for what is described in the later chapters. The place where I was born and grew up, West Virginia during the 1930s, was harsh and depressing, at least from the perspective of coal mining families like mine. My father, being a coal miner, appeared to have relatively few options in life and possessed very little in the way of resources with which to deal with the harsh circumstances that the day-to-day living offered in those times during the Great Depression. With only a second grade education there was no such thing as upward mobility—only downward—down into the coal mines—an occupation that took his life at a very early age.

Life was very difficult as well as highly dangerous for the coal miner. The violent coal mining strikes of the 1930s "harshened" further the already bleak existence that coal mining families like ours experienced. Most miners were paid very low wages for their hazardous and backbreaking work and many with large families were forced to purchase the necessities of life from the stores owned by the coal mining company. Interestingly, coal miners were often not paid in American money but in mining company script; it was good only for purchase of goods in the company store. Needless to say that coalmining families often became fully dependent upon the coal company, and as the amount of money they owed to the company mounted many families found themselves stuck in the mining towns. Tennessee Ernie Ford's popular ballad of the '50s about the lives of coal miners rang true about our family owing their "soul to the company store" and was certainly true about most of the miners in those circumstances.

The coal mining strikes of the 1930s were vicious and unsettling events in the lives of these families. Some of my earliest childhood memories centered around the long picket lines of rough and rowdy miners with their pick axes and shovels walking and rousting about the picket lines. I also remember the meager food parcels that were doled out by the Miners Union once a month to tide the miners until the strike ended. Food baskets containing the necessary staples for living were provided by the miner's strike fund and were meager indeed—with dried apricots, rice, some fat meat, flower, corn meal, and potatoes. When I was a small child my father, Glen Butcher, told me that I should never become a coal miner. He said to me one night, "This coal mining is a bad life!"

It was equally difficult for women. Georgia Neal Butcher, my mother, was only thirteen years old when she married my dad (he was seventeen.) My memory is that she left school after the 4th grade. The men in her family also worked in the coal mines, as well as in the lumber industry. My oldest surviving sister, Gloria Brannon, was born when my mom was sixteen years old. She had two other children before Gloria. A daughter, disabled at birth, died at two and a half years and another died within days of his birth. By age twenty-two, she had me, her fifth child, and two more followed me.

My mother's days were consumed with laborious tasks: childcare, cooking, cleaning, and gardening. We had no running water in the house. Coal mining is a dirty occupation and the company did not provide showers for men at the end of their shifts. Every day my mother would drag a large tin tub into the living room, draw water from the well, heat it on the stove, and carry it to the living room for my father's return from work. The stove was coal burning and required wood and coal to be carried into the house.

One Sunday afternoon, I had just turned eight, the daily routine of our town, Winifrede, West Virginia, was shaken by the announcement on the radio that America was at war—the Japanese had bombed Pearl Harbor. Almost everyone who was alive at the time remembers what they were doing when the heard the news flash. It was one of those vivid shared memories that accompany tragedies of that magnitude, like the Kennedy assassination or the terrorist attacks on 9/11. My brother Jerry and I were playing with our toy cars on the back porch. The rest of the family was listening to the radio. I remember hearing yelling about "the Japs" and being "bombed." Everybody gathered near the company store and talked about what would happen next.

My dad, like many of the other men, wanted to join the Army right away. However, when he tried to enlist, he was deferred because of his large family and his essential occupation—the country needed coal to operate its steel mills.

****

One day, not long after the Second World War began (January, 1942), as I was returning from school, the little town was again alerted by the mournful whistle of the mining company's siren signaling—this time there was a serious problem at the coal mine. As I ran down the dusty road away from the school I encountered my Uncle Bub (Delbert Butcher, my father's younger brother) who also worked in the mine. He told me to go home because there had been a terrible accident and that my father was badly hurt and was being taken to the hospital. Later, I learned that my dad had died as he lay in the hallway of Charleston General Hospital. For some reason that I was not told about he was not admitted into the hospital for treatment.

A few months later we left the mining town and moved to Charleston, the capital city of West Virginia, which was about thirty miles away, because my mother could get work in one of the growing number of war production plants in the area. This enabled her to supplement the less than adequate work compensation payments. We received a total of $36.00 per month for the family plus $18.00 per month for each minor child. There were five children at the time. My mother and the five of us moved into a three-room house on the Westside of Charleston and she began working in a glass plant that produced military materials. Consequently, due to the "around the clock" production schedules of the plant, she could work as much overtime as she could handle, enabling her to make a down payment on a small house.

The house we lived in wasn't much of a structure; it was quite old and in a general state of disrepair. We always worried about it being somewhat of a fire trap, but this house was actually a cut above the homes in which we lived in the coal company towns where my dad had worked at Bergoo, Clifftop, or Winifrede. The little house had one bedroom, where my mother slept, and a living room where my two sisters slept. There was a small glassed-in sun porch on the side that served as a bedroom for the three boys. The room was at first unheated, and then we were able to get a small natural gas stove that provided some warmth in the winter. For a long time there was a broken pane of glass that allowed cold air to creep into the room.

I was in the second grade when we moved to Charleston. The living situation in the city was different—we actually had an indoor bathroom! I liked living in town better and I enjoyed the lower grade school (Littlepage) I attended near home. I liked the teachers and the school had several rooms, unlike the two-room school that I attended at Winifrede, where one room held grades one through three and the other held grades four through six. The war intruded into our lives when we learned an uncle, Jay Tilley, was killed at Cherbourg, France in 1944 leaving a widow and several children.

When I was in the 5th grade my mother became quite ill. We thought it was the flu, but it did not clear up. Her doctor began a treatment for pleurisy that involved putting a very tight binding around her chest. This caused a great deal of pain. After a few days of this misery she went to see the doctor to have the binding removed. Shortly after he removed the binding, while she was still in the doctor's waiting room, she had a massive coronary and died. She was only thirty-two. My mom did not see the end of WW II and left behind four minor children: Dickie, age seven; Jerry, age nine; me, age eleven; and Joan, age fifteen.

The four of us lived in our house with our older sister Gloria, who was eighteen years old. Our grief was overwhelming and we lived in the almost constant fear that we would end up in an orphanage. Within a few months of our mother's death, Gloria married a recently discharged Navy sailor, Russell Chandler. They lived with us for a few months, but our house proved to be too small and the arguments too loud, so they left. We were four children living alone. Although we were underage we were determined to continue our lives as we had been living. We did not want to be separated. My fifteen-year-old sister Joan was a very determined person and provided the glue to make this arrangement work. We prepared our own meals, got ourselves off to school, paid the bills (when we could), and tended to our own business.

The fact that we were without adult supervision did not mean that my sister, my two brothers, and I lived as feral children such as the Wild Boy of Avignon—not be any means. We tried to maintain a home life of sorts: we went to school, stayed at home most nights, maintained reasonable hours (every one of our friends had to go in at night so we didn't have any one to play with), and cooked our own meals—and did everything we could to avoid being separated as a family. We were well aware that if we failed at these tasks or called attention to our unusual situation we might wind up living in an orphanage, which to us was unacceptable. We formed a very close unit; it was us against the rest of the world.

Growing up without parents or any adults in our home was filled with many uncertainties and voids. There were times when we felt isolated from society and alone. It would have been valuable to have some adult advice and perspective. It would have been comforting to have a parent's touch in times of troubles or uncertainty, not to mention having help with creature comforts. There were many nights that we went to bed with empty stomachs and more nights in which we went to bed with an emptiness in our souls. Although children living alone can do a lot to support each other, there are many things that they cannot do.

In some respects, however, we fared pretty well. The closest thing to adult supervision that my brothers and I ever had was our older sister, Joan, who tried to provide guidance; but she asserted little in the way of control over our activities, especially as we grew older and she had her own worries to contend with. We had a guardian, my Uncle Mark, who was a bachelor and had his own life to lead. His duties as guardian were few and he was seldom bothered because we wanted to be left alone.

At first we needed Mark just to sign papers but when we learned to reproduce his signature, for example, to sign our report cards, we didn't need to call on him at all. (I can still do a pretty good job of signing his name even after all of these years). Mark lived a few miles away and we rarely saw him, although he was handy a few times that we needed to thaw our pipes when they froze. In a pinch we could get a bit of advice from our maternal grandmother who lived a few miles away (with Mark). She was in poor health (diabetes) and could not provide much help except occasionally taking my baby brother Dickie in for a meal and a bit of temporary company.

The absence of adult role models was not something that we were particularly concerned about. We thought we were getting along just fine without them. An interested outsider, if there had been such a person, would likely have disputed this. Our deportment suffered somewhat from not having a proper model to follow. We didn't always have clean clothes to wear or particularly good table manners, but we pretty much avoided major problems.

We did have some "adult" influence, however, because we went to every movie that we could. Movie characters were the people from whom we learned adult roles and adult behavior. There were times that we spent the entire day on Saturday and Sunday in the movies watching and re-watching whatever was playing; these were most often western movies with Gene Autry and Roy Rogers, and we especially liked the war movies that appeared to be plentiful at the time. I think the times we "imitated" movie characters, such as the Three Stooges, our behavior problems might have been more evident.

The movies were essentially free for us. Jerry and I would usually take an extra job of passing out fliers, show bills as they were called, in return for free passes. If we had one free pass my brothers and I could get everyone into the show quite easily. We soon got to know the people that took up tickets who might let us pass through the line. Or, if that did not work, then one of us would go into the theater on a pass and then, in a few minutes, open the fire exit to let the others, including friends, inside. We watched movies and ate popcorn and candy for lunch and supper. It never bothered us that sometimes when we left the theater we had splitting headaches. Movies were a great escape for us; and besides, we had nothing else to do with our time. I remember one time that we simply stayed all night in the theater after the last show played and hung out until the next morning when we went home.

Some Sundays, when we were short of money, we had a way of getting a little change. The three of us would go to Sunday school at a small church near home. At the end of the lesson the teacher would draw names from a hat and the winner would get a quarter. Since there was only one other boy in the class and we were three we had pretty good odds of winning the quarter. We would take our quarter and go to a local drug store where there was a pinball machine. Getting five nickels change we would use one nickel in the pinball game and spend the rest on treats. One nickel usually sufficed for the pinball because we were pretty adept (my brother Jerry being most facile) at putting our toes

(*Left to right*): Dickie, Jim (the author), and Jerry playing
with "Butchie" the dog in Charleston, West Virginia.

under the front legs of the pinball machine to slow down the ball so that we
had better control over it. We were able to run up a lot of games. When we
tired of playing the pinball machine we would sell the remaining games at a
discount to anyone who was interested and we'd wind up with a few extra
quarters to spend. We managed to have fun and earn a little extra cash in the
process.

We also devised another way to have some extra coins to play the pinball
games. One day we found a few broken records in a garbage can at a store.
The records were made of a plastic-like substance (wax) that was quite shape-
able. We broke the records into smaller pieces and sat on the pavement rubbing them to the size and shape of various coins. Not realizing, or at least not
caring, that what we were doing was actually illegal counterfeiting, we found
that these slugs worked well for a while. Our little project ended not too long
afterwards, however, when the machine owners realized what they were get-

ting and fixed the machines not to accept slugs. By then, however, we were on to other things.

The four of us stuck together quite closely in order to maintain a family. We really asked nothing of anyone and kept a pretty low profile. This living situation may be very difficult for anyone to comprehend from today's perspective. How could the social system allow four minor children to live alone, essentially by their own wits, without adult guidance? Without some welfare assistance? Perhaps this situation could not happen today with the social welfare system that we have now; however, in West Virginia in the 1940s there was no such system. What about other family members? One relative or another indicated that they would take one of us (usually my brother Dickie because he was so cute!). But we declined their offers, choosing instead to try to make it on our own.

There were times when we had no food in the house—particularly towards the end of the month before the paltry compensation checks arrived at the first of the following month. This was the only money we had coming in on a regular basis after my mother's death—the small, monthly miner compensation checks. So, it became necessary for me, and later my brother, to obtain paper routes to provide additional money for the family; usually we needed all the money we could earn delivering papers just to buy food. When I was eleven years old (in the winter of 1945) I went to talk with the station manager of the Charleston Gazette about the possibility of taking over a paper route that I had heard from one of the other boys was vacant. The manager seemed very sympathetic toward my home situation and my need to earn money but had some genuine concerns as to whether I was going to be big and strong enough to carry a heavy load of newspapers and whether or not I could learn the route so he gave me a test. He put a load of newspapers in a sack and told me to pick it up and carry it up the hill (Charleston is a very hilly city and it always seemed that we were going up rather than down hills!). Then he showed me the houses on several streets that subscribed to the Gazette. After a while we stopped and he backtracked with me to see if I could remember the correct houses. When we were through he told me that I had the job and could start tomorrow.

I worked at carrying papers for the remainder of my school years and for the last few years I was given the job (along with my friend Bob Baker) of assistant manager for the sub-station. We opened up early in the morning, counted out the papers necessary for each of the routes, and supervised the other boys. If they failed to show we needed to handle their routes. Bob and I split the salary for this job. This income was direly needed when we were growing up and although it was insufficient for some things we needed, at times it enabled us have food and some clothing (not the most fashionable) for school.

Most of the time my sister and I discouraged any assistance from other family members such as aunts and uncles. That is, we refused what we saw as "charity" and wouldn't have anything to do with it. The Christmas of 1946 stands out as a good example of the closed and resistant attitude we developed toward receiving help from family. Two of my aunts visited our house a day or so before Christmas one year and brought with them some food for us. My brother Dickie, being too young to be defiantly proud, as Joan and I were developing to be, was quite excited, especially about the pies they brought. Joan and I refused to have anything to do with them and after they left we refused to eat the pies! As much as I try to figure why Joan and I took this stance with respect to gifts from the rest of the family I can only say that it likely had something to do with my sister's refusal to accept anything because they did not initially offer to help us in our plight. It was a matter of defiant pride. I was really too young at the time to understand much about the source of Joan's negative attitudes toward some of our aunts and uncles. I only knew that it was imperative for me to back up Joan to maintain the integrity of our foursome. I knew that I could not accept those pies—though even as I think of it today they sure looked delicious!

My brother Jerry and I wanted to make Christmas 1946 a good experience for Dickie, who still believed in Santa Claus at the time. We bought him a couple of presents although there wasn't much money to go around, even for necessities. After we had the little tree up in the living room (my sister was now sleeping in our mom's room and we had the front room as a family room) Dickie was very excited about Santa coming and wanted to stay up and wait for him. We did not think this would be a good idea so we talked him into watching Santa from a hole we drilled through our porch room door looking into the front room. On seeing this peephole Dickie wasn't totally convinced about it because he realized that Jerry and I would not be able to see Santa. So, he insisted that we drill two more holes in the door; though it was a bit silly now as I look back, we did so just to keep up the ruse. Had we had an adult living in the home I am sure that we couldn't have gotten by with such property defacement. These three holes in the door, each at a different height, stayed there until we all eventually moved from the house.

Jerry and I also realized that we had to have some kind of presents to open ourselves to continue the "Santa deception" so we purchased a cheap paper airplane model so that every one would have something to open on Christmas morning when Santa finally came. To this day, when my brother Jerry and I have our annual conversation over the holidays, we always inquire as to whether the other has his "Christmas holes" drilled yet.

****

Despite our life circumstances, or perhaps because of them, my brothers and I found some escape from our cares by retreating to the woods north of our house. We went there whenever we could and sometimes we would actually skip school to build our hideout in the woods. We learned a lot about taking care of ourselves and living on our own in nature—woods skills, stealth, and avoidance of unpleasant things in the outside world. On some occasions, when rumor had it that we were going to be placed in an orphanage (Witherow's Home for Youth), we hid out in the woods until the threat blew over. No one could ever find us if we did not want to be found! The truth is that no social agency was ever involved or interested in our case. We basically sailed through our adolescent years without much pressure from the outside.

Early social and material deprivation can have a wide range of effects on children, usually negative. There were many times in our youth that we did not even have the basic necessities of life. How did these emotional and material deficits affect our development? In the case of our small family I think the answer would be that the lack of support and the lack of resources that we

experienced as children was not entirely negative—at least insofar as gener-
ating a powerful motivation to succeed in life. We were very painfully aware,
most of the time, the differences between the "haves and have-nots" in our
society and we were determined that we would have a better life when we
were older. We lived with the belief that we had to simply survive and bide
our time. The future had to be better!

During these times we had a loyal and constant four-legged companion—
a wonderful mongrel dog we called "Butchie." She tagged along with us everywhere we went (even waited for us outside school at times). She
unconditionally loved us even when we had no food to share with her; she
loved us whenever the world seemed to have forgotten us. Butchie followed
us everywhere and ate whatever we had to eat that day, and of course some
things we wouldn't. Sometimes the meals were pretty grim but she never complained. Her favorite treat to share was an RC (Royal Crown) Cola and Moon
Pie, which we managed occasionally even when we were low on cash.

One of the darkest days of my life up to that point came when one of our
neighbors, who we disliked forever after that, called the dogcatcher on Butchie
when we were at school. This was a terrible blow to us because she meant so
much to us. We did not, of course, have the money to retrieve her and we felt
horrible that we could not help her because she had been so loyal to us. My
brothers and I cried through the evening when we found out that the dogcatcher had "disposed" of her. This was a pretty bad thing to do to us and we
did not have much to do with those neighbors after that.

****

It was difficult for us to know what to do when one of us was sick. Even a
minor cold or the flu, without a parent to guide one through the miseries,
could produce great anxiety and our imaginations might run wild as to what
the illness meant. We had a group fear of illness, largely induced by the fact
that we had been conditioned to expect the worse. Death was a common event
in our family—both parents and an older brother and sister had died earlier.
These were anxious times with only ourselves to turn to.

One day when I was about thirteen, my sister Joan became quite ill with
stomach cramps and had to go to the hospital. She had to have her appendix re-

moved. My brothers and I were quite upset over this situation because the health care system did not have a very good track record with our family so far.

Joan was in the hospital for several days and the other boys and I were on our own but we took pride in being able to handle the situation without help from others. In addition to carrying my paper route in the morning, I took on Joan's usual task of preparing meals for my younger brothers. I took this responsibility very seriously and made sure that we all ate three square meals every day. I developed a plan for providing the meals that we needed yet also included saving some money at the same time. So, I cooked the same thing for lunch and dinner—macaroni and cheese—even though my brothers complained about the sameness of it all.

When my sister got out of the hospital she was concerned that we had not been taking proper care of ourselves. (She was excellent in home economics at school and actually won an award in high school for food preparation). I proudly told her that we had eaten well and that I saved some money from our reserve as well (I had spent less than $1.40 of our food money for the week). She was curious about how I had done that and was shocked that I had fed the family so well on so little. She asked what we had prepared for meals. When I told her that we had macaroni every day she almost laughed and cried herself back into the hospital. I didn't realize what was so funny to her at the time, I only felt proud that I had gotten by with such a savings.

FOR THE RECORD: A SLIP IN JUDGMENT

Even without adults to provide guidance to our daily living we walked a pretty narrow path and usually avoided major problems; Joan's influence on us was powerful and all she had to say was, "Don't get into trouble," and we knew to steer clear of mischief. For the most part we heeded her words and stayed away from the darker side of the street. We did not take up habits such as swearing or smoking cigarettes or drinking alcohol that seemed to be practiced by some others our age. We made a great deal of effort not to call attention to ourselves and tried to do what "the good kids" in the community did—we went to school, did what odd jobs we could. Our rule was "No problems, no orphanage!"

This rule got side tracked early one dark Sunday morning when I was fourteen. One morning, after we delivered ours papers, my brother Jerry, Gordon Bostick, and I were hanging out with nothing to do on the corner near where our routes intersected. Gordon had just discovered that a certain type of cap that fits over the air valves on tires had a particularly interesting function—if reversed, it actually let the air out of tires rather than inflate them. We were marveling over this finding when our problem started. Gordon thought that it would be good (and just) to let the air out of one of the tires on the car belonging to a man on his paper route who had cheated him out of money. We went along and helped out—revenge was certainly sweet at the time. It felt good to remedy the wrong in this way. We had a brief, momentary sense of doing something worthwhile.

Then I thought of someone on my route that had failed to pay their paper bill also so we remedied that great injustice as well. Then we got into the swing of the moment and thought of other people who might have caused us problems (like the ones that called the dog catcher) or that we thought were grouchy to kids in the neighborhood. We pretty well settled every score there was to settle at just about the time that the police car wheeled up and scooped us into custody. Charged as delinquents, we were pretty sure they were going to throw the book at us because we were caught in the act.

One of the most troublesome aspects of the situation was that questions were being raised by the judge about our ability to take care of ourselves. When our day in court came we did not know what to expect and we feared the worst—that we would be sent to Pat Witherow's home for the wayward. But our guardian, Uncle Mark, came to the rescue and went to the juvenile court with us. We were uncertain at first as to whether Mark was going to make the court appearance. He did not take well to such duties and it did require that he take time away from this favorite activity—shooting pool at the Smokehouse Pool Hall on Washington Street. His appearance in court on our behalf gave the judge the clear impression that we did have adult supervision and that we had just made a slight deviation from our customarily good path in life. Mark assured the judge that we would be punished for our transgressions when he got us home. The judge gave us probation.

Mark told us to go home and wait for him. Jerry and I, thinking that we were going to be punished severely, of course headed for our woods hangout where we were sure no one would find us. We hid there for many hours in spite of being hungry and thirsty. After some time, Dickie brought us some bread and a bit of good news; we were told we could come home because Mark wasn't going to punish us.

FAILURES IN THE SCHOOL SYSTEM

By agreement among ourselves (mostly to keep the authorities from getting interested in us) we usually went to school. The school that I attended in the 6th grade (Tiskelwah) was not a very pleasant or supportive place nor were the teachers at all understanding of our living circumstances. Admittedly, I probably was not a particularly well functioning student academically. I was also usually pretty tired, having to get up at 4:30 A.M. every day to deliver the papers. The unsupportive school environment can be characterized by a couple of circumstances that happened to us—one to me and one to my brother.

The most appalling lack of sensitivity that I experienced at this time was during what was called a Parent-Teacher's Association or PTA "Drive" when I was in the 6th grade. The school and the teachers were interested in having 100% membership in the PTA chapter and began to pressure the children to register both parents by bringing in .50 cents dues for each parent. Because I did not have any parents at the time I thought I was exempt from the PTA so I did not bring any money in to register.

How wrong I was! Not only did they expect 100% registration but also the teacher actually put the names of the students on the blackboard of those who had not made their contribution. Every time I looked and saw my name on the list I got embarrassed. So, in order to remove my name from the infernal list I took some of my paper route money and went to the teacher and paid for one parent registration. She accepted the money and erased my name from the blackboard.

Years after we grew up and made our way in life my brother Jerry showed me one of his report cards from school that I think gives you the picture of how thoughtless and insensitive the school system was that we attended. Jerry—who managed to do pretty well in life having obtained a couple of

Ph.D. degrees and a successful career as a minister—obviously had some talent that went unrecognized by any of his teachers. His grades in school were pretty abysmal though and his report card showed it. But what was most pathetic about his report card was a hostile note scribbled by one of his teachers that said: "Do not release this report card until this student's shop fees have been paid!" These certainly were not the kind of experiences that promote personal growth and self-confidence.

I would say that there was somewhat of a black cloud over my school experiences during these middle years, but not every day in school was bad. I had a few good moments too. One day our school was engaging in a scrap metal and paper drive in order to help the war effort. We were very enthusiastic about this project and enjoyed doing this—not just to get out of school for a bit but because we felt as though we were doing something worthwhile by going out and picking up junk and old papers that could be used in the war production. One of the brightest moments of my early school days was when I took some of the papers that I had gathered up into the basement of the Tiskelwah School where the papers were collected and I started to read some of the pages of the old newspapers that were stored there.

I found one bundle of papers that had been published in 1887 and I started reading them. I found the topics fascinating and the old pictures intriguing. I found myself reading several of the papers and forgot about the time, returning quite late to the classroom. All through the scolding that I received I kept thinking of how more interesting those old papers were compared to this stupid school routine.

That was not my last trip to the storage basement. Soon afterward I went to school, but instead of going to the classroom, I decided to read newspapers instead—all the way through the lunch hour (I had brought a sandwich to eat) and into the afternoon. Unfortunately, before long all the papers were taken away and I had to return to the regular school program.

A second bright spot in my rather meager early days occurred when I found an intriguing object in a junk yard that I passed on the way home from school—it was an old Army airplane, just sitting there beckoning to be explored. This was shortly after the war ended and a lot of military hardware began to be dismantled and sold as scrap. I was fascinated with this old plane.

I had heard a lot about these Army planes on the radio, now here was one right up close! A friend and I planned an adventure and discovered a way inside the fence and climbed up on the airplane wing (it was an T-6 Army Air Corps trainer) and into the cockpit. Even though it was incomplete and damaged, the left aileron was missing and the instrument panel had been mostly cannibalized, to us it was still a warplane! We went back a few more times before the honorable bird disappeared from the junk pile. We were never caught by the junkyard owner who had the reputation of being aggressive in keeping people away from his junk.

You may wonder where a youngster of twelve would acquire such strong interest in the military that I was beginning to develop, but I think the explanation is quite simple. I was taught these values. World War II was a time of total mobilization and many Americans were fully immersed in the war effort. Everything that happened seemed to relate to the war and to a devotion to the objectives of the military. Most families had loved ones in the service and proudly displayed the "stars" in their windows signifying how many men and women were serving in the military from the family. This was a critical period in my development, from ages eight through fourteen, and I think I "imprinted" on this national obsession and societal goal.

It was not simply that I was an impressionable youngster but rather that the whole social order was abuzz with the war effort: the radio, and of course, the newspapers that I delivered constantly presented stories about the war and updates on its. Many of the headlines that as a newsboy I yelled out on the streets of Charleston trying to sell papers related to the war. This included the one announcing VE Day and the end of the war in Europe (incidentally, VE Day, May 8, 1945, was one of the most profitable evenings that I had selling papers—people were paying a dollar or two for a single copy!).

During the war years, even some of our school lessons carried with them a heavy emphasis on the war. Geography lessons even included names of such exotic places such Tarawa, Guadalcanal, Anzio Beach, and many other places where our troops were fighting.

In simple terms I believe that I was taught by society to respect and value the military—through the schools and the media. I have discussed my impressions, if not obsessions, of these early wartime attitudes with other people my age and have found similar feelings—the social context at the time seemed to imbue interest in things military. How could we not value such things? They were of the utmost importance. Even President Roosevelt encouraged us daily to devote ourselves to the military effort!

What a person is or what they become is often set in motion in their early years. I was perhaps more extreme in my identification because I had no other effective adult role models to learn from. To me a military career was a direct route to being accepted or even important.

Throughout junior high and high school my academic interests and experiences ran lukewarm to cold. There was little incentive for us to do well much of the time; so the goal was to pass the classes and get promoted and not to call attention to ourselves.

A DISCOVERY THAT SOME MATH CAN BE USEFUL

Although school was generally pretty bleak for us, there was an occasional discovery that learning could be fun. There was one bright spot in high school—a teacher that made a difference in the way that I thought about something. In the ninth grade I performed pretty miserably with mostly "D's" and a sprinkling of "C's" until I encountered a particularly effective teacher, Mr. Thomas Hill, who happened to get my attention. Mr. Hill was a math teacher at Stonewall Jackson High School who also taught a course in aviation navigation. Being interested in flying at the time, I took his class and earned an "A."

Mr. Hill told me that the stuff that I had learned about navigating an airplane was actually a branch of math called geometry and demonstrated that the procedures we had been using to plot an airplane's course was simply plane geometry. He encouraged me to take that math class and told me that he thought that I could do well in it. The next semester I took the course in geometry from him and was surprised how much I enjoyed it; there must have been some spill over to other courses because I actually got all "A's" that term.

Mr. Hill was also involved in the High School branch of the Civil Air Patrol Cadets and invited me to join. This was an outstanding experience in several respects. It was somewhat like the Army in that we wore uniforms and I also learned a lot about aviation. I actually had the opportunity to get a couple of flying lessons and spend some time flying an old Link trainer. Mr. Hill's classes were certainly the highlight of my high school days. He also showed a personal interest in me and invited me on a few family outings; he had a son that was somewhat younger than I. The problem with the public schools at that time was there were not enough Mr. Hills to go around.

A FALSE START TOWARD A MILITARY CAREER

I couldn't wait until the time that I could join the Army and be a part of things that were important. Then in 1950, a new war started in a place called Korea and American soldiers were being sent there to stop the aggression of the North Koreans toward the South Koreans. I was not quite seventeen, the minimum age for enlistment (I was actually several months short of it), but I identified with the underdog in the conflict and thought that it was important that Americans stand up for the South Koreans in their troubles. I also saw my opportunity at last to enter the military so I mentally increased my age a bit and went to the recruiting office in the Post Office Building on Capitol St. in Charleston to enlist in the service. I am afraid that my enthusiasm and exuberance must have been showing too much in that I had taken in with me a packed bag—I was ready to go! After a brief and somewhat unsatisfying discussion with the recruiter he informed me that I did not qualify because of my age and that I would have to wait until I was seventeen to volunteer when I could enlist with parental permission (which I knew that I could sign myself if I couldn't get permission from my guardian.)

I was disappointed by that turn of events. So I waited. By the time I reached seventeen, my last year of high school had begun and I had gained a bit of perspective on life, thanks to Mr. Steadman, the Dean of Students at Stonewall Jackson High School, and Mr. Hill who had encouraged me to stick it out a bit longer, until May, when I would get my high school certificate. I compromised my burning ambition to go in the active duty military with an alternative option that I thought could tide me over until May. On my seventeenth birthday, I joined the 100th Division of the U. S. Army Reserves. I enjoyed playing the part of being a soldier for the six months that I had to wait to go on active duty. Graduation from high school finally happened on May 23, 1951 and my departure for the Army was scheduled for the next day. This time I waited until I had my ticket before I packed my bag. Finally, the day came and I was ready; I even bought a new shirt and pair of pants to wear on the trip to my new life.

AN EMERGING IDENTITY, COMPLIMENTS OF THE U. S. ARMY

I said goodbye to my sister and brothers, and my uncle drove me to the Charleston railway station. My train was scheduled to leave Charleston at 7:00 P.M. on May 24th. A couple of friends from Stonewall Jackson High "Class of '51" wanted to come down to the station to see me off but I felt it best that they did not, so I discouraged it. It was an uneventful sendoff; I waited on the station platform looking across the Kanawha River at the bright lights of the city until my train came. Especially visible were the lights from the Pastime Bar on Kanawha Boulevard blinking out its neon welcome to passers by. I was feeling very excited but not particularly sad about leaving; I was anxious to get my life under way.

The Baltimore & Ohio Railway conductor ushered me to what I considered to be very fine sleeping car accommodations that the Army had arranged for my overnight journey to Maryland for my indoctrination. Though quite small, scarcely larger than a railway seat, it was comfortable and, for one who had never been on a train, "top class." As Charleston disappeared in the evening and the train began its long journey through the winding mountain trail on the way to Maryland, I anticipated what the next phase in my life held for me. I sat in my cabin on the train for a while savoring the novel experience of being on my own and taking a night train to what I considered such an important destination, the beginning of my military career. It felt good to be someone at last—finally to be part of something worthwhile and heading for the Army. Later that evening I walked around the train to get a bite to eat with the meal voucher that the recruiter had provided. I chanced to meet a couple of friendly guys who were about my age, both recent graduates from South Charleston High, and following the same venue that I had chosen. They even planned the eventual path of going into the airborne that I had set for myself. We hit it off right from the beginning. One of them, Gary Baker, and I followed the same course for a quite a while—being eventually assigned to the same Army indoctrination company (the Army does things alphabetically) and we wound up going to the same basic training program at Indiantown Gap, Pennsylvania, getting assigned to the same basic training company, and then eventually going on to Fort Benning, Georgia for Army parachute training in the same jump school company. Our parallel course changed after jump school, however, when we received different permanent duty assignments. This was the first of many brief transitory friendships that characterized military life. We enjoyed sharing each other's company and some of our new experiences for a time.

When the train pulled into the station in Baltimore we embarked on our new adventure. Our first Army duty involved having to wait a long time to get picked up—a phenomena we would soon become accustomed to because the terms " Army" and "waiting" are almost synonymous. However, at that time we were very impatient. As we waited in the little station town for the Army transportation that would take us to the Ft. Meade replacement center we could hear loud music coming from a juke box across the road playing a very familiar refrain of the day that I will always associate with those times— Rosemary Clooney's "Come On-A My House."

Our little band of recruits was finally picked up by a somewhat worn Army truck and we were on our way. We soon passed by a large sign that read "Fort George G. Meade Army Training Processing Center"—we were finally there, a welcome sight. After we dismounted the truck with our small bundles of earthly belongings that represented the world that we had just departed, we were taken to a "holding" barracks for processing.

We were informed by a corporal on duty at the reception center that the recruit processing administration was closed for the long Memorial Day weekend so we were to be given a temporary duty assignment—kitchen duty, better known as kitchen police or just KP—for the weekend.

Thus began our first exposure to the Army. Gary and I were instructed to "fall in" (although we did not know what that meant yet) and we were marched by the corporal to our assignment—a giant, consolidated mess hall. We were still dressed in our civilian clothes because the Army had not yet provided us with military issued clothing. We assumed our new duties, initially with great vigor.

Like some fiendish punishment for an unforgivable crime we were assigned to clean the long accumulation of soot and grease from all of the stoves in the consolidated mess. Ours was indeed an incredible entry into Army life. Or, could this simply be the Army's way of letting us know that we had passed from one life into another? We spent the entire weekend cleaning out coal and wood burning stoves and grease sumps. By the end of the two days we looked like bedraggled chimney sweeps—covered from head to toe with ashes and feeling muscle aches that only accompany the most grueling marathons.

Undaunted by this somewhat unpredictable aspect of our new home we eagerly awaited our next assignment. We wondered if we should feel fortunate to have been allowed this extra training experience so early in our Army career—perhaps we had already made great strides in becoming soldiers. In addition to learning a bit about how the Army works in our initial exposure in the consolidated mess hall, we also began to learn a little of the language of the Army—those strange sounding expressions that rang in our ears that long weekend: "Ye gawwdamned recruit sombitch!" "Yo'ur lower than snake sheeet!" and other such invectives that oozed through the somewhat chubby, balding mess sergeant's southern drawl and could be loosely translated as "Fellas, I'm not very happy with your work!" These were terms that would haunt us for many nights during our indoctrination and basic training.

As our unhappy, brief but intense, bout with our first KP ended, the less than benevolent mess sergeant gave us one last bit of information about ourselves as we left to return to our company. He said, "You'ens are more useless than tits on a snake!"

Following my long stint at KP on my first weekend in the Army I was beginning to learn that there were two kinds of minds—the human mind and the Army mind. I realized at the time that I had a lot of work to make the transition to the Army mind—it was not going to be easy!

Gary and I were, however, determined not to allow this unfortunate indoctrination experience diminish our desires to make it. We had committed ourselves to be career solders and we could hardly wait for the next phase of character building given that we had now survived the first one. That Monday we received our whirlwind recruit processing with all the trimmings: another physical, several vaccinations, some lectures about comportment, and what to avoid in town if we were ever lucky enough ever to get a pass, and some new clothes (all brown or olive drab and none of them fitting much). I simply threw away the new civilian clothing that I had purchased for my entry into military life. Somewhat like my initially overly idealized view of the Army, they were in shambles.

We also received what was called "the flying twenty." This was a $20.00 advance on our pay to allow the recruits to buy the stuff they wanted us to have but were not going to give us, such as shoe polish, Blitz cloth for cleaning brass, shaving gear, and so forth. We were next then herded onto a troop convoy westward toward Pennsylvania and our proper introduction into the Army—to basic training at Indiantown Gap, Pennsylvania.

Indiantown Gap, near Harrisburg, was nestled in the northern Allegheny Mountains—an old Army base that first saw service during the Civil War as a Union Army training base. The camp had also been used as a basic training facility during the First and was re-opened during the Second World War; it had proudly served as a National Guard base in between the wars. A large part of the military base had been closed down during the de-mobilization after World War II in 1946. The camp was reopened again in order to provide hilly terrain to condition troops for the mountainous conditions of Korea. The Blue Mountains of Pennsylvania certainly provided an appropriate match.

When the ragtag group of civilian solder wannabees arrived at Indiantown Gap we were loaded onto other smaller trucks to take us to our assigned company areas. We were assigned to Second Platoon of Company C of the 169th Field Artillery training command company. When we arrived at the company street and off-loaded from the trucks, we were instructed to form into ranks in front of the Company Headquarters. At last we had arrived! We were finally at home in the Army.

Our first official duty in basic training was to take the hammers and crowbars they provided us and remove the boards from the doors and windows to the barracks we were assigned. We entered the dirty barracks, still lined with the cobweb covered steel Army cots from another era. One of the NCOs then held a formation and explained that we were going to have a party to celebrate the beginning of our basic training, but his tone of voice and manner of speech had less than a festive air. We were about to learn what a "GI Party" meant.

The remainder of the day, night, and a portion of the following day were devoted to a general and thorough clean up of our new home. The pushy corporal counted out a certain number of men for each specific detail such as mop detail, broom detail, window washers, bathroom scrapers, painters, and so forth. Many of us were, for the first time, introduced to the infamous Army lye soap that was used for every cleaning purpose. Many hours later we began to feel as though we were making progress on the re-make of the barracks. At one point late in the evening we were marched to the supply center and issued our brown Army blankets and mattresses. In spite of the less than pleasant chores we found ourselves immersed in, some of us recruits, the younger ones, were enjoying the adventure somewhat as one might a summer camp; others in our group it seems were not so enthusiastic.

2

Merger of the Human Mind and the Army Mind in Basic Training

AS I ENTERED INTO THE ARMY INFANTRY Basic Training Program in 1951 I was exactly where I wanted to be even though I, like some of my buddies, had definite rough spots on us when it came to adapting to the military way. We did not always see eye-to-eye with our non-commissioned cadre. The one ingredient, however, that was not lacking from my thinking at the time was motivation. Even more, I wanted to excel in "basic" and then go on to other more challenging assignments—particularly airborne (parachute) training.

As we settled into our routine, I quickly learned that it was unwise to inform my fellow trainees that I had enlisted in the Army. Having enlisted was an invitation to ridicule, and my somewhat frail self-concept could not deal with too much joshing around at the time. Most of the men in basic training had actually been drafted into the service and were very disgruntled and unmotivated. They hated everything the Army stood for. Most of the recruits were older, in their twenties, and many had college degrees. Several draftees in the training company even had Ph.Ds. and would have rather been elsewhere other than in Army basic training learning about such things as the Garand M-1 rifle and night compass reading.

I quickly learned that "liking the Army" was invitation for becoming the butt of jokes. I actually had to learn to bitch about things that happened in order not to appear out of step with my buddies. Enlisted men had a derogatory term applied to them, they were called "RAs," a term that was referred to as "Regular Army." Army serial numbers for enlisted men were of two types, those beginning with the letters "RA" denoting regular Army for enlistees and those beginning with "US" for men who were drafted. Draftees had every right to bitch and complain while RAs, so the belief went, deserved none of those privileges because they were stupid enough to enlist therefore they deserved what the Army handed them… and more.

Of course, the military had ways of inciting anyone and everyone to the great act of griping because "the Army way" usually meant extracting a bit more pain or inconvenience out of the troops than was actually called for by the circumstances. The Army seemed inefficient beyond imagination, for example, the way the military organized outings. The Division Commander might want a march to begin by 8:30 A.M., which most of us agreed is a civilized hour. The Regimental Commander, in order to arrive at this time, would order the call-up to be at 7:30 A.M. Next, the Battalion Commander, fearing SNAFUS (military slang for "Situation Normal: All Fucked Up"), would set the call-up for 6:00 A.M. Finally, the Company Commander, knowing that the troops needed to be fed, had police call (the necessity for soldiers to line up, bend over, and pick up everything that doesn't move in a radius of several hundred yards around the company area) would modify the call-up to be at 4:30 A.M. Every soldier knows the result of military logic to be "Hurry up and wait."

SGT. SCARFACE AND HIS IMPACT ON CHARACTER DEVELOPMENT

Usually a grizzled combat veteran headed up each platoon in the training command at Indiantown Gap. Our sergeant was well suited for the job of shaping raw recruits. He was one of the toughest looking people I have ever met, although most of us recruits were afraid to actually look him in the face. Scuttlebutt had it that he received his horrible facial wounds either during the Second World War or in Korea. No one dared to inquire directly about how he got disfigured, because, in addition to looking mean, he was generally mean spirited in all of his interactions. Everyone referred to him (behind his back, of course) as Sgt. Scarface.

Sgt. Scarface was medium in height, athletically built, and had a flat top military-style hair cut. He never smiled, although some guys on the front rank one day thought they detected a tiny little smile on his lips. However, he was not being soft or friendly at all and as they shortly found out that it was simply because he had just passed gas! His manner and appearance defied anyone from commenting or looking displeased about it.

Sergeant Scarface and the noncoms were away from the barracks for the day (I thought) and there were only a few guys sitting around writing letters. It was very quiet and I was feeling sort of bored so I decided to have a bit of fun at the expense of the others. I was usually a well intentioned but certainly not a perfect soldier. The situation that followed was not one of my better moments for good judgment; in fact, it was a judgment error that I would regret for weeks to come. In order to see how quickly people could react, I stood at the top stoop to the front doorway of the barracks and loudly yelled into the room, "Fire! Fire!

I chuckled as the loungers all jumped to their feet and tumbled down the steps toward the company street and moved sharply away from the building that they assumed was burning. They waited; I watched their surprised expressions with some momentary enjoyment.

As I was enjoying my little prank, out of the barracks door in a frenzied rush, came a half-dressed Sgt. Scarface. I was astonished to see him as he burst open the door, accidentally tripped on the top step, and fell unceremoniously on his face (as one recruit described it later "ass over elbows") into the dust of the company street below.

A hush came over the troops as the flustered non-com looked around to see that everyone got out of the "burning" building. He stood, brushed himself off, and then took stock of the situation. After a brief period, he realized that there was no fire and began an impromptu investigation into the circumstances of the unauthorized drill. He hurriedly formed the platoon remnants and in a somewhat angry tone of voice yelled, "Attention!" And he certainly held our attention with some characteristically unauthorized language.

Then he asked, "Who yelled fire?"

The ranks were silent as though nothing had happened.

"Well, speak up! " he screamed.

Then he blurted "Eh! You won't say then! Then By God it's time for some good old collective punishment!"

As he was about to call forward all of the collective wrath of all sergeants past and present against the whole platoon, I decided that I had better confess to the deed and face the punishment or else I would be ostracized for life. I timidly stepped forward and confessed, "I yelled fire, Sergeant."

He marched in rigid military fashion over to where I stood at attention. He glared at me in disbelief. I was not feeling very comfortable at first; and my mouth became quite dry as I found myself staring deeply into his mouth at the spit oozing from it as he yelled various random obscenities. His yelling made the cumulative scars of battle appear more pronounced as his jaw wagged endlessly—yelling words and invectives that I do not remember.

Everyone else in the ranks was dismissed back to their pleasurable evening of relaxation while Sgt. Scarface and I got to know each other better—he yelling and me reflecting on my considerable inadequacies. After a time he marched me to the company supply room and showed me a rather large wooden box filled with Army pistols, not spiffy clean Army pistols, but dirty, grimy, cosmoline smothered pistols. He described in some detail how my new off-duty hour routine would consist of reporting to this box and cleaning these weapons until they passed a "white glove inspection." Many hours were subsequently whiled away in this fashion. To this day I can field strip and put back together a U.S. Army .45 caliber pistol blindfolded in short order.

Periodically, and for the remaining weeks of basic training, Sgt. Scarface kept this event in memory and would frequently turn his attention to me. For example, when the platoon would be standing at parade rest awaiting a new activity, he would remember his embarrassment in stumbling down those steps and point angrily to me and yell: "You, soldier, double time! In place, double time HO!"

Difficult times pass. In spite of my occasional persecution by the cadre, I found myself actually enjoying basic training as the course proceeded. I was determined to get through this damn hurdle called "basic hell" so that I could get on with the rest of my Army career.

****

My situation steadily improved as I learned my lessons and I even had a fleeting fantasy, from time to time, of getting through the program with distinction (even though my little escapade with the fire drill pretty well deterred any kind of honorable mention in the final basic grading). I began to think about the next challenge—airborne training. But, first I had to get accepted into the airborne training program, a task which, we were told by Sgt. Scarface, would not be possible unless we were tough "sonza bitches," which he doubted.

We were told that the PT (physical training) exam was to be held in a few weeks and that the airborne physical was more grueling than the exam that was required to successfully pass basic training. So, a few of us eager airborne hopefuls began to prepare for the big airborne PT test by doing extra exercise sessions. At the end of the long training day, that sometimes included long marches with full field packs, we would fall out on our own and do additional physical training (fortunately all of the pistols were by then cleaned).

Gary and I were pretty steady with this small group of regular Army volunteers. I felt that it was necessary because I was not exactly built like the sturdy, muscular paratroopers that are depicted on the recruiting posters, given that I weighed only about 150 pounds (soaking wet)—somewhat slim for my six-foot height. The extra PT drill we put ourselves through may not have done much to assure that we would pass the airborne fitness test but one thing was assured—there was not an ounce of fat on my bones. (Of course, there hadn't been an ounce of fat on my bones since I was six months old!)

Regardless of the amount of will and sheer determination that spirits can muster, the human body has limits. The military has a flexible and shifting view of what those human limits are and the role of the non-commissioned officer is to find the breaking point—then stop just short of that in their demands on trainees. The plan doesn't always work that way in reality. On one of those long marches designed to test our psychic mettle and physical back strength, our sergeant attempted to turn me into a pack mule with equipment weighing nearly as much as I did. My back was insufficient for the task and the next morning I couldn't stand erect. I was sent to the Battalion Medical Dispensary for "sick call." I was very reluctant to follow this course because I did not want to be seen as a laggard but I had few options; I was hurting too much to make the duty formation.

My first experience with Army sick call was not optimal—at least from the perspective of one who was experiencing great pain. After a rather long wait with other "suspected laggards" I was sent to see a medic, not a physician. Without a word he watched my awkward and strangely bent entrance into the examination room and nodded in a sage manner. He appeared to have an intuitive understanding of my problem. He reached on his shelf and pulled down two medicines—one a white bottle of APC tablets (better known as aspirin) and the other a reddish-brown liquid, which was referred to by one of my buddies as "horse piss." This was a fiery designed to quell the desire to report pain in man, if not actually cure the problem. Rumor had it that the red-orange liquid is also used on the backsides of Army horses to promote docility, enhance speed to satisfy man's determination, and to infuse the desire to carry heavy loads. I avoided sick call whenever possible after that. Thanks to a quiet weekend and the opportunity to lie on the barracks floor for long periods of time I was able to return to duty on Monday (though with the remnants of pain) in my company and not be "sent back" in training to another company. For decades hence this back problem has resurfaced from time to time as a reminder, through returning pain, that I am not well built for equestrian pursuits.

THE DUAL CHALLENGE

I wanted to make a strong finish to my basic training with a couple of major tasks that the Army used to "weed out" the unfit: one was the infiltration course often referred to euphemistically as the "confidence course"; the second was the thirty-mile forced march with full field packs. These were the crown jewels of Indiantown Gap basic training. It was important to finish them in strong fashion.

One of the highlights of basic training or, depending upon one's perspective, one of the most horrendous hurdles to get through was the so called confidence course, aka as the infiltration course. This course allowed the basic trainee to put together a number of elements of his training involving crawling through difficult terrain, much of it under low barbed wire while live machine gun bullets whizzed about overhead. This course required a great deal of physical stamina plus a willingness to move forward with explosive charges going off around us and machine gun bullets whizzing a short distance overhead. Gary and I decided that we would be first to finish the course even if we had to stand up to run the thing. A little competitiveness went a long way and our trek through the course went as planned and we were the first through—needless to say it probably was as much the result of the draftees lack of motivation to do the course as it was our abilities to handle the grueling course. We didn't care—we finished tied for first anyway and that was all that mattered. With the infiltration course out of the way, our training course took a nicer turn and we felt that we were on the last lap of basic training.

The final big hurdle for recruits in this basic training program was a thirty-mile march with full field packs up into the Blue Mountain. We all looked at this trek with some trepidation because of the tales told about the experience from other recruits who were ahead of us. The day before the grand march my turn came up to have "dental call" and the dentist promptly removed all of my wisdom teeth and returned me to duty.

The next morning the march began on time. The pace was swift and the loads heavy. We marched throughout the day and began our climb up the Blue Mountain in the afternoon. My teeth, or rather the packing where my teeth had been, had given me a lot of trouble throughout the march but became worse as we began our climb up the mountain. By nightfall I was in great pain and was having a lot of bleeding from the gums. I did not say anything to anyone about my problem because I wanted to finish the march so as not to be sent back in basic training.

By the time we finally arrived at our bivouac area, cut the brush, and pitched our tents I was in considerable misery. I slept very little that night but still kept quiet to the non-coms about my problem. In the morning my tent mate, against my protests, went to the captain and informed him of my condition. The company commander expressed genuine concern over my condition and ordered me to ride back to camp on the chow truck. I was discouraged about not completing the march because I thought it might be taken as "dropping out." No one said a disparaging or joking comment to me about getting out of the last part of the march. Secretly, I was pretty relieved that I did not have to make the march back—I was feeling weak and miserable.

We were given a pass into town with our completion of this major hurdle in basic. Even I, who had wimped out on the last lap of the march, received the honor of the basic "success" pass. Our mood was running high and this was our first opportunity to go to town as soldiers since we had left our civilian days.

A TASTE OF AMERICA IN THE 1950s

The society I grew up in was racially segregated. African American soldiers primarily served in "All Negro Units" during World War II. In January 1948, President Truman decided to integrate the military through executive order (Truman Library, 2012). MacGregor (1981) described the resistance by senior officials and their predictions that racial conflict would occur at large U.S. military bases if integration were implemented. However, other senior officers like Army Chief of Staff J. Lawton Collins, thought otherwise and, given the situation in Korea, argued that a segregated army was militarily inefficient. As MacGregor (1981) explained, gradual integration occurred because local commanders found it necessary. Commanders of the nine training divisions in the continental U.S. realized it was impractical to maintain separate white and black training units. I got to basic training about two months after the Defense Department's March 1951 announcement that all basic training units were no longer segregated.

During my basic training at Indiantown Gap we encountered no problems among racial groups. We got along well, mixed well, and seemed largely to have a common enemy—the non-coms like Sgt. Scarface that treated all of us with equal disdain. My experiences were not uncommon. According to MacGregor (1981), no racial incidents were reported during the conversion to integrated basic training. Furthermore, my experiences working with African Americans in basic training (three out of seventeen in our platoon were African-American) influenced me for the rest of my life. I developed low tolerance for people who discriminated against others based on race.

One evening our platoon received a pass to go into Harrisburg. One of my buddies and I decided to go into town and invited another good friend, an African-American, along. We wandered into a beer joint, stepped up to the bar, ordered three beers, and laid down our money. The bartender, looking somewhat dismayed, took one look at us and brought back only two glasses of beer. He said, "Boys, I'll serve you but I am not serving a darkie. I'm not going to encourage them to come here!"

We were angered at this treatment, not expecting it in a northern state. My friend and I looked at each other and without speaking a word in agreement we simply tipped our glasses upside down on the bar and walked out with our arm around our friend. We found ourselves another bar where the three of us were served.

Of course, the problem with discrimination against some of our buddies was not as great in Pennsylvania as in Georgia where some of us went to jump school. One of the most disgusting and surprising things that I noticed when I arrived in Georgia on my way to Fort Benning were the numerous "Whites Only" signs that were located at bus and train stations. This was the first time I saw such blatant discrimination. My Army buddies thought that our country had no place for such bigotry. We would have completely endorsed General Ridgeway's conclusion described by MacGregor in 1981: "...it has always seemed to me both un-American and un-Christian for free citizens to be taught to downgrade themselves this way as if they were unfit to associate with their fellows or to accept leadership themselves."

Despite the success with changes in basic training, desegregation of units in Korea was much more gradual and still ongoing by the time I got there in October 1952. The Eighth Army, confronted with battle losses in white units and a growing surplus of black replacements, quietly began assigning African American soldiers to understrength white units, just as they had already been doing with South Korean soldiers. General Ridgeway officially requested that the Army allow him to integrate African-American soldiers into units under his command in Korea in April 1951 (McGregor, 1981). However, it was only after the end of the Korean War that the Army announced that 95% of African-American soldiers were serving in integrated units (Truman Library, 2012).

ARMY JUMP SCHOOL

Infantry basic training tends to have variable effects on its victims. Some who are repelled by the experience tend to conclude that for the remainder of their lives "they will not walk any further than the corner pub or carry anything heavier than a six pack of beer" while others thrive on the situation. It was clear, however, that graduation from basic was a great day for all of us in the training command; even the draftees seemed to feel proud of their accomplishment during the sixteen-week infantry basic training program. Everyone, even the draftees, stood a bit taller than they did at the beginning of the program. Toward the last days of basic training rumor had it that all of the duty assignments were posted at the company orderly room bulletin board. I dropped what I was doing and ran to the company bulletin board to read the posting. I waited my turn to get my assignment and to find out whether I had made it into airborne training. I had. Others in my group were less ecstatic on finding out that they were on their way to Korea. One of the most sullen and vocal Ph.D.s in our command, one who was usually razzing the RAs, found himself on his way to Alaska.

Getting into jump school was a lot easier than getting through it. The airborne physical education program was extremely grueling—especially doing the entire PT in the hot Georgia sun in the summer. Fitness was, and still is, considered to be the sine qua non of airborne training. Physical strength and endurance were the themes running through the program whether it was getting to the mess hall or receiving indoctrination on the various elements of a jump. It was running, push-ups, and other harsh muscle building exercises. Most of us hurt in places we did not know we had throughout the course. A number of trainees failed to make it through because of the long runs and the grueling exercises. Most of the people who dropped out or were eliminated from the jump school program were excluded because of their failure in the physical training. Our "extra" PT sessions in basic training probably served us well in conditioning us for the airborne course.

The airborne training cadre was fully as aggressive and demeaning to the trainees as those in basic training. One day one of the picky corporals was jogging along with the other cadre to the front of their respective formations and, as on other days, hurdled over the wire fence as they usually did in a showy manner. This time, however, he failed to make the leap successfully, and fell flat on his face.

A few of us (perhaps those of us who learned our discipline from the Three Stooges movies) thinking this was very funny, laughed aloud. The corporal did not appreciate our finding such enjoyment at his expense and loudly requested that we step forward and remove sawdust from the pit a mouthful at a time ("No hands soldier!") and carry it over to the next one. This accomplished, we were then told to move another mouthful of sawdust from pit number two back to the original pit. Our mouths, already dry from the hot Georgia sun, now had a horrible, rotten, wooden taste. We took all of this harassment in stride; we did, however, carefully note for future reference that corporals do not have much of a sense of humor.

Some people, of course, dropped out when it came time to leap from a perfectly good airplane into the Georgia sky 1,200 feet above mother earth. Each element in the training program was designed to acclimate the trainee to some phase of the parachute jump, whether it was the physical exercises, the PLFs (parachute landing falls), the thirty-four-foot tower (where door exiting procedures were perfected), or the 250-foot free fall tower where we practiced and mastered descent and landing procedures. All of these elements were honed to perfection so that the actual jumps were simply a routine culmination of the disparate skills that had by the time of the first jump become routine.

The actual parachute jumps were the easiest part of the program, once one made the first step into space; however, some of our fellows were disqualified because they froze in the door. The five training jumps went smoothly and those who remained at the end of jump week earned the coveted "jump wings" of the airborne corps.

The successful completion of jump school included an obligatory visit to one of the most decadent cities in the United States: Phoenix City, Alabama, better known as "Sin City, U. S. A.," across the river from Columbus, Georgia and near Fort Benning. Phoenix City held a special attraction for soldiers—especially those who had just completed jump school and were "feeling their oats."

It was obligatory for new jumpers to spend their well-deserved pass in Phoenix City. If one happened to get into a fracas of some sort then the more deserving they would be of the honor to wear the prized jump wings—symbol of toughness—at least as young jumpers were led to believe. If the jumper survived a night on the town then one's final placement in an airborne division was supposed to be a snap.

After we got dressed for our visit we strolled by the Company Headquarters to read the listing of "Off Limits" places where a GI would get arrested just for walking into the joint. We read the list and discovered the most vile and wicked of places was called "Carlton's Fish Camp." The notice read Strictly Off Limits! This was exactly the kind of place we had in mind. (The "Off limits" designation was where adventuresome GIs looked to find places where people tended to have fun. We had heard about this establishment as a "place to drink, carouse, and gamble.")

As it turned out, Carlton's Fish Camp was somewhat of a bust. It was pretty tame and we left after dropping ten bucks in a dice game that was likely rigged. The town of Phoenix City did not have a great deal of excitement for us that evening so we returned to camp feeling somewhat disappointed that we had not raised much of a fuss in town and pondered whether we really deserved to be called paratroopers.

****

For my permanent duty assignment I drew the 82nd Airborne Division in Fort Bragg, North Carolina. I was excited about this assignment to the famed 82nd—to which I would report after my five-day furlough. This would be my first visit home since I had enlisted and I looked forward to my return—this time as a soldier. Very different, I thought, than when I left more than six months before. I felt as though I was a different person than when I left and it was a good feeling walking around my home town in the uniform of an Army paratrooper. Even though, underneath, I was not much different than when I left, my appearance was certainly different. I found that going to bars and taverns was a much more exciting and rewarding experience—lots of free drinks and plenty of friendly up-beat conversation. And, it seemed that if one put an airborne soldier's uniform on a fire hydrant it would attract young ladies. What a fantastic transition in just six short months!

LIFE IN THE 82ND AIRBORNE

My assignment in the 82nd Airborne was initially somewhat disappointing. In point of fact I was pretty discouraged with the unit to which I was assigned— the Quartermaster Corps—destined to become a parachute rigger, that is, the person who packed parachutes as a full time job. I was slated to remain at Ft. Bragg for only a few weeks then I would be sent to another facility to attend a three-month Parachute Rigging School; this I was told was because of my test scores on the Army entrance examinations that I had taken at Ft. Meade.

When I reported for duty in the Rigging Company I found it to be a pretty plush facility compared with all of the other duty stations I had been in since my enlistment. The barracks to which I was assigned had two-man, semi-private rooms instead of the large squad rooms, and the guys actually had them fixed up pretty nicely, even with non-military style decorations! The company size mess hall was homey and actually had a jukebox that seemed to play constantly. The one song that was most popular at the time and seemed to get the greatest play was a tune called "Slow Poke," by Pee Wee King. This seemed to me to be an apt theme song for this outfit and one that was a bit too tame for my liking.

As I was being briefed on other aspects of the assignment, I was informed as to how lucky I was to be assigned to the Parachute Riggers for several reasons:

- No field duty
- All work was 8:00-4:30; no night problems.
- No KP—parachute riggers were too well trained and possessed very vital skills to waste on KP. Such routine duty was performed by lesser troops.

• No harassment from the officers and NCOs because everyone was treated as a valued employee.

This outfit sounded too good to be true but I was assured by guys in the company that it was a great place to be. Why then was I not happy with this assignment? Why did I request a transfer to the infantry? I told the First Sergeant that I was not really unhappy with the riggers but that I simply had enlisted in the Army in order to be in the airborne infantry. He couldn't believe what he was hearing but agreed to process my request nevertheless. But, if I turned out to be unhappy there (as I surely would, he surmised) I would not be able to return to the Quartermaster Corps. I acknowledged my understanding but I assured him that I still wanted to transfer to the infantry. He wished me luck and signed my transfer.

A few days later the 325th Infantry Regiment sent a jeep for me and a soldier who was also being sent to an infantry line company. An Italian-American named Mazzetti, who was sporting a black eye and seemed to me to be a bit subdued, also awaited the transport to the 325th. Mazzetti was a "straightleg" or "leg," which is a somewhat derogatory term referring to a soldier who has not completed airborne school and is not authorized to wear bloused boots, that is, must wear their pants straight. From time to time some legs get temporarily assigned to airborne units in order to fill slots if the unit is under strength. Some then go on to jump school. Others, like Mazzetti, just drift through their assignment without a desire to qualify. They usually end up in a regular infantry outfit somewhere.

We tossed our gear in the jeep and headed out to our new company; I, at least, with enthusiasm. As we drove along, Mazzetti was uncommunicative and I was in a good mood; I tried to talk to him but he was sullen and withdrawn. Finally, after we got near the 325th Regimental Area, he asked me, "What did you do wrong back there to get sent down to the goddam infantry?"

"I requested to be assigned there," I said.

"Are you crazy? You are going to be sorry for that! Those bastards there are going to kill us!"

I found out later that Mazzetti had gotten into some trouble in the Rigging

Company and was sent to the infantry as punishment (of course, only after he had been punched out by one of the people in the company) because he had been caught stealing from the other guys.

After getting my platoon assignment and bunk in the 325th Infantry Regiment I began my life as a parachute infantryman. The company to which I was assigned was an elite one and had great NCOs—men who had experienced considerable combat in the Second World War and who knew well what they were doing. Sgt. Wolf, a soft-spoken yet firm individual, had been in one of the infantry battalions in the first wave of troops during the Normandy invasion. He seemed to be very knowledgeable about handling troops and was well liked and respected by the guys in the platoon. I was excited about the duty and enjoyed the activities, believing that I could learn a great deal from this organization.

For the next few months, we made frequent training jumps and engaged in a lot of field problems. In some ways it was a continuation of basic training except that everyone knew what they were doing. It was, of course, somewhat repetitive. We ran, did PT, ran, did more PT, and then ran some more. A basic rule in an airborne infantry division is that everyone runs everywhere you go if you are outdoors. No slouching, no walking. Any infraction such as an unbuttoned shirt or dusty boots would result in punishment that always involved knocking out pushups—usually fifteen.

I loved this life—the feeling of involvement with something worthwhile and enjoyable. That is, except for those times when I might have been the target of some practical joke or mis- directed energies. For example, from another guy's misfortune, I learned to sleep with my boots under my pillow on those nights when some guys went to the PX beer hall and came in late looking for a place in which to urinate.

After a few months in the 325th Regiment, my desire to experience a broader and more exciting military career began to get to me as I settled into barracks life in the airborne in a division that was considered to be the "Honor Guard" of America and not one likely to be sent overseas. This outfit was a "dress rehearsal" or "show and tell" division but the "spit and polish" was a bit much. There were frequent inspections to assure that we had our gear clean and tidy and, of course, laid out properly in a military fashion. Inspections were very serious business in the 82nd.

One day we were having an Inspector General's review of the barracks that we were told had to be passed with flying colors in order for us to receive our promised weekend passes. One of our guys, Jim Jude (another West Virginian), was a friendly, sociable, fun loving guy who might be found on either end of a good natured practical joke. This particular time he was the recipient of an evil deed that caused the whole platoon to lose their weekend passes. Just seconds before the General was scheduled to inspect our barracks someone slipped a piece of paper in Jude's mess kit that was otherwise laid out neatly on the bed as prescribed by protocol. As the General entered the room and the platoon leader yelled the obligatory, "Attention!" the whole room full of sharply dressed soldiers snapped to in preparation for the review.

As the General began his inspection, he made very sharp military style movements down the line of troops, occasionally stopping to look closely at items on a trooper's bunk to assure that they were evenly placed, neat, and of course according to regulation. Three bunks down the row he stopped in front of Jude's bunk and noticed something sticking out of the mess kit. He picked it up, saying, "What's this? A piece of hamburger? What the...?"

He unwrapped the note that read, "Fuck you, the Phantom strikes again!"

The General snapped to attention, did an abrupt about face, and hurriedly left the room. His face showed a considerable amount of redness with the veins in his neck protruding in an unmilitary fashion. It was quiet in the squad room except for some muffled chuckles; outside the room voices were dismayed and loud.

Any survey taken during our two-week long restriction to barracks would likely have found great satisfaction in the prank even though no one liked the outcome. It seemed a small price to pay for the slight crack in the spit and shine of the 82nd Airborne routine.

After a time in the 82nd things became so routine that there seemed little challenge. The training jumps were usually interesting and fun but the most dangerous activities we encountered in the 82nd at this time involved the risky social lives of the troops. One dangerous sport involved going to the Enlisted

Men's Club where pent up energies, lots of alcohol, and young macho aggressiveness often erupted in physical free-for-alls. I have a vivid memory of sitting with three friends when, out of the blue, one of them used his fist to smash in the nose of the guy sitting across from him. It was eye opening to see the loss of control in someone who was typically pleasant and passive. This gathering ended abruptly with a trek to the medic.

Another break in routine was to going to "Fatalburg," the GIs slang term for Fayetteville, NC. There was a notorious bar in Fayetteville called The Towne Pumpe with a bawdy floorshow consisting of five scantily clad obese women who danced demonstratively on a center circular bar. The other attraction was a bevy of prostitutes who openly described the sex acts they could perform. Although this popular watering hole was off limits for the 82nd Airborne Division, GIs regularly frequented it, so, of course, I had to go. Shortly into my visit with a couple of buddies, the M.P.'s conducted one of their periodic raids to scare away the clientele. As whistles were blowing, we could hear voices in the front of the bar yelling, "This is a raid! Everyone out in the street! Fall in!"

At the same time, other excited people inside the bar were shouting, "MPs! MPs! Beat it!"

I hurriedly ran to the back of the bar, accidentally bumping into one of the dancers on the way. We were both laughing hysterically. I cautiously crawled through the bathroom window into an alley and found myself a safe place to stand, out of the hustle and bustle in front of the bar, across the street where I could watch the raid progress from a distance. I remember commenting to other bystanders, some of whom had also been inside, "I think it's a shame that 82nd Airborne soldiers—America's Honor Guard—would go into such a dive!"

That turned out to be my first and only visit to The Towne Pump. Upon sober reflection, and at the ripe age of seventeen, I concluded it wasn't worth risking my Army career for something that really wasn't that much fun after all. Apparently, the off limits designation, M.P. raids, limited off duty time, and watching others behaving foolishly or violently did have an effect on some of us.

I enjoyed serving with the guys in the 325th and always felt a sense of camaraderie, even at times when I would rather have been left alone. One night we were on a field exercise and one of the guys had somehow wandered into town and come back late at night to where our tents were pitched. I was sleeping soundly when all of a sudden I felt my sleeping bag being dragged from the tent. I rubbed my eyes and found myself staring at Jude leaning over me with a quart fruit jar filled with "white lightening," a homemade, illegal corn whiskey sold on the sly. Thinking that it would taste like turpentine I declined the offer. He was uproariously drunk and kept laughing, saying, as he held the potent substance over my head, "In you or on you, b'God. In you or on you!"

I made some appearance of drinking the stuff at least enough for Jude to satisfy himself that I had cooperated and went off and find another reluctant drinker to roust out of bed.

A SOLDIER'S LIFE CAN BE A DOG'S LIFE: WE GOT "RUN OUT OF TOWN"

Soldiers are not always desirable company; in fact, they are sometimes viewed as very unsavory characters. And, if the truth were known, we were certainly open to trouble though not particularly courting it. One spring day two other troopers from our outfit and I decided that we were tiring a bit of going down to "Fatalburg" and drinking beer until we couldn't see straight and we were tired of hanging out in places with so many troopers around, so we decided that we would give ourselves a geography lesson and learn a little about the great state of North Carolina. We decided to go on a weekend pass to the City of Charlotte, some distance away in the western end of the state.

Charlotte was not a soldier's town and no one that we knew had ever ventured there on pass; it was simply too far a journey for guys who were out for immediate fun. Stopping at a friendly appearing tavern on the outskirts of town we started in on our partying at the first watering hole we could locate. We thought we could ask directions and get information about the "hot spots" in town from the folks in the tavern but we couldn't get much out of the bartenders so we stuck around there until the evening wore on.

This seemed like a pretty good spot and there were a lot of women drifting in and out so we settled in for the duration. Late in the evening as we were getting comfortable in the place, and a bit loud as I recall, our table got jostled accidentally by a good looking but quite drunk woman and a man leaving the dance floor. We were simply going to ignore the incident until the woman turned to one of our guys and dumped the glass of beer she was carrying on his head—all the while laughing in a somewhat hysterical manner trying to pull the chair out from under the other trooper. I watched in amazement as the events began to unfold until I, too, got into the fracas. In a flash we found ourselves surrounded by a pack of local ruffians who were now set on clearing their town of solder riffraff as we were referred to. After a few minutes of scuffling around, a police squad came on the scene and broke up the engagement well before much damage was done to anyone or property. Only we solders were hauled outside. The civilian perpetrators were allowed to continue their fun.

As the police sergeant, a balding chubby, red faced man with a rather gruff personal style, and his cohorts were about to drag us into the station the bartender from the tavern came to our rescue and explained to the officers that we had pretty much been drawn into the situation and that he did not think our actions warranted our being arrested. The policeman thought for a moment, looked us over, and pointed to the highway back toward Ft. Bragg and said, "See here! You fellas get out of town while the gettin' is good! Don't ever come back to Charlotte again! And tell all your buddies if they know what's good for them stay out of Charlotte. This aint no solder's town!"

We happily left town, vowing to ourselves never to return to that "Hick Place." After we drove a few miles down the road we stopped the car and slept until morning, a most uncomfortable sleep. It was good to get back home, back to the barracks with a comfortable cot to sleep on, back to "Fatalburg," a town with many blemishes but one that knew the value of being a soldier's town.

FROM QUIET VOLUNTEERING TO POLITICAL INFLUENCE

It was a lot of fun being in the 82nd Airborne. Although I enjoyed the comradeship of an airborne infantry line company after I had effected my transfer from the Parachute Rigging Company I was, nevertheless, somewhat bored with stateside duty and wanted to serve overseas, preferably in a combat unit; obviously this would not be with the 82nd Airborne. I then began to submit my parade of transfer requests. Each week I went into the First Sergeant's office and requested that I be transferred to a combat unit in Korea. Each week

Top Sergeant Swedish, a gruff but very well liked older soldier, told me that our company was under strength and, because I was parachute qualified and was government property, I would remain with the unit. (Sergeant Swedish was an interesting and colorful soldier in that during the time that I was there he set the record for the number of parachute jumps in a single day, something like 120.) Undaunted, I continued my overseas transfer requests for several months.

In the spring of 1952, the entire 82nd Airborne Division was detached to the state of Texas for a grand military maneuver that was dubbed "Operation Longhorn." We rode all the way from Ft. Bragg North Carolina to Lomita, Texas by Army convoy—a trip that lasted many days (since we traveled at only thirty-five miles per hour). The trucks drove about twelve hours a day and each day the cooks provided us a packed lunch of one cheese and one baloney sandwich (dry, without any dressing) and a carton of milk.

The trip was interesting, with lots of scenery, although traveling hundreds of miles sitting on the wooden seats of an Army two-and-a-half-ton truck was sometimes uncomfortable and very hard on the posterior. One interesting aspect of this trip was driving through the little towns along the way with people watching us by the side of the road. Occasionally, when we were stopped, we'd see pretty girls along the way and invariably someone would strike up a serious conversation with one of them.

One of my best buddies at the time, a Ukrainian fellow named Taras Zacharco, even made a date with one woman through a note that he wrote to her and threw alongside her feet tied to a rock. She threw back her phone number. Another friend, Jude, bought a puppy from one of the bystanders along the road. The puppy became a platoon mascot for a while until it soon became ostracized because it had the bad habit of urinating on one's lap. Periodic yells from troopers could be heard, "Great pails of puppy pee, Jude, take this damn dog!"

Another interesting part of the drive down to Texas involved the periodic bathroom stops better known in the Army as "piss calls." Picture this scenario: A long line of Army vehicles are traveling in a caravan several miles long. When the officer in charge in the front jeep finds a likely spot to stop for a handy bathroom trip, that is, when he finds a somewhat deserted section of road where he can find privacy, he then stops his vehicle and dismounts. All of the other vehicles following the commander take this cue as the signal that the long awaited bathroom stop has arrived and they begin to come to their sequenced halt—a halt regardless where the remaining vehicles find their spot, for example, along residential parts of the town, on city streets, next to a church, in front of a girls' school! Where to find a potty? Of course, any spot along the road had to suffice. The 82nd Airborne's nickname was changed from America's Honor Guard to America's "Watering Division" as we made our way through the South.

The soldiers en route to Texas in this long caravan likewise did not have the opportunity to find accommodations in motels or hostels along the way as one might do on a vacation drive through the country. Rather, the sleeping accommodations were carried attached to our own field packs in the form of shelter halves. Each soldier carried a piece of canvas that when combined with his buddy's tent half became a pup tent, which was pitched along our course of travel—usually in wooded parts of the states. In true military fashion the tents were typically pitched in rows facing a common front or company street. Not palatial by any means but considered adequate to offer enough shelter to keep us dry for those rainy nights—a climatic situation we encountered several times during our journey.

During one of our many evening stops we pitched our tents on a wide, flat, open field near Jackson, Mississippi. This large expanse of flat ground was excellent in that we did not have to clear brush in order to set up our company tents. We pitched our tents, dug the holes in the ground to house our latrines and deeper garbage pits, set up our mess tent, and the cooks prepared a nice dinner. All was good: a nice home, a nutritious Army meal, and good companionship as we built our campfires and sat around talking. It was good then to be in the Army—a fun camping adventure!

After lights out and the camp began to settle in for the night it began to rain, slightly at first then in a tremendous downpour. I was awakened, at first by a slight feeling of cold on my backside, then by distinct feelings of wetness all through my body. I began to hear curses and grumbling from the tents in the company area, as the large flat area (which had apparently been only a dried out swamp) became a lake.

"AAAGH! I'm soaked"

"Head for the trucks!"

My buddy Taras and I began to quickly roll up our gear in the shelter halves trying to retain all of the tent pegs (the Army charged us if we lost them) and headed for the trucks. I was running, falling, splashing, and laughing all the time trying to hold on our equipment.

In front of me, running in an equally awkward manner holding his gear under his arms, was our platoon sergeant, Sgt. Wolf, all 6'5" of him. Suddenly he disappeared completely from sight as he fell headlong in the deep garbage sump now filled with filthy water. We made it to the truck nearly dead from laughing at the Sarge trying to pull himself out of the inundated pit. When he finally made it to the truck with potato peelings and carrot tops protruding from his hair and equipment he did not look the part of a tough infantry platoon sergeant but more like a drowned garbage rat. Even he, setting aside his usually serious manner, found much to laugh about in the drowning of the 82nd Airborne.

When we arrived in Texas, we camped near the town of Lometa (nowhere near anything we had ever heard of), pitched our tents, and busied ourselves getting our gear in shape after the long drive and the horrendous weather we had experienced getting there. Most of us were pretty naive about desert living but found great fun in throwing cactus burrs at each other, playing with armadillos, and talking about rattlesnakes, which were thought to be quite abundant in the desert.

As the sun sunk over the western prairie, the sky began to take on the appearance of a deep purple haze with ever increasing points of light as the stars became more visible in the darkening void. What beautiful sunsets there were in the desert! That night I slept soundly until about 2:00 in the morning when I was awakened by a distinct rattling sound in the tent. I moved slightly and immediately felt a very sharp pain in my thigh—a snakebite I hastily concluded!

I lay there awake for a while not wanting to rile up the snake any further. I contemplated moving about, getting up, and getting help for the snakebite. But instead, I just waited in silence—concluding that the snake would only bite me more and I would only die sooner. I thought about dying there in the desert for a long time, finally I fell back to sleep not expecting to be alive in the morning.

As the light began to dawn and I awakened with noises coming from outside the tent signaling the beginning of a new day. My eyes popped open in amazement—where am I? I'm not dead! What happened? I thought to myself. Maybe the poison from the rattler was not enough to kill me but I actually felt pretty good. What happened to the snake? Was it still here in the sleeping bag? I began to slowly unzip the bag being careful not to stir whatever was in the bag with me. After a time, I quickly leapt from the bag nearly trampling Taras as I crawled from the tent. What happened? Was it all a dream?

Actually I figured out pretty quickly what had made the sharp jabbing pain in my thigh—a few very small needles from the cactus that we had been playing with the day before had stuck in my leg. I had somehow rolled on them in the night causing what I thought was a "snakebite." The most troublesome aspect of this situation was when I later evaluated my own reaction to it:

"Why did I not yell for help?"

I have thought about this situation for a long time and have never resolved in my own mind that even though I was pretty convinced that I had been bitten by a poisonous snake I very complacently resigned myself to do nothing about it and simply accept death. Even today I am more than a bit surprised by my crass resignation not to go for help and my apparent willingness to accept "signing off" from life so readily.

****

We obtained our briefing on the field operation a couple of days later. Our job in the three-week maneuver was to serve as "aggressors" in order to provide an enemy for National Guard troops that had been recently activated to prepare them for combat. During the maneuver we made two parachute jumps in the desert and walked around among the cacti for seventeen days playing war games. It was a lot of fun and we surprised the "enemy" (National Guardsmen from the Dixie Division who had recently been called up to active duty) on several occasions, capturing units that our script told us we should allow to win.

I especially liked being in the desert and enjoyed seeing the wild horses running free on the range. My favorites were two white horses that leaped over our heads as we were lying in a skirmish line early one morning, playing the aggressors and awaiting the designated enemy in an ambush. But, as Operation Longhorn came to a close I began to look forward to new adventures.

The truck convoy journey back to North Carolina was tedious and did not offer us the humorous episodes that our trip down had done. After the maneuver was over and our long olive drab convoy finally made its way back to North Carolina and home base, I became even more determined to obtain my transfer to a combat unit in Korea.

One evening I sat down and wrote a letter to the senator from West Virginia, the Honorable Harley M. Kilgore, indicating that I was from West Virginia and that I had volunteered a number of times to serve in Korea but that my request had always been turned down. I pointed out to him that I was eighteen years old and single. "Why not send me to Korea instead of someone who is married or has family responsibilities?" Within a week a response came from Washington—a very nice letter from the Senator indicating that he was proud that a fellow West Virginian was so patriotic as to volunteer for Korea the way that I did and that he would see if he could do anything about my request. He indicated that he might not have much influence in such matters as Army personnel movements but that he would inquire into my honorable request.

Senator Kilgore was a powerful member of the Senate Arms Appropriations Committee which, among other duties, voted on the promotions of general officers. His letter to me clearly understated his influence with the military and what he might do in terms of my request. Within hours after he made his inquiry with the 82nd Airborne Commanding General, I was called into the company day room (CQ). Sergeant Swedish was in a bit of a rage and told me that he did not like soldiers going over his head to get their way. He indicated that my request to go to Korea was being granted and that I was to be processed for immediate reassignment to a Korean combat unit. But, in the meantime he had a number of jobs to keep me busy. Obviously he thought that I had too much time on my hands so he provided some additional tasks for me to do to limit my letter writing. I was given a permanent KP assignment for the remainder of my time in the company.

****

The 82nd Airborne paratrooper was, for the most part, a pretty Gung Ho guy and most of the men in my platoon were envious of my orders to go to Korea; several of them told me that they wished they were going also. One day as I was running through the company street from the mess hall to my barracks I passed by the Company Commander. As regulations required, I slowed and saluted sharply. The captain walked over to me and said, "Soldier. Never mind what the sergeant says. I know he's stuck you on extra duty. I want to tell you something else. Good job! I wished I were going to Korea, too!"

I was on my way to FEACOM—or, in official terms, Far East Army Command. I felt pretty good now. I knew that I had done the right thing.

I was given a one-week stopover in Charleston on my way to Seattle and the port of embarkation. I had a chance to say goodbye to my sister, Joan, and my two brothers, all of whom seemed to be doing pretty well. My sister Joan had married a good man, Corky Hissom, and had just recently delivered a new baby. I felt reassured that everything was going well at home.

GOODBYE TO THE STATES

The train ride across the northern states was exciting. I took the train from Charleston to Chicago, then hooked up with a Great Northern Railway train that went all the way through Minneapolis-St. Paul and on to Seattle. The whole trip took several days. During the layover in Chicago I met a couple of guys ("straightlegs" but friendly) that I spent a lot of time with on the trip. They enjoyed going to the club car of the train where drinks were served and one could while away the hours playing cards.

We arrived in the processing center in Fort Lewis, near Seattle, and went through the usual military processing—we had to update our records, insurance forms, allotments, wills, and so forth. Just before our departure we traded in all of our dress uniforms for Army fatigues. The message that we were getting was that we would not likely be needing all of our pay where we were going; and that there would be no fancy parades.

There was a lot of waiting time at the center and the troop ship we were waiting for was not yet prepared for embarkation. So, we were given a pass on the weekend prior to our departure. We were authorized to go into Seattle for an overnight. I hooked up with my two buddies from the train and we caught a bus into town. We found that Seattle was a nice town and the people were friendly enough; we walked around a bit until after dark and decided that since we were going to be departing the good ole USA for overseas we would have ourselves a farewell party at one of the local joints.

We sauntered into a very likely spirit house and asked for a table. It was very crowded and loud with what seemed to us to be just the type of exciting, fun entertainment we deserved and there were a lot of attractive young women. Aha! We thought our uniforms would be a very fine attraction. Then, the manager checked our identification and, unfortunately, I fell short of the legal age to be admitted. I felt a little embarrassed that I, one of the rugged paratrooper types, could not even be admitted into a drinking establishment because I was too young, a mere child! My buddies tried to convince the manager that I should be immediately let in the bar because I was going off to fight for our country and could die there. The manager did not buy the argument and I was unceremoniously kicked out. My buddies, being loyal comrades, chose to go with me—a tough decision given the ample supply of attractive ladies we could see laughing and dancing inside.

We did manage to find another bar that was less discriminating; it was called the Chinese Beer Gardens, and seemed to specialize in beer with no questions asked. It was tough for a soldier to actually buy a drink because every time our glasses emptied one of the local Seattle citizens would buy us another round.

Getting up the next day was not a pleasant experience. My head felt as though there were jackhammers working inside and my mouth tasted like the floor of a bat cave. Later in the day our heads began to clear, and as we were strolling down the street just killing time until we needed to return to post, we approached a man standing by the open door of his car. He had apparently seen us walking and drove ahead of us, stopped, and waited for us to walk by. He asked us if we could talk for a moment. Soldiers were a bit wary of strange men approaching them on the street, but we stopped to hear what he had to say. He said, "Would you boys like to come out to my house and have dinner?"

Somewhat taken aback, we looked at each other.

"I'll bring you back to town afterward. My wife, daughter and I would like to have your company for Sunday dinner. What do you say?"

We agreed, thinking that there was probably no problem that could result. We went along. and it turned out to be a most enjoyable afternoon. Our friendly host told us that evening that they had lost a son in the Second World War and now made a point to befriend soldiers who were likely to be bound for overseas. His wife and fifteen-year-old daughter received us like we were part of their family. The dinner was excellent and we enjoyed their friendly spirit.

When he took us back to camp he, recognizing that the other two guys smoked, gave them each a cartoon of cigarettes. I (the mere child of the trio who didn't even smoke) was given a batch of candy bars. A few days later when we boarded the ship to leave for Asia we had very pleasant memories of our brief stopover in Seattle and all of the people that we had encountered there. It was as though the folks had adopted us as their own. Our pleasant thoughts of this seacoast town would not soon die in our memories. These were the kind of people I thought we were going overseas to defend.

LIFE ABOARD A TROOP SHIP

Our ship, the *Marine Phoenix*, was definitely not a luxury cruise liner either in terms of accommodations or cuisine. It was known as a troop ship, aka a tub or a floating sick bed. The accommodations for sleeping were sparse and crowded for the three-week trip. Compartments were over booked and the men slept in vertical stacks of bunks about six high with just a couple of feet between rows. Each bunk had only about a two-foot crawl space between it and the bottom of the next bunk above. Most of us (except for some seasick ones) preferred the darkness of the evening and quiet of the deck rather than staying in the stale atmosphere down below. At night one of the larger decks was rigged with a screen and showed recent movies. One beautiful, starry evening on deck we watched the movie "High Noon"—for about the third time.

Everywhere you looked on the continually rolling and overstuffed troop ship there were brown, Army fatigue dressed GIs all trying to do the same thing—kill a lot of hours until we reached our destination. Finding a quiet spot on the crowded ship took some ingenuity but I managed to find a niche on the aft deck or fantail and whiled away some hours looking for flying fish and whales in between drifting thoughts. At times we gathered on the top deck in small groups, at least those of us who were not sick. There our conversations usually gravitated to the question of whether the war was going to last until we got into it. We did not get much news about the war except an occasional announcement on a bulletin board near our mess hall. There was usually little of substance in those few vague, mimeographed lines that mysteriously appeared and then disappeared just as anonymously.

Sitting alone on the deck of a ship overlooking an expanse of rolling sea provokes one's thoughts and images. In my case a constant preoccupying concern was that the war was going to end before we had our chance to get into the action. A few other guys that I hung out with who were volunteers shared these thoughts. The draftees among us had different anticipations. They prayed for an end to the hostilities before their arrival. Their wishes and prayers were, of course, aimed at canceling out those of the volunteers. As the ship plied the waters on its sluggish trek toward the Far East, it was a nip and tuck battle of minds as to the outcome of the war—whose prayers would have the greatest influence to the fate of the war? Would the draftees best us in their quest for an end to the war and will it to be all over before we arrived? Would the RA's get their wish? The time dragged on.

Those fortunate GIs who felt well enough could eat all they wanted but most found the Navy meals unappetizing and boring: tasteless breakfasts consisting of plastic pancakes or watery scrambled eggs, a comparably unpleasant lunch comprised of beans and weenies, and suppers repeating the theme of beans but with variation in some other unidentified meat-like substance.

One form of entertainment for those of us who, perhaps due to sheer luck did not get sick, was watching others handle the task of dignified barfing on a miserable ship. The only time that I came close to getting seasick myself was one day when the fellow standing (there were no sitting tables) next to me at lunch puked directly into his plate of beans and weenies. When I glanced at his plate I found that the resulting combination actually looked more appetizing than what I had been originally served!

3

Arrival in the Land of the Morning Calm

WE STOOD ON THE CROWDED DECK AND WATCHED with interest as we made our grand entry into Yokohama Harbor in Japan. It was just a few short years after the end of the war between Japan and the United States and extensive rebuilding was in progress. However, there were still many places in which post-war reconstruction had not yet taken root resulting in many conspicuously vacant blocks where buildings once stood.

After disembarking from the troop ship, most of the sick GIs were to say with considerable relief, we were transported to a processing center where we went through additional vaccinations, paper processing, and checking whether we had our dog tags, weapons, and winter clothes. During our brief stay at Yokohama I developed new friendships with other paratroopers who were also in transit to Korea—all but one of whom had volunteered. Some had stories similar to my own difficulties in getting transferred to the Far East. One of these troopers had been given the option of going to the stockade for some crime he had committed or volunteering for Korea; he reluctantly chose the latter. Several of the guys, like Stan Stinson, wound up in the same infantry unit with me. Stan and I had a parallel course for a while in the same infantry company until his wounds later in the war required his evacuation.

I became close friends with one other former paratrooper, James Sullivan (he went by the name of Sully), who had just come over from the 11th Airborne. With a hint of mystery, he admitted that his company did not really put up much of a fight to keep him. Sully was outgoing, friendly, somewhat impulsive, and a gutsy fellow. He was savvy in that he managed always to be first in the chow line and last in the vaccination line. He was adept with a deck of cards and not always trustworthy in the way he dealt them; we played hearts almost constantly during our waking times while we waited for the boat to take us over to Inchon, Korea.

In two days, and about five hundred Hearts games later, we were loaded on another troop ship; this time we all had arms that ached with what we were told was our final cholera shots. This troop ship was a bit more crowded and more run down than the one in which we made our ocean crossing. It was now only a short jaunt across the Sea of Japan to Inchon: our final port of embarkation. Our thoughts were often of anticipation as to what the situation would be like when we finally arrived at our destination.

We really did not know a great deal about the place we were going—Korea, a rugged peninsula that juts down from Manchuria into the Sea of Japan on the east and the Yellow Sea on the west. The land mass is divided into two halves politically and many would say arbitrarily. The Northern part, that is the portion above the 38th Parallel, was taken from Japan and given to Russia in 1945 for its part in defeating the Japanese in the Second World War. North Korea, originally a highly industrialized section of the peninsula, was by the 1950s a communist nation under the harsh leadership of Kim Il Sung.

South Korea, the nation in which we were investing a lot of our youth to defend, was originally a predominantly agricultural region of the country. From seacoast to seacoast—on the east and west shores of the peninsula—steep cliffs rose from the sea and met in the center carrying the hilly theme across the country. About two-thirds of south Korea's territory is hilly and the remainder is flat plain. Korea is blessed (some might say damned) with a wide range of climate from extreme cold in winter to extremely wet in the spring and extremely hot in the summer. Many of the hills and valleys are luxuriously terraced with paddies, which in season provided bountiful harvests of rice, the predominant crop.

Our final destination would be a foxhole somewhere along a trench line that cut a jagged 255-mile path across the peninsula separating these two warring countries. I was up on deck when the transport made its stop near Inchon and dropped anchor some distance off shore because of the treacherous tides at Inchon. I could not see the shoreline in the distance but, interestingly, I could smell the offensive odor of fish distinctly coming from shore. Our entry into Inchon Harbor was in style indeed: military style. Since the troop transport could apparently not go all of the way into the harbor our troops had to embark over the side, down rope ladders, and into small bouncing landing craft that would take us the final distance to shore. We had been briefed that this was not going to be an easy transition since we had to carry our packs and M-1 rifle over the side of the ship with us. These warnings were an understatement; what the naval briefing officer should have said was, "Your disembarkation on to the landing craft carrying all that gear is not humanly possible but you have to do it anyway!" Most of us made it on to the erratically bobbing small craft without a severe dunking, but not without an ample supply of sprained limbs, rope burns, water in the face, and abrasions.

As the landing craft approached the dilapidated pier at Inchon our nostrils became increasingly sensitized to the odor of fish that had been laid out in the sun to dry, a form of food preservation. It was a dramatic entrance on to Korean shores. We were glad to be ashore even though our immediate destiny was uncertain. We stayed only briefly at Inchon Harbor before boarding the trucks that would take us to the replacement center near Seoul.

LIFE IN A REPPLE DEPOT

The Army did not seem to be in much of a hurry to get us up front; we mostly sat around inside the barbed wire enclosed replacement camp known as a Repple Depot until they decided our division assignments. Being young and energetic, and somewhat open to experiencing novel things, some of us decided to wander into town for a visit even though it was "off limits" or absolutely forbidden. The compound was surrounded with barbed wire fence and concertina wire and there were armed guards posted every so often, walking post in order to assure that we did not wander into the surrounding civilian areas.

Although it was not much of a town, some of the guys who had done the same thing the night before said they had a good time, finding some girls and booze. "Why not try the same thing ourselves?" Sully suggested.

"Sure, I'm game," I replied not hesitating.

At nightfall, with blankets tied around our waists, we crawled through a hole in the fence and headed to town. The blankets were needed to use for barter for different commodities since we had no money. We found the location where the other guys had told us all of the action was. It really was not difficult to find since there were others headed in the same direction and the trail was well marked.We were greeted at the little makeshift hut or "hoochie" by a very friendly Korean man who bade us to come inside. Once seated, we began to discuss our wishes in specific terms. Our conversation appeared to be proceeding in the proper direction we had hoped when we heard some noises and loud voices coming from outside the house. A military policeman stuck his head into the doorway and brusquely ordered us to step outside and into the lineup.

We found ourselves prisoners among a line of other guys, some laughing others cursing softly to themselves. We were marched back to camp and held at attention, with all of the trappings of disgrace, until the camp commandant came to our formation and took down our names and serial numbers—information readily available on our dog tags. We were all provided with a written notice (called a DR or Delinquency Report) that we were to receive "company punishment" when we arrived at our final duty assignment because we had disobeyed orders, violated a prohibited area, and destroyed government property (this is a catchall charge that can be applied to anyone who even cuts himself while shaving or stubs his toe while marching).

In addition, for our misdeeds, we were all assigned to punishment duty that consisted of a work detail that was ordered to dig a large garbage sump for the post. The garbage sump was quite an ambitious undertaking. The corporal in charge of the work detail marked off an outline on the ground in the shape of a square that was 24 x 24 feet. The ten GIs who had been rounded up in the dragnet began to ply their new trade as sump digger—under orders to turn this rocky Korean earth into a functioning garbage pit. We began this ominous chore not knowing how far we would get before the Army had other duties for us to fulfill.

The next afternoon we were ordered to stop our digging and fall into formation to receive our permanent unit assignments. We thought that it was just as well that we quit digging because in a day and a half the proposed huge sump hole had barely gotten started (it was only 1/4 inch deep in one corner).

We formed a ragtag circle around the high wooden platform. The duty sergeant informed us that he was going to read out our names and our duty assignments and we were to move our gear into a designated area for the divisions to which we were to be assigned. He shouted out names and assignments for a long time until most everyone had a placement. Sully and I went to the area designated for the 17th Infantry Regiment of the 7th Infantry Division. We milled around for a bit as the sergeant's reading droned on. He paused for a breath when, in a moment of sheer elitist bravado, Sully shouted out to the duty sergeant, "Hey Sarge! What is the chance that us airborne guys will be sent to the 187th?" The 187th Airborne Regimental Combat Team was the only parachute infantry unit in the Far East Command that spent most of its time in Sasebo, Japan, and was presently attached to the 7th Infantry Division for a brief tour.

The sergeant stopped his reading from his list and peered angrily into the crowd as though to burn holes through the questioner. He then shouted, "You're goddamn in the 7th now!" "Fall out and get your gear together. You're asses are moving up!"

We boarded a train to the front, a journey that would take about three days. The train traveled to Chunchon in Central Korea then north to meet up with the 7th Infantry Division holding down the central front in the Kumhwa Valley, east and south of Panmunjom. We had been assigned to the 17th Infantry Regiment, known in Korea as the "Buffaloes." Sully and I received an almost identical set of orders that also contained the small red "DR" attached. The train moved along toward Chunchon, Korea at a snail's pace. (This inch-by-inch travel was thought by some to be how the city of Inchon received its name).

As we passed slowly through the sections of Seoul, I was struck by the incredible destruction that the city had suffered since the war. It was Hell's landscape! Originally a large colonial city of over a million and a half people, it was now almost devoid of commercial activity and human life. There were burned out buildings and piles of rubble everywhere.

One of the most vivid memories I have of Seoul city was a large building face, really only a wall remnant, of a large structure that had once been a public commercial or government building. The wall contained three large pock holes running in a diagonal line from the bottom left to the top right of the building, in all likelihood direct hit shell holes from a high powered cannon, probably an 85 mm from one of the communist T-34 tanks that advanced on Seoul at the beginning of the war.

The train slowly made its way toward our final destination, the ancient city of Chunchon, stopping periodically—probably to fix the rails up ahead we thought. Our train resembled one of those antiques that we had seen in Western movies or in films about the Orient in the 1920s with open-sided cars. Periodically, when we slowed to a stop we were mobbed by civilians, many of them young children who looked to us like street urchins in terms of their clothing. They reminded me somewhat of myself in the past running around the streets of Charleston. Hundreds of thousands of civilians, especially children, were displaced during the Korean War; it was astounding. The tattered children appeared to be suffering from malnutrition, and most of the GIs on the train were suckers for their smiles, their sorrowful faces, and their ever-present outstretched hands. We tried to fill the dirty little hands with anything we had to eat from our packs and our ration tins. One of the youngsters, who couldn't have been more than six or seven years old, kept holding his fingers to his lips asking for cigarettes. I didn't smoke cigarettes at the time and motioned that I did not have any.

Someone said aloud, "He's too young to smoke anyway!"

Someone else pointed out, "He's not interested in smoking them stupid. He's only interested in trading them for food so he can stay alive."

Someone handed him a couple of cigarettes and he moved toward the back of the crowd. Seeing these kids was perhaps the saddest part of the ride toward the front.

THE FIRST NIGHT AT THE FRONT

The long journey from stateside through countless processing centers, vaccinations, paper trails, and assignment rosters finally ended at my ultimate arrival at the company rear of Fox Company of the 17th Infantry Regiment. Company rear was little more than a wide spot in the road with a few storage and supply tents and some sandbagged trenches which could serve as a refuge in the event of incoming long range artillery shells. In a short while, the Company Executive Officer and the company clerk met us at our truck. The lieutenant directed us to leave our duffle bags in storage and only take exactly what we needed up front, which was not much—a bedroll, pack with rations and some extra clothing, an M-1 rifle, and the most important piece of equipment—an entrenching tool (a combination shovel and spade carried by each infantryman). He looked at Sully and me with some dismay when he saw the Delinquency Report attached to our orders saying, "A couple of screw-ups huh?"

The Exec told us that the DRs would be given to Captain Vaughn when he had time to deal with them; he then briefed us about the company positions as we marched up toward the forward positions.

It was getting dark when we arrived at the company command post (CP) on the hill. Sergeant Casper, the platoon sergeant, welcomed us in a very friendly and reassuring greeting. He was a calm combat veteran from the Second World War and had been with the 7th Infantry for several months. He seemed to know quite well what he was doing and projected an air of confidence to others. We were a bit on edge and did not know what to expect and his introductory words were very quieting.

He told us that a lot had been happening the past few days with the Chinese apparently stepping up their offensive. However, we were in a relatively quiet sector for the moment and that we were not expecting anything from "Old Joe" tonight so we shouldn't have any problems getting some sleep. He assured us, "Don't worry about pulling guard for a few days. We'll give you a chance to get used to it up here." We immediately liked the sergeant and were disappointed to learn later that he was a short timer and only had a week or so to go before he rotated back to the States.

Fox Company sign at company rear area.

The night sky as seen from the front—the end point of the long string of military stopovers—created a lasting impression on my mind. It was beautiful in a strange sort of way. I was impressed at first by the dark night stillness that seemed to creep in around me as I surveyed the valley floor below our trench line. There were no searchlight units operating close to our positions, consequently the sky retained to some extent its darkness for a time. As I watched the outline of the enemy hills, some several thousand yards in the distance, my gaze was attracted to a sudden sequence of lights emerging from a place near the valley floor traveling upward into the sky. The red lights cutting a distinct skyward path were tracer bullets from a machine gun below—they etched the night sky with colorful dots as if being placed there by a master painter.

Occasionally in the distance we would see a flash of light followed a few seconds later by the sound of an explosion. As I studied the valley with interest, my thoughts centered on the practical question of what was the procedure for estimating distance to targets by counting the seconds that elapsed between the flash and sound of an exploding shell that we were taught in basic training. Practical reality always had a way of intruding into moments of reverie at the front.

I found myself a wide section of the trench line and bedded down on the hard, cold ground in my sleeping bag. In spite of the sergeant's reassurance about the "relatively safe place," I did not sleep soundly that night. On several occasions incoming artillery shells on our side of the lines startled me into wakefulness, and I must add created some anxiety. I was reassured by the lone sentry standing a few feet away that the rounds were a good distance away. I was awakened on two occasions with parachute flares bursting overhead and drifting toward the valley floor where someone thought they had seen movement. It was a long and generally restless night.

In the morning my new squad leader showed me around our trench line and introduced me to the other guys in the squad. Everyone looked pretty ragged and unshaven, and their clothes were about the dirtiest things that I had seen since my stove cleaning stint at the consolidated mess hall at Ft. Meade. I was introduced to another rifleman and told that I would be standing watch in shifts with him and sharing the bunker near by. The bunker was in a slightly widened part of the trench a few yards away and was covered with about six layers of sandbags. The routine was that one man would sleep and the other would stand watch—two hours on, two hours off. The other soldier, whose name was Mike Yancik, had been in the platoon for a couple of weeks. He seemed to have a pretty good grasp of the tactical situation we were holding at the time so I settled in to learn how to be a combat infantryman.

Later in the afternoon, Sgt. Casper came by my new foxhole with Sully in tow and said that he wanted to show us the third platoon's positions over the ridge so that we could get an orientation to their situation. Their positions were a bit more precarious than ours and they had received some probes from the Chinese a couple of nights before and had killed two of them on the wire (barbed wire and concertina wire that was strung out in front of our positions.) The worst part of the visit to the third platoon was that one had to make his way across an unprotected area to get there—by running. If I ran in a crouch, I was told, then the sniper on the Chinese hill would not be able to see me clearly. An upright stroll across would be a sure invitation to wind up on a Graves Registration listing. I watched as the sergeant made his way across the open area and I mimicked his movements, rather awkwardly, but it worked. A few minutes later, I heard a rifle shot from the Chinese sniper as one of our guys made his way in the other direction. The sniper missed but it was a clear reminder that this place was dangerous!

Although our present positions were relatively well defended because of the steep rock ledge below them, we were not immune to artillery fire that was periodic yet regular and intense. The Chinese Army regularly threw harassing artillery and mortar rounds into our positions to keep us down. We had a good vantage point overlooking the trails that the Chinese were using to bring up supplies and to launch patrols against our front. Another attraction for the Chinese artillery fire were the two tanks that were dug in about 100 yards on our left to provide support for our forces and to fire their howitzers at the Chinese positions from our post. One thing that infantrymen learn pretty quickly on the front lines is that tanks and machine guns draw return enemy fire. It's best to bed down in an area that is somewhat distant from these attractive targets!

Even though the Chinese artillery shells hitting this sector were of the general harassment variety, even random shells could have a disastrous effect. That evening, two men from another platoon were killed as a result of a direct hit on their bunker. Both were sleeping at the time and never knew what hit them. Though dying in one's sleep at the end of one's life might seem to be an attractive and welcome way to go, it is not, by any stretch of the imagination, considered an acceptable alternative to experience at such a young age and with so much life left. Direct shell hits were ominous and mentally unsettling events—a danger that I had not factored into my desire to experience military combat. I did not like to anticipate such possibilities.

After a week on the line, dodging artillery shells and playing chicken with the sniper across the way, it came our turn to run a patrol into the valley, an ambush patrol near the Chinese positions. I volunteered to go on this trip into no-man's-land and the platoon sergeant hesitatingly agreed because I was pretty green. It was a fourteen-man patrol whose mission it was to go out into the valley as soon as it became dark, make our way to a preselected location, and set up our ambush along a worn path in hopes of surprising the Chinese (who were probably planning to do the same thing to us somewhere out there.) Patrols in our outfit always had an even number of troops so that the each man was responsible for knowing where his buddy was at all times.

I had the job of assistant bazooka man for the patrol, which essentially meant that, in addition to my M-1 rifle, I was carrying an extra pack containing several bazooka shells. The bazooka, an anti-tank or anti-pillbox weapon, looked like a collection of wide pipes when it was dismantled. When it was put together it resembled a stovepipe or that musical instrument from which it derived its name. Because I had not fired one of these contraptions since basic training, the platoon sergeant thought it wise that I get in a few practice shots in case I had to take over the job on the patrol. We went to one of the forward firing positions and I took aim on a burnt out tank on the valley floor some distance away. Either the long range to the target or my bad aim resulted in two misses but the desired practice served to remind me of the procedures.

The moon was full and the lighting in the valley such that one could see our formation pretty clearly for about ten yards. We moved into the valley quickly and quietly finding the location we wanted just across a knee-deep stream that we waded through. The walk out into the valley took about two hours. Once we were in position we simply waited in silence hoping that our hunt would be successful. Once we settled in I began to notice that the night was really getting quite cold and I was beginning to shiver. Damn, I thought to myself, this is only October and it's already freezing. In trying to take a drink of water from my canteen I discovered that there was a thin coating of ice on the surface. What kind of winter lay ahead? I wondered if I had made a mistake in submitting my parade of transfer requests and leaving the pleasant climate of North Carolina for this cold place. Could it be that I might live to regret my decision to go overseas?

We waited in ambush for six shivering hours then carefully began our trek back across the valley to our own positions being wary of falling into a trap set by Old Joe that might be awaiting our return journey. The return, following a different route, was uneventful. When we got back to our positions we went to the platoon Command Post (CP) for a cup of coffee and some C-rations because we were famished. After chowing down I started back to my foxhole when the platoon sergeant stopped me and held out his hand. He handed me an official paper indicating that I was now eligible to wear a CIB (Combat Infantryman's Badge). The CIB is one of the most prized possessions that an infantry soldier can own. The only way that a soldier can wear the CIB is to spend six days under fire as an infantry soldier. After all of my journey and frustration getting into a combat unit—at last, I had something to show for my efforts.

****

The major offensive that the Communist Army launched against the U.N. forces beginning around October 8th was beginning to spread into the Kumhwa Valley on the Central front. The entire valley had been a boiling caldron of activity from mid-September through October of 1952. Several slopes became embroiled in what was referred to as the "Battle of the Hills," with Sniper Ridge, Whitehorse, and Triangle Ridge being prominently displayed in the dispatches. The ROK army, our South Korean Army allies, got the initial brunt of the attack on White Horse Hill but soon several other hills were in the path of the enemy aggressive initiative. Jane Russell Hill, actually a pair of hills named after the actress with the buxom figure, was a part of Triangle Ridge.

The military historian MacDonald (1986) described the Battle for Triangle Ridge, in October, 1952, as a Chinese effort to make a point during the U. S. Presidential elections by assaulting White Horse Hill. The American general, Van Fleet, then responded with an attack on enemy positions in the Triangle Hill complex, in an effort to relieve Chinese pressure. This effort involved the American 7th Division committing a battalion a day to the fighting. When the battle ended, with only portions of the positions in American hands, Van Fleet's Division had suffered 9,000 casualties.

In early October our unit was ordered to defend a section of the line in the Kumhwa Valley and after a long rainy march we arrived at a reserve position behind Triangle Ridge near White Horse and Sniper Ridges. This reserve duty, referred to as a "blocking position," was designed to guard against a breakthrough on any of the hills that were under direct assault from the Chinese. Should the Chinese capture any of these hills we were prepared and in position to counterattack. Since we were not in direct positions facing the enemy this reserve activity was considered somewhat easy duty. It was easy duty, if you discount the intense and almost incessant artillery barrages that fell onto our midst.

We were scattered about foxholes, hastily dug along the sloping hill. There were also a few huts that afforded only minimal protection from the shelling because they only had a layer or two of sandbags on the top. During the long day of shelling several hundred rounds fell in our vicinity killing several men and wounding a score of others. One hut received a direct hit killing or wounding everyone inside. Neither the foxholes nor the huts provided much protection from direct hits but I decided, after picking up several small pieces of shrapnel in my hand, that I would take the risk of moving into one of the huts for a while. Perhaps one could avoid the smaller pieces of shrapnel inside even the thin walls.

Once inside, however, I regretted my decision because one of the ten or so guys in there was having a very loud religious experience. With each screaming incoming shell he let out a shriek calling out for God to spare him, in return for which, he promised loudly that he would forever be his dutiful servant and change his wicked life. I had heard the expression "There are no atheists in foxholes" before and I supposed it referred to our friend. Most people, however, simply took the shelling with a designed resignation minus the showy religious fervor. Most of us doubted the sincerity of our friend's promises given the vile language and behavior he generally demonstrated, but if it made him feel more secure, more power to him. His screaming and running about the hut became more intense and he had to be restrained by a couple of guys at one point to keep him from hurting himself. Unfortunately, he was killed just a short time later when he received a direct hit on his bunker while asleep.

I was almost to the point of deciding to return to the open foxhole when someone yelled out that there was hot chow being set up at the bottom of the hill for anyone who was hungry. I was starved so I grabbed my mess kit and started to go toward the area where the food was supposedly located. At that instant a series of incoming shells whistled their approach and I dived back in the hoochie for cover as they burst, spewing their maiming fragments around the company area. It became quiet for a moment and I gathered up my mess kit once again and headed out.

Someone shouted, "Hey, Where are you going?"

I tried to appear calm, saying, "To get some supper."

"You're crazy to go out in that!" someone else said.

Another guy handed me his mess kit and said, "Would you please fill mine up too?" I agreed, taking his mess kit in my other hand.

On reaching the bottom of the little hill I soon found that I was all by my-self—no one else had ventured out. I hurried down to the line of thermos type chow cans and looked inside finding the one with the main dish—creamed chicken—and quickly filled up the two kits. As I topped off the last one I heard the now familiar and ominous whistle of an incoming shell and I crouched to the ground as it exploded a hundred yards away. I hurriedly stood up and ran quickly and a bit awkwardly back to the hut just as a series of shells burst on the scene, this time near the food area. I dived into the bunker, pre-serving the precious cargo of chicken stew (which tasted wonderful, by the way). A moment later, we looked out to where the chow line had been set up and saw instead a large crater where the once inviting food containers had once stood. The remainder of the supper had been destroyed. The artillery and rocket fire continued into the night; and early the next morning we left the reserve position and returned to the Main Line of Resistance (MLR).

****

We soon found ourselves back in frontline positions occupying a relatively quiet sector of the Missouri Line. We settled in with some relief after the in-tense shelling in the blocking position behind White Horse Hill and had hopes for a quiet breathing spell. Then, our Regimental Commander, Col. William Hardick, took a page from Robert E. Lee's book during the American Civil War and initiated a lateral troop movement in order to concentrate forces in a small sector of the line—a move that turned out to be an effective mobilization of force in an attack against Jane Russell Hill. The Second Battalion of the 17th Infantry Regiment was alerted that we were being moved over to the right side of the MLR, about twelve miles, from which we were to launch an assault to re-take a position on the Triangle Ridge. We prepared to launch our attack early in the morning and moved out at about 6:00 A.M. We marched in a quickstep formation, carrying all of the equipment needed to assault a hill, and moved into position to make the assault by 1:00 P.M. in the afternoon.

4

The Battle for Triangle Ridge:
Our Assault on Jane Russell Hill

THE BATTLE FOR TRIANGLE RIDGE, REFERRED to as "Operation Showdown" among American forces, began on October 14th and was designed to straighten out the MLR by removing the Chinese forces from the gap in the U.S. lines (referred to as the Missouri Line). General Van Fleet, commander of the 7th Army, viewed this attack as a means of pressuring the Chinese and Korean leadership to more seriously pursue the peace talks at Panmunjom that had recently broken down. The Battle for Triangle Hill (referred to as the Shangganling Campaign by the Chinese in books and movies) was the largest and most costly Korean War battle during 1952. The operation involved elements of the 7th Infantry as well as the 2nd Republic of Korea (ROK) Division against the Chinese 15th and 12 Corps.

Triangle Ridge was a V-shaped range of hills in the Kumhwa Valley. Pike's Peak was the northwest ridge, to the northeast was Jane Russell Hill, and off a short distance north of her was the towering hill that we referred to as Papasan, a 1,062 meter high mountain, because it dominated the valley. Papasan, like other hills in this valley, contained a number of tunnels in which the Chinese Army housed their troops, artillery, and supplies. Throughout this region there were complexes of caves and old gold mine shafts—remnants of bygone times. Historians for the Chinese Army, as a result of the eventual outcome of the battle and their victorious retaking of the hill from the South Korean Army, highlight this campaign as one of the most influential victories that impacted their military development. In 1956, a Chinese film, "Battle on Shangganling Mountain," honored this engagement.

FOX COMPANY ASSAULT ON JANE RUSSELL HILL

Our time to move against the Chinese forces had come and Fox Company was assigned to attack Jane Russell Hill; we were going to go up the right slope. We were told, euphemistically speaking, that we would be "reinforcing and relieving" a unit that had been chewed up by the Communists' attacks. This description neglected to inform us that most of the hill was actually in Chinese hands—at least the parts that counted—i.e, the top.

The march up the hill was silent and long. Our column snaked up the steep and winding slope that was nearly devoid of vegetation. The air was filled with the heavy smell of cordite from exploding shells that still rained occasionally from the skies, bursting at random across the landscape. As we worked our way up the steep trail toward the crest of the hill, we passed a few straggling GIs from another company sitting alongside the trail on their way down the hill. They had gone up the hill earlier and had taken heavy casualties in the process.

At one point, our column stopped for a brief break to rest our legs and backs, which were laden with ammunition and water. We saw coming down the path two seemingly downhearted captive Chinese soldiers with their hands above their heads. I was surprised by the height of one of the soldiers who appeared to be about 6'4" and well nourished. "Whoever told us the Chinks were short!" someone yelled out. The prisoners were from a regular Chinese infantry company that had substantial military experience. The shorter of the two prisoners, we later learned, was a veteran of decades of military service in China; he had been carrying the same weapon in the same company for nineteen years—as long as many of the American GIs had been alive! This was a rather unsettling concept for our young minds to contemplate. What kind of people were we up against?

Battles are rarely as neat, clean, and unambiguous as those depicted in movies—they are, in reality, dirty, confusing, and often chaotic events without a sense of direction or purpose. Our mission on Jane Russell was clearly of this sort. In the briefing we were told that we were going to "reinforce in assault," that is, we were going to go into positions that were partially occupied by other Americans. Our tasks were to relieve and reinforce them and go on to take the remaining part of the hill that was still in Chinese hands and hold until relieved. Other than a few men leaving the hill as we climbed up the trail, I didn't see anyone else. Our company was basically the entire show on the hill.

"Secure the hill" we were told. Easily stated, simply explained, but it was not as easy to see or to clearly accomplish. Before we were far into our mission we were taking fire from the crest of the hill that was owned by the Chinese (and a pretty aggressive lot at that). We moved up the reverse slope of the hill in a skirmish line as far as we could go, trying to remain out of the intense fire from the Chinese machine gun that was peppering our lines whenever we presented a target. We located a point beyond which only Chinese was being spoken and dug in near the top of the hill.

It was impossible to hold the north face of the hill because of the commanding elevation of the Chinese positions on Papasan (on the map called Hill 1062) that allowed them to annihilate any positions they saw on the military crest of our hill, the point at which American infantrymen usually prefer to take up residence in times like these. Most of our platoon remained on the reverse slope while a few observers were in locations on the military crest to serve as lookouts for additional Chinese assaults. There was a trench line across the front of the hill that served as nighttime positions when we would likely come under assault from the enemy infantry; otherwise we stayed in trenches on the back slope to reduce casualties from shelling.

We dug foxholes in the rocky soil because the trench line was not deep enough to provide protection from the shells that came in from Chinese positions on Papasan. On the far left of the platoon's positions they were experiencing additional problems in the form of hand grenades that were being lobbed over the ridge line from a Chinese bunker on the other slope of the hill. Every so often someone would yell out, "Duck, there's a grenade!" and we would see one of the Chinese hand grenades roll down the slope. There were two common types of Chinese grenades. One looked like a potato masher with a round pin in the handle. The Chinese would put their fingers in the pins and lob them— one motion would send the grenade flying and pull out the pin at the same time. The grenades would explode about four or five seconds later, if they did not misfire. Fortunately for us they had a high failure rate. The other grenade type was larger and more rounded, somewhat like a gourd but with a similar pin arrangement.

One of our platoon leaders, tired of having these grenades roll down the hill making everyone run for cover, decided it was time to get rid of that nuisance. He instructed our platoon sergeant, Sgt. Casper, to try and get men over there to knock out the bunker. In the afternoon, our squad leader sent Sully and me up the ridge to reconnoiter and discover where the grenades were coming from. We crawled up the slope of the hill, taking our time and keeping as low to the ground as possible to make it up the knoll without being observed by the Chinese across the way. When we reached the top and looked across the valley toward Papasan for the first time we were stunned with its appearance. It was a very high hill that towered over our little knoll like a big brown dirty giant. We made our way as stealthily as we could across the top of the hill overlooking the trench line to try and get a good look from the spot on the ridge from where the grenades seemed to be coming.

We couldn't see much of the lower trench from our vantage point, as we laid side by side with our heads about a foot apart so we could talk quietly, looking for the best way to make our way to the Chinese positions. Sully, pointing down the hill, turned to me to say something but before he got his words out a Chinese sniper bullet crashed into his head and blood gushed from the ugly hole between his eyes. He was silenced instantly. In a state of shock and excitability, I half pulled and half dragged Sully's lifeless form across the hill top yelling, "Medic! Medic!"

One of our medics, the reliable Corporal Buckley, who had a pronounced stutter when he tried to talk, was there quickly. Buckley had risked his life many times on that hill to attend to the wounds of others. The stress of battle wore perhaps more on him than the rest of us because his job often called for exposing himself to enemy fire to reach wounded men. It is interesting that Buckley's hair turned almost completely white over night on that hill—a situation that I had heard of but had never seen before. In Sully's case, there was nothing Buckley could do. When he reached him, it was too late; he apparently died instantly.

I was badly shaken. My friends were not supposed to die—certainly not someone like Sully whom I knew so well and who had so much to live for. Sully had become a very close friend in the few weeks that I knew him and to see him end up this way was a severe jolt—one that crept up on me later at moments when I tried to fall asleep or at times when nothing else occupied my thinking. For a while I had a strange mixed feeling about the situation. On one hand, I was troubled that I had lost someone so close to me. But, on the other, there was also a feeling of relief—not relief that Sully was dead, but a sense of relief that it was not me. I was experiencing intense guilt over the fact that I had lived and that Sully was dead. What I was feeling at the time was that I was glad I was still alive and that the sniper, in his decision to fire at one of the two heads, had chosen Sully's rather than mine. These were very troublesome thoughts—thoughts that would remain with me for years—always carrying with them a cold, chilling sensation and a strange sense of wonderment.

But, on the hill there was no time for worry or reflection. We had to try to knock out the Chinese bunker before the enemy soldiers killed everyone in our platoon. The next attempt to get a closer look at the Chinese positions took place about an hour later. When Sully and I were lying on the ridge line earlier, I had seen a trench running along the hill toward the Chinese positions. I told Sgt. Casper that I thought I could get to the bunker by crawling along the lower trench. He wished me luck and assigned a BAR (Browning Automatic Rifle) team to provide cover to my rear from the crest.

I crawled down into the trench, which though shallow, provided cover from the direction of the sniper that had shot Sully. I crept along opposite to our platoon's positions—toward the place that the grenades were coming from. About thirty yards ahead the trench took a slight jog to the left; I paused and took a look around the bend to see what I could observe. I found myself staring into an open cave only a few yards away.

I waited for a few minutes, slowly loosening the pin from a fragmentation hand grenade. I had a good view of the trench now. It ran toward the cave and up toward our platoon's positions. I could see how the Chinese had been able to lob their grenades so easily at us and how our return fire had been so ineffective at getting back at them. For an instant I took my eyes off the cave entrance to survey the trench line running away from the bunker door. When my glance returned to the doorway I was shocked to see a person standing in the doorway, dressed in his quilted Chinese uniform holding a large "potato masher" grenade in his hand getting ready to loft it toward our platoon's positions.

The Chinese soldier appeared to be just as stunned as I was—when he saw me moving my rifle into firing position. We stared at each other in utter amazement for what seemed like ages! Suddenly, he jumped abruptly back into the cave before I had a clear shot with my M-1. Recovering from my surprise, like the neophyte hunter who freezes when he spots his first deer (referred to as "buck fever"), I emptied the clip of the rifle into the cave and lobbed in the hand grenade through the cave opening.

As the grenade exploded I quickly made it back over the crest to the safety of our platoon's digs. I felt relieved to be back over the top in the relative safety of our side of the hill. Strangely I also felt a bit relieved that I had not had to fire directly into the face of the man that I had stared at so long in the trench. The image of his face was still burning in my memory. I don't know if the grenade I threw into the cave had gotten any of the Chinese inside but maybe at least it would give them a headache!

More importantly, my little visit to the cave provided a more clear and effective plan for getting at the cave doorway. Our third attempt proved to be highly successful. Three of us made the attack, this time from the far left side of the platoon's positions adjacent to where the Chinese bunker joined a trench that had been visible to my observation before it was so rudely interrupted by the appearance of the Chinese infantryman. The plan was pretty simple. I volunteered to go into the trench first and toss two grenades into the cave; when they exploded, the other guys were to rush into the trench firing an M-2 carbine (which threw out 750 rounds per minute) into the doorway. Then we would all three enter the cave.

The plan was not perfect because we failed to take into account some basic laws of physics, but it worked well enough. The first part of the plan proved a bit more difficult than anticipated because of the concussion of the grenade traveling through the narrow trench. When I crawled down the trench to the left of the cave (which was deeper and narrower than I had experienced on the other side of the cave) the concussion from the two grenades that I tossed in knocked me against the wall and sent my steel helmet tumbling down the hill out of reach. When I recovered, my friend, Carlos Coleman, from Oak Hill, West Virginia, was already following the smoke into the trench and firing incessantly into the cave. As he approached the cave he received a spray of bullets into one of his pants legs from a burp gun from somewhere below. Fortunately all he received was some frayed trousers; all of the bullets missed his leg. When his ammo gave way the second rifleman, Tommy, who was later to die on the hill, took over.

The cave was quiet as our weapons fire ceased. We heard nothing from inside the cave and timidly entered into the cluttered room that was high enough to almost allow us to stand erect. We saw only some motionless forms that had once been human, now misshapen from the concussion and the onslaught of slugs from the automatic weapons barrage. The bunker was ours. The grenade lobbing into our positions was stopped at last. As we explored the cave we found a number of interesting things, particularly some unusual weapons. One of the souvenirs was an American-made .45-caliber pistol, perhaps a weapon that the Chinese had obtained from an American soldier (or it could have been a remnant of the World War II weapons that were provided to the Chinese Army). After I captured this weapon from the Chinese I felt that it no longer belonged to the U. S. Army but was really my souvenir. I did not, however, negotiate this fact with the government. Instead, I decided that I would send it home. About thirty years later I donated it to a museum in my hometown of Charleston for their exhibit on the Korean War.

I also captured a rather unusual rifle that I was later told was a Czech built, bolt-action weapon that was quite long with a long, sharp bayonet attached to the end. Unfortunately this weapon was later lost and I was unable to bring it back home. Also in the cache of unique weapons were a couple of burp guns (the favorite weapon of the Chinese and also of American souvenir hunters) and an unusual machine gun on a wheeled platform that resembled the old Maxim machine guns from the U. S. Civil War period. It contained several barrels around a central ring. Because of its weight and because it was non-operative we left it. Coleman also found a small personal diary in the cave that he kept. Many years later, I asked a Chinese colleague from Hong Kong, Fanny Cheung, to translate the notebook into English for Coleman. There was not much of interest or any personal information about the soldier in it. He was apparently trying to learn how to write and was practicing his writing in Chinese.

THE FIRST NIGHT ON JANE RUSSELL HILL

Our defensive lines were thinned now. As a result of the shelling we had taken a lot of casualties throughout the day. Sergeant Casper placed us in positions along the trench about twenty yards apart. In each foxhole, he assigned an American and a ROK (South Korean soldier). Our company had, prior to coming up the hill, received about thirty ROK replacement soldiers to fill vacancies. We knew little of what was going on around us beyond our position perimeter.

I was assigned to a foxhole with a young South Korean man named Kim, probably my own age or younger, who could neither speak nor understand English. I knew only a few words of Korean, and none of them useful in polite conversations or in important military communications. We were uncertain as to what was going on around us and both of us were anxious as to what to expect during the night. We watched the field to our front, not really being able to communicate well our innermost concerns as we peered into the confusing night of battle.

We were on full alert so neither Kim or I slept a minute all night. We spent the time scanning the slope in front of our foxhole for movement. Nighttime on the front was scary in the best of circumstances, but under threat of imminent Chinese attack with no one to talk to, it was beyond frightening. My new friend and I talked in whispers trying to learn something about each other's language and culture. Parachute flares exploded overhead in an almost continuous parade throughout the night, floating slowly to earth and casting eerie shadows across the battlefield below. We compared words for things you could point to in the frail light such as "flare," "rifle," and so forth. We also found that we had a common language in which we could communicate—math. We gave each other math problems to work and as it turned out, his skill at algebra was a clear step above mine. We were, however, not able to share many of those inner feelings that creep up on you when you feel cast in a sea of danger.

The ear-piercing whistling sound of incoming 76 mm rounds both terrified the infantry soldier and initiated a chain of reflexes that resulted in an automatic dive for safety in a trench or to the ground if no deeper sanctuary was nearby. One had only a matter of seconds to get to cover when the screaming sound was first heard. The shorter the amount of time one heard the shell's scream the closer it came. It is commonly believed that "You never hear the shell that directly hits you!" So we took slight comfort in hearing the sound and thus the ability to avoid its consequences. At least it was a warning to take cover.

The Chinese Katusha rockets, on the other hand, had a rather different sound and provided little warning (it was more like a "whoosh"). The most terrifying aspect of rocket attacks was the fact that they usually came in waves, a sequence of bursting shells along a line. The rocket gunners firing onto Jane Russell Hill had almost perfect and deadly aim on our trench line and periodically sent a salvo into our midst. The devastating rocket fire prompted our leaders to move the line to the reverse slope during all but direct attacks on the hill. This evening the entire force remained on the frontal slope because of imminent counter attacks. As a result we suffered a number of casualties from intense rocket fire.

At one time during the evening, the Chinese artillery also fired some white phosphorous shells (WP shells). This horrible variety explodes with a beautiful white/blue burst of flame that looks somewhat like a more sinister version of 4th of July fireworks back home. White phosphorous, however, brought no expressions of joy or awe from the close observers, only terror. Unlike shrapnel from high explosive shells, white phosphorous particles would stick to one's skin and could burn all the way through the flesh. The best way to put out the flame was to pack the hole with mud and smother it. I was much more afraid of white phosphorous shells than the mortar or artillery high explosive fire.

One artificially comforting aspect of the intense shelling we were receiving this night on Jane Russell Hill was the thought that as long as the shells fell on our positions we would not have to face a direct assault from the Chinese infantry. In the night when the shelling stopped, or rather was strategically moved to our rearward slope, we knew that an infantry assault was imminent and we became more watchful when things became quiet.

Our company mortar platoon performed extremely well all evening projecting flares, lighting the slope toward the valley. We were comforted, as we waited in our trench line, by the fact that we could see what might be coming up the hill toward us. The parachute flares gave off a strange, eerie glow as they drifted toward the ground. After a few moments another flare was sent aloft lighting up the night sky.

After what seemed like an eternity of waiting we heard the eerie sound of bugles playing in the distance—a sound that Americans learned to associate with a direct frontal assault by the enemy. The sound of shrill whistles could also be heard on the slope below, sounding the troops into desired formations. We waited, peering into the night at the shadows manufactured by the drifting antics of the flares winding their way earthward. We watched for the visible shadows to move and take form in the sights of our rifles. Finally I could see on the finger of the knoll below our positions the Chinese counterattacking force rushing upward toward our positions. The shadow figures came toward us, the bugle blaring, as our lines opened fire into the moving figures below. The machine gun and rifle fire from our lines must have been horrendous as seen from the valley floor looking up toward our positions. None of the Chinese soldiers reached the top. The shadowy figures disappeared into the night and we returned to our shadowy world to wait and see what fate offered next.

The remains of the night were spent in a period of relative quiet after their counterattack failed to unseat us from the hill. For the moment, at least, in this deadly game of "king of the hill," we were king—we would need to see what happened next. Early on the second day on the hill my job as a rifleman with the 2nd Platoon took on an expanded element as I was assigned to forward lookout duty. Before daylight my squad leader instructed me to go to a somewhat protected spot on the military crest (near the top of the hill facing the enemy positions) to look for enemy activity and to sound a warning to our troops on the reverse side in the event Chinese infantry engaged us. As the first light of morning began to provide a more clear focus on old Papasan Hill, the ominous mountain that peered down on our humble knoll, someone on my left detected some movement over 1,000 yards away in the valley floor and began to fire. As I looked in that direction I could make out figures moving stealthily across the front toward a ravine at the base of Hill 1062. I fired an initial shot (I had learned the trick for obtaining an estimate of the range to a target by placing a tracer cartridge into the chamber of the rifle; one could actually see where the bullet hit). The figures kept moving as the tracer shell struck against a rock in front of them, ricocheting abruptly in a different skyward direction. I yelled for others behind me to begin firing at the figures now moving faster across the valley floor and continued to fire at the Chinese soldiers. In a few moments a BAR man on my right also opened fire into the group of figures. Others who had awakened from their sleep to join in the action soon joined us. In a few minutes the entire section was alive with firing into the force below. In less than two minutes a wave of 60 mm mortar shells were also hitting the target when our mortar men got the range. It is very difficult to imagine how anyone could have survived the firepower that was soon laid into the small section of real estate at the base of Papasan. We did not see any further movement at or away from the area when the rain of fire trickled to a halt.

We learned the next day that some of the positions on our line had been overrun and other GIs had withdrawn during the night to positions to our rear. The platoon leader, a very well liked and trusted officer, was killed. We were later to learn that one of the officers in our company, a lieutenant, became so frightened that he could not speak and would not come out of his foxhole. The condition that he experienced is referred to in the field of abnormal psychology as a "hysterical aphonia" or a psychologically based inability to speak. He was only able to speak in whispers and unable to "give commands." After we left Jane Russell

Hill, he was transferred back to the rear. During his wait for a transfer he became the mailman, a low level of duty for an officer. His condition today would have been diagnosed as a Post-traumatic Stress Disorder (PTSD).

INCREDIBLE KENTUCKY WINDAGE OR A LUCKY SHOT

Given our success with intercepting and eliminating the Chinese patrol, I received a new assignment, officially this time, as a sniper. Another rifleman (a Connecticut Yankee named Mike Yancik) and I were sent across the top to a new sniping position on the military crest of Jane Russell Hill, a couple of hundred yards to the right of the position from where we found the earlier bevy of Chinese infantry. Here, because a finger of the ridge took a sharp rise then flattened in front of us, we did not have as clear a picture of the valley floor as we did from our prior position. However, we were in somewhat of a more protected spot from incoming fire. We also now had a good view of the opposite side of the finger and, of course, a broad perspective of Papasan that loomed ahead and over us. For most of the morning we laid motionless behind a rock that had a tree stump resting slightly on it. Because our position on this knoll was visible from Papasan, we were still somewhat vulnerable to sniper fire if our position were given away to the Chinese positioned on the distant heights. Remaining motionless was important as dawn's light turned to day. We waited patiently for some movement on the ridge ahead much like deer hunters might await their unsuspecting prey from a tree or a deer stand. The day dragged by without much activity. We watched a couple of hawks or vultures circle in the blue-sky overhead; we watched the sun trace its reliable arc across the noonday sky. This was a relatively easy life because we were escaping the constant digging taking place on our "home side" of the hill to improve our positions.

As we watched the ridge line on Papasan in the distance we noticed some movement about two thirds of the way up—slowly at first, their pace seemed to increase as the two Chinese soldiers moved rapidly toward the crest of the hill. The range was a bit too distant for an "iron sights" sniper to reach effectively. The figures running steadily up the hill appeared to be only an inch or so high on our visual field. I decided to try a shot and, with an air of confidence I said to Yancik, "Watch this!" In one quick twist of the knob on the sight of my M-1 I ran the setting as high as it would reach and raised the rifle to a position a few inches above and to the right of the first racing figure and pulled the trigger. This move was often referred to as "Kentucky windage" but it really was sheer guesswork. The sound of the lone rifle shot seemed extremely loud to us in our somewhat tight nest and we pressed ourselves against the ground all the while keeping our eyes on the quilted figures working their way to the top of the hill. In a few seconds, one of the figures stopped then tumbled to the ground where he remained motionless. Yancik yelled, "You got him! You got him! What a shot!" I couldn't believe my eyes. The man actually dropped. Could he have simply stumbled? No. He laid there inanimate for the remainder of the day.

There was considerable discussion around the company over the next few days about this rifle shot. I guess I just let it go because I was getting some pretty good acclaim for the deed, although, at first, I tried to say that it was just a lucky shot. But the other guys seemed to want to believe that this was an incredible, intentional shot. (If they had only known about the mediocre marks that I had made on the rifle range back in basic training then this reputation would not have gone very far.) But for a brief moment in time I was hailed as a kind of "Sergeant York" of Fox Company in terms of marksmanship. For all I really knew, the poor guy could have died of a heart attack simultaneous with my single rifle shot!

There was a downside to the acclaim that I experienced, however. It was shortly after this event that I came to be hounded by one of the other riflemen in the platoon to do him an odd favor. Al Dyckoft (not his real name), a somewhat uneducated if not outright stupid man, kept asking me to shoot him! "Shot me!" he would say, mispronouncing the verb. He kept pleading with me to shoot him in the leg—to give him a million dollar wound when no one else was looking. "Would you just shot me in the leg without hitting the bone?" he would say. We had all heard of the frightened soldier who shoots himself in the foot in order to get evacuated to the rear, but this was a new twist. I had difficulty avoiding him. He would find out where my position was and crawl to it with a very whinny voice and ask, "Shot me, please." He told me he had a wife and kids and wanted to make it back to Ohio. I had never encountered anything like it before and tried to ignore it. But, he kept coming.

Finally, I told him, "No, I can't do it. I'm not that good a shot and I might put it through your heart instead." He finally got the message that I wasn't going to shoot him and he left me alone. That was the best outcome for him because he had been working another angle to get off the front with Captain Vaughn. "Please let me be your jeep driver back in company rear. I used to be a chauffeur in civilian life," he told the captain. Fortunately, he was more persistent with the captain than he was with me and shortly after we got off Jane Russell Hill he was transferred to the Battalion motor pool. This transfer was best for everyone concerned; he was pretty worthless in combat.

SHORT SUPPLY OF FOOD AND WATER

We had taken with us on the hill two days of rations and water. After the third day there was no relief in sight and food and water became scarce to non-existent; we began to get very hungry. Because we had no communications to and from Battalion, we were unaware of the reason for the lack of supply. The Chinese had broken though to our rear areas, or had brought the approaches to the hill under intensive artillery fire, so that no supplies could be brought forward. Our hunger and thirst grew as time wore on and we began to scavenge through the packs of the men who had died. Another one of my buddies shared some rations that he had found in a somewhat bloodied field pack. This seemed like an unseemly thing to do, but rather necessary under the circumstances. I had some difficulty eating C-rations out of cans that had blood and dirt all over them but there was nothing we could do about it. The path to survival is sometimes an ugly one indeed.

The fact that we were cut-off from the rear also meant that we could not get wounded men off the hill. On the third night one of the men from our squad who was gravely wounded cried out in pain throughout the night causing frightening and terrible feelings of uneasiness among the others. There was no morphine to ease his pain. We listened to his anguished cries throughout the long night. Mercifully, he died of his wounds before the sun came up.

THE ABANDONED GOLD MINE AT THE BASE OF THE HILL.

The Chinese Army was well blessed with a labor force that was impervious to harsh working conditions—digging seemed to be their strength. The Chinese

People's Army included many men from peasant farms who were not unaccustomed to hard work. They dug enormous underground living and fighting positions deep into the earth. Some tunnels have been discovered on abandoned Chinese positions that could sleep hundreds of men. The Chinese forces developed a double system of tunnels. In addition to their main line positions they also constructed a network of tunnels behind the current positions in the event they had to fall back under enemy attack. The tunnels were dug deep into the earth, assumedly to be able to protect the troops from nuclear attack—a situation that they considered likely given the loud threats that had been made by General MacArthur and President Truman earlier in the war about the possibility of using nuclear weapons. The Chinese apparently took this talk seriously.

Once the Triangle Ridge complex was secured, an American patrol into the surrounding valley near where we kept seeing the enemy infantrymen made an interesting discovery—a series of tunnels including a deep mine shaft, a remnant of an old gold mine, beneath the Chinese hill. The Chinese had effectively operated out of these caves during the Battle for the Hills and returned to them during the daytime in order to avoid artillery barrages and air strikes. Needless to say, a demolition team from the 13th Combat Engineers soon placed explosives in the shaft and detonated them in order to close off access to these safe havens of future enemy operations.

AIR POWER IN THE BATTLE FOR THE HILLS

I have had little to say so far about the role of air power in the Korean War. We occasionally saw high-level flights of fighters or fighter-bombers heading northward—this was where the air war was largely directed. We generally did not see much of the Air Force or Navy. Most of the air assaults were made on targets far away to the north of the front lines. However, in this period of time we had the occasion to witness some of our airmen at work, close to the ground, with air strikes.

It was occasions like the Battle for the Triangle, when there was daytime ground movement of Chinese forces, that the fighter air war was most effective. Much of the tactical air war in Korea was directed against "assumed" targets where bridges, wagon paths, or trench lines appeared to be occupied or used by the enemy based on aerial photoreconnaissance maps. So often "Old Joe" was simply holed up in caves and tunnels deep under ground, safe from the blazing guns and napalm showers from the fighters or artillery fire. The Chinese infantry simply waited until cover of darkness allowed them to move about undetected.

The night skies of mid-September and October 1952 were a little different in that, from the air, ant size targets could be detected crawling around the slopes moving to or from home bases in caves on Papasan or the T-Bone. One afternoon from our trench post we watched with great excitement as a formation of four Saber jets made a bombing and strafing run against Chinese troops trying to reach the safety of a cave on Papasan. The jets made two passes on the area and the third time through dropped napalm into shadowy crevices along the valley floor—an impressive sight as the flames from the tins of jellied substance leaped into the air.

It was also during these close air-ground operations that the possibility of accidental strafing was a genuine concern. From the air, infantrymen looked somewhat alike and it might be difficult for a jet traveling at several hundred miles per hour to make a ready distinction between friend and foe. American ground forces carried with them brightly colored plastic panels to mark their positions and to point the direction of the enemy to the fighter pilots above. The air-ground engagements that I witnessed were generally effective and only on one occasion did I know of an accidental bombing of our forces by a Navy jet.

****

On days like those on Jane Russell Hill, there was often no clear line between Chinese and American forces. Old Joe would hold one part of a trench and we would hold an adjacent niche. Overall, we typically had more of a problem with long-range artillery fire than we did with the air-to-ground operations, in large part because these were rare and generally well directed. Artillery operations in Korea, like any war in which there is a stabilized main line, were a constant and dreaded activity. GIs quickly learn the difference between incoming vs. outgoing rounds and when to duck for cover. But, artillery sometimes misfires and short rounds are a constant fear for infantry troops.

After five days on Jane Russell Hill, three of which were without food, we left the slope down the same windy, steep grade that we had come up several days before—a number of us with shrapnel wounds that needed to be treated by the medics at company rear. The weakened state of the company occasioned some to question the worth of the week's expenditures in human life. This piece of barren real estate had clear nuisance value for the Chinese if not real military significance, sticking out the way that it did like a thorn in the side of old Papasan that towered so powerfully above it. Holding our little hills like the Russell peaks seemed as though we were challenging the Chinese at their strongest point—announcing to them that we can take what you throw at us and not give you this ground! The actual military value, however, was not apparent to the average rifleman.

We were relieved from our positions on Jane Russell and were noticeably happy to leave although the departure was not uneventful. We had to dodge through an area of the road that the Chinese artillery had zeroed in with 76 mm's. Once a squad of ROKs had made its way up the knoll to the trench line we hurriedly moved south, dropping to the ground periodically with the familiar sound of incoming artillery rounds. As we made our way off the hill, we passed a column of fresh troops on the way up heading for our old positions. We razzed them a bit as we passed warnings to them of all the terrible things waiting ahead for them. The truth was that we were very relieved to be off the hill and heading to the rear for a rest.

After we came off Jane Russell, Carlos Coleman and I became close friends and spent a lot of time together when duty allowed. Even though he was almost six years older than I, we seemed to hit it off well. After our little adventure on Jane Russell, and the fact that he was from Oak Hill, West Virginia, near where my family had originally lived, seemed to cement our friendship. I also liked it that Carlos was a pretty gung ho type. He was even more of a volunteer than most of us since this was his second tour at the front. He had been in Korea for about fourteen months when I arrived in the company. He spent nine months with the 2nd Division when the front was stuck down around Taegu, and he was with them when they pushed the line north of Seoul to where it stabilized. He volunteered to go for a second tour from the replacement center when he was rotating back to the States. When we returned to Sniper Ridge we hung out together in the trenches and once we even slipped off into town at one point (when we were back in a rear reserve) for a little excitement. He was game for anything!

****

When we came off Jane Russell hill and went back into reserve, our ranks had been thinned considerably and there were a lot more cots available than there were men to sleep on them. We only had four men left in our squad so other guys joined us—we had plenty of room. Our large squad tents would usually sleep eight to twelve guys depending upon whether we had a full complement and how long we were going to remain in that location.

Buckley, our platoon medic, sporting his newly developed spotted white head, was not assigned to a particular squad but usually took a bunk wherever he chose. He was so well liked (and everyone wanted to be good friends with the medics for obvious reasons) he could find a welcome place anywhere. After we moved off Jane Russell Hill, he stayed in our tent for a while.

Once settled into our tents, the idea of having some beer and laying back was foremost on everyone's mind. That evening our PX beer rations became available. There was plenty of beer because there were more cases of beer than there were soldiers. After the traumatic days on Jane Russell Hill we felt an overwhelming need to re-hash what had occurred. The spontaneous recapitulation of the events was aided substantially by the beer ration, which went down smoothly and appeared to mellow out the group. As darkness came, we drank by candlelight. We always placed candles on tin cans that were affixed to the high poles that held up the tall squad tent.

Buckley sat for a long time, deep in reverie, with his back leaning against the tent pole. As the evening wore on the candle tilted slightly at one point and melted wax began to drip off the candle, falling inconspicuously on his newly whitened head. After a time he recognized that there was a foreign substance sticking on his head—he ran his hand through his hair and, not realizing what it was, was shocked and complained out loud yelling with his characteristic stutter, "GGGGod DDDamnit!! NNNow mmy head has lumps on it!"

The author (*left*) and Carlos Coleman cleaning up some spoils of war after capturing the weapons on Jane Russell Hill, October 1952.

THE DISAPPEARANCE OF THE DELINQUENCY REPORT

The next day Sgt. Casper came to my squad tent and told me that he was happy with the way I had helped the platoon secure the hill and said that he was promoting me to corporal and, if I wanted, he would like me to replace one of the squad leaders who was killed on the hill. Surprised with his offer and feeling pretty proud that he had confidence in me, I readily agreed. I was a bit hesitant to tell him about the situation with the delinquency report on my records and the recommendation from the Repple Depot that I be reduced in rank to private for my misdeeds there. He told me to report to the commanding officer for further briefing.

When I found Captain Vaughn, the company commander, he asked me to come to the command tent for a meeting. He looked sternly at me and indicated that he had looked over the delinquency report that I had been given and the recommendation that I be busted down to private from my present rank of private first class.

"I have torn up the delinquency report you had from Seoul," he said, "and I am tearing up the recommendation that you be reduced in rank. You have been promoted to the rank of corporal at the recommendation of your platoon sergeant."

He congratulated me on my actions on the hill and said that he was proud to have me as a squad leader. He said that my promotion to corporal had already taken effect and that he wished Army regulations allowed my promotion to sergeant right away, but I would have to wait for three weeks to get the next promotion.

Then he added, "That is, if you can just behave yourself now that you are away from the front for a few days!"

I liked Captain Vaughn and we got along well. He seemed to have confidence in my ability as a potential squad leader and let me know it. A couple of weeks after we got off Jane Russell Hill, he was transferred to the Division Reconnaissance Company, known as Recon. This unit spent a good bit of time in the rear areas but occasionally was used at the front for reconnaissance—usually traveling in jeeps or half-tracks. Captain Vaughn called me over one day and asked me to transfer with him to the Recon Company. He indicated that he was trying to put together a special Recon unit and wanted to recruit some guys who were not afraid to take risks.

I felt honored that he thought enough of me to extend this invitation but I was reluctant to accept. I thought it would involve too much rear echelon duty and also I was a bit over sensitive to the fact that I had never had the opportunity to learn how to drive a car—something that might be required in a mechanized unit. I reluctantly declined saying that I thought that I should stay in the infantry. This may have been an enormous career mistake because the kind of duty could have been very interesting. But, I felt that the infantry was my destiny. My friends thought that my mind had drifted somewhere to the south side of lunacy when they heard my decision to stay in Fox Company.

Shortly after my corporal stripes were sewed on they had to be removed to make room for my new sergeant stripes. In just a few short weeks I had been transformed from a private with a proclivity toward trouble to a staff sergeant squad leader.

THE FIRST SQUAD

I liked being an infantry squad leader in the U. S. Army but I am afraid I had a lot more motivation for the job than I had experience or training for it at the time. But the guys seemed to accept me anyway. They were all older than me in years but that did not seem to matter to them; actually, in combat everyone looks pretty grungy so it is difficult to know exactly how old anyone is anyway. I wanted to be the type of leader that led by example rather than just bossing others around, and I vowed to myself that I would not send anyone else to do something in action that I would not or could not do myself.

I also decided that I was not going to give the guys a bunch of "spit and polish "crap but only the essentials. I was not always able to live by the last resolution because that is not the way of the Army.

Although it might appear so from the outside, American Army units were not alike. An infantry unit is more than the sum of its parts—more than just a collection of individuals. However, the unit, whether a squad, platoon, or company, takes on a distinctive character depending upon those components. An incident, an opportunity, a challenge can help to form an infantry unit's personality.

Our squad, with many new men, jelled quickly into a high morale organism that was "all for one and one for all." One event that I think served to develop our bond happened when our company was marching back from a brief stint on Sniper Ridge to the rear area and as usual we were hungry. Infantrymen are marked by excesses—they are either starved, sexually deprived, or in extreme danger. Extremes seem to provide the circumstances that generate the necessary glue for unit cohesiveness—and on this day we were extremely hungry.

As we marched along, a column of trucks from another company was making its way through our formation of marchers—two columns of men moving along both sides of the narrow road, ten yards apart. The trucks were not moving very fast.

One truck that crept along between our columns was filled with crates of assault rations. Two of our guys, without saying a word, leaped up on the vehicle and "borrowed" a large crate of rations. In a flash, and without skipping a step, the container was opened, with the aid of a trusty bayonet, and its con-

The author's new squad, November 1952: *Front row, left to right:* Watcott, Schoen, Daggett, Field. *Back row, left to right:* Pinkham, the author, Kenway. Photo taken by Dale Moss.

tents distributed to the guys in the squad with a few leftovers for others close by. In another flash, can openers appeared from our belts along with the trusty Army spoon and we went about the job of reducing one of our deprivations. The new guys assigned to the first squad seemed to hit it off well. The laughter, the lively step, and more than a few raunchy limericks were constructed for the rest of the march. Even the new guys, not yet tested in battle, seemed to feel a part of the group.

One of the best additions we had to our platoon after Jane Russell was another former paratrooper—Frank "Vito"" Field. Recently arrived in Korea, he was a transfer from the 11th Airborne Division. Fortunately, Vito was assigned to my squad. He was certainly one of the main reasons for our squad's combat

Dale Moss smiling as usual.

effectiveness over the next months and I am sure one of the reasons that I made it back from Korea. Other new members of the company included Ray Daggett, Don Schoen, and Del Kenway. They all blended well into the squad and made outstanding contributions to our success over the next months.

This squad became one of the most gung-ho collections of soldiers in the Battalion. Over the next few months any dangerous or questionable mission, through numerous combat patrols in the frozen valley, we were the first to step forward in unison to volunteer. There seemed to be a chemical reaction that occurred in the squad members that led us to volunteer to walk down one of the riskiest paths available in the Battalion. Those in Battalion and company headquarters were quite willing to give us the venues we wanted.

REFLECTIONS ON THE TAKING OF HUMAN LIFE

It is safe to say that when I volunteered to go to Korea, I gave little thought to the fact that I would be killing others. Obviously I knew that in war an infantry soldier is expected to kill the enemy. But, the admonition "Thou Shall Not Kill" was also well engrained. At ages seventeen and eighteen, I had neither the skills nor inclination to question the philosophical justifications for what I was expected to do. Without any clarifying discussions, I came to accept, but not fully understand, that it was not only OK to kill the enemy in war, it was expected.

It was the infantry's duty to kill others before they killed you or your buddies—that is the code of the infantry. If the code was broken, you faced extremely negative consequences—yours or your buddy's death or the humiliation of a court martial by your country. A poem I memorized in high school, Alfred Lord Tennyson's *The Charge of the Light Brigade*, frequently entered my mind because it resolved my dilemma by clearly pointing out my role:

> *'Forward, the Light Brigade!'*
> *Was there a man dismay's ?*
> *Not tho' the soldier knew*
> *Some one had blunder'd:*
> *Theirs not to make reply,*
> *Theirs not to reason why,*
> *Theirs but to do and die,*
> *Into the valley of Death*
> *Rode the six hundred.*

Other methods are used in the military and society as a whole to reduce the concern over taking a human life during wartime. The enemy can be characterized as subhuman or simply as targets. In Korea both officers and enlisted called the North Koreans "Gooks" and the Chinese "Chinks." Such attributions helped me to frame the enemy soldier as different and not human.

When enemy soldiers are seen a distance away through the sights of a sniper rifle, the bombsight of an airplane, or the computer screen for a drone, they look microscopic and less human. It is much easier to fire a shot at a diminutive target than life-sized people. I encountered this directly when I faced the Chinese soldier in the bunker right after Sully was killed. I quickly saw him as a real person, not just a target "Chink." Both the Chinese soldier and I hesitated before acting, but I recovered first and survived. He died.

Army chaplains were available to talk if a soldier sought them out. However, I was not raised in a religious family and did not seek such support. Instead I found comfort that I was still alive and able to continue on with my surviving friends.

Shortly after the war I attended and graduated from Guilford College, a Quaker school in North Carolina. I learned how Quakers believe that it is wrong to take the life of another, even in wartime. Both in the classroom and out we had numerous discussions about pacifism, as well as my experiences in Korea. I gained a great appreciation for Quakers and their worldview, especially their tolerance for someone like me with such different experiences and beliefs. But, even after four years at Guilford, I still believed duty came first for soldiers.

5

Life in the Trenches

A GREAT DEAL HAS BEEN SAID ABOUT TRENCH warfare in bygone eras. Prolonged stabilized battlefronts and sieges are not new and go all the way back to the beginning of mass warfare. Regardless of the war, regardless of the era, trenches hold many things in common for the infantry soldier—not the least of which are the constant danger, the filthy existence so inherent in trench living, and the incredible boredom at times.

One can find many reasons for armies engaging in trench warfare. First, some past situations of trench warfare came about because the armies pitted against each other were relatively equal in strength or determination, or both, and one side was not able to prevail over the other, thus a static or stagnant front emerged in a war of attrition. Examples include the Siege of Vicksburg and the Battle of the Wilderness in the American Civil War and the trench warfare in Europe during the First World War, to mention only a few.

In Korea, the stagnant front line trench warfare during the last two years of the war was seemingly by choice (our choice)—a stalemate determined by political decision or a political commitment not to go further to prevent escalating the war. The stabilized front resulted from our rules of engagement. In other words, we were in a programmed stand off. We were not allowed to go further forward; we were not allowed to retreat backward. We were stuck somewhere around the 38th parallel while the politicians and negotiators tried, seemingly in vain, to bring about peace. In this way, our stagnant trench war was different from past wars. Not better but just different.

The Chinese did not particularly like a stabilized MLR (Main Line of Resistance). Having a static front took away a major element of the Chinese People's Army's strategy of military engagement. Earlier in the Korean War, and in their war against Nationalist China to wrest the large country from Chaing Kai Chek's control, the communist army was a night infiltration force beyond comparison. They traveled at night in force and holed up in the daytime to avoid detection. Their formations and strategies were designed to infiltrate and flank or gain the rear of their enemy where they could do the most damage. They were effective in the early stages of the Korean War to break through American and ROK forces, move to the rear, and set up ambushes against relatively undefended units and personnel. The Chinese were able to trap entire divisions in their ambushes as the American forces disintegrated after their push to the Yalu River had weakened and over extended their fighting units. After the American and ROK forces were able to establish themselves across a broad front and effectively tie-in their flanks the Chinese strategy was less effective and breakthroughs were on a smaller scale. The stabilized war or trench warfare was more in keeping with Western tradition and allowed the superior firepower of the United Nations forces to be employed more effectively.

The infantry soldier was actually told very little about the overall plan of the war in Korea. The lack of general information really mattered very little since it was only what happened in his immediate front, his own small sector of the MLR that counted most. It mattered most whether there was enough ammunition for the task at hand and that rations were reasonably regular.

DEFENSIVE POSITIONS

The essential purpose of the trench works that zigzagged across the roughly 255 miles of Korea was to defend against assaults by the massive Chinese and North Korean armies that tried to capture strategic or desirable pieces of real estate. With fewer men in place it was necessary for the UN forces to defend with superior and effective use of firepower. Each section of the MLR was a citadel of armament—an arms manufacture's dream.

Fox Company spent a considerable amount of time on Hill 327 of the MLR in positions that overlooked the Yokkokechon Valley and several smaller hills. The Chinese held T-Bone Hill with the exception of a small foothold of the American forces. The American occupied string of positions leading out from 327 to the T-Bone included the outposts Yoke and Uncle. These knolls were platoon-sized circular trenches at the crest that were well covered with sandbags that could resist heavy shelling, a common occurrence.

Typically an infantry company would have an assigned section of the line and would, at any one time, have two platoons of infantry (about eighty or so men)—reinforced with heavy weapons such as mortars and machine guns stretched along the trench line. One platoon would be held in reserve to allow for a counter attack if the lines were breached by an enemy assault. It is easiest to visualize an infantry company's line defense if you think of two slopes of the hill: the forward slope along which firing positions would be dug in and usually connected by a trench; the reverse slope which was not in direct contact or line of sight of the enemy hills and would contain command and support personnel.

The weaponry was spaced along the trench line in such a way to have overlapping fields of fire. Every thirty yards or so there would be a Browning Automatic Rifle (BAR) or a .30 caliber machine gun—weapons that fired both rapidly and accurately at good range. Interspersed along the MLR were also 57 mm recoilless rifles and an occasional "quad or twin fifty," a set of two or four heavy machine gun that fired .50 caliber ammunition. These weapons were effective against troop concentrations, machine gun positions, and mortar positions. On some sections of the line tanks would be dug in usually in such a manner as to provide indirect fire but with positions in place to enable them to move up to fire directly at approaching enemy if necessary.

Below the defensive positions and covering the entire front was placed an important line of defense—barbed wire and concertina wire to slow any advancing enemy. Within and/or below the barbed wire GIs would place trip wires attached to flares and mines that might be set off by enemy troops walking in the area.

Also below the trench line and concertina wire, and some distance from the line itself, each platoon would set up a listening post or LP. The job of the

Yoke and Uncle outposts, near T-Bone Hill.

LP was to observe the approach of the enemy and warn the line of impending attack. The LP was usually a foxhole disguised and camouflaged so that the enemy would not determine its location. Often, the LP would be made up of four foxholes, in a diamond shaped formation, to provide 360 degrees visibility and protection. The LP would likely be wired for communication by a microphone attached to the platoon Company Command Post (CP) by communication wire. The men serving on LP would be rotated each night so that this sometimes scary duty would be shared. In the event of a major attack, the LP would be "called in" to the company defensive line.

The rear slope or the reverse slope of the hills contained the support troops. Any man in a rifle company, even a cook, was subject to combat duty. On more than one occasion the cooks were issued ammunition and employed in direct combat.

The reverse slope of the hill, usually out of direct firing range but vulnerable to mortar and artillery fire, were the administrative units of the infantry company such as the CP and the chow bunker. The CP usually housed the Company Commander and Exec Officer and the radioman and runners. The reverse slope of the hill also contained an offensive force—mortars. Both 60 mm and 81 mm mortars from the weapons platoon could cover the target area. Further back in the rear was the enormously effective Division Artillery.

****

Many units attempted to provide hot meals to the troops at least once or sometimes twice a day if the position on the MLR allowed. That is, if food could be brought up. At times, we were in places where artillery barrages preempted any effort to provide hot meals.

In some situations there were "chow bunkers" actually on the rear slope of the line. Hot meals were prepared and served to the men in shifts on the line. Even on outposts where the GIs were far out beyond the MLR some hot meals were served (see photo on next page). Being a cook in a line company was not necessarily an easy and safe job. Cooks were in as much danger from artillery shells and other dangers from the skies as anyone else. On one occasion the Navy accidentally bombed our MLR positions; the rockets hit the mess bunker killing a mess sergeant and two others.

The chow bunker held the heart of the company (at least as far as the hungry GI was concerned)—the cooks and the utensils needed to prepare meals. It was fairly typical for an infantry company on the line to provide two hot meals a day—usually breakfast and supper. The GIs would have C-rations for the noon meal. Breakfasts might consist of scrambled eggs or pancakes, or my favorite: ground beef on toast often referred to as "shit on a shingle" or SOS for short. Dinners often consisted of re-constituted mashed potatoes, some variety of beef, pork, or chicken, and a vegetable like canned lima beans—pretty basic cuisine but warm and nourishing. Many GIs would take their mess kits, fill them up at the chow bunker, and dine in the quaint atmosphere of their gun position or foxhole.

It was not easy to wash one's mess gear out in the field with warm soapy water, as the technical manuals suggested. Experienced GIs learned that it was

The platoon on Outpost Yoke having a hot meal in a protected area of the hill.

important to remove the food particles from their kit and spoon (all we used for eating was a spoon, which was usually carried on one's belt.) The eating utensils were cleaned with dirt. One would simply take the spoon and plunge it into the ground a couple of times and then wipe off the dirt on one's pants leg. The mess kit was also cleaned by rubbing dirt on it then brushing off the dirt particles. This way they were ready for the next meal. One learns not to be squeamish about the lack of cleanliness in the infantry!

****

Another important component of some sections of the reverse slope in some companies along MLR was the helipad—a clearing where Air Rescue Operations brought choppers all the way to the front to evacuate wounded. Medical evacuation efforts often would get severely wounded soldiers back to a MASH hospital and into surgery within an hour after they fell from shot or shell. The survival rate of seriously wounded soldiers was much greater during the Korean War than during WWII, largely due to the rapid evacuation provided by Air Rescue Services. A frequent sight in Korea was the little Air Rescue chopper with its twin pods containing stretchers moving to and from the front on their life saving missions.

KOREAN SERVICE WORKERS

Attached to our fighting units, usually stationed far in the rear areas out of artillery range, were the Korean Service Corps (KSC) personnel. These men were Korean civilians, nicknamed "Choggies," who performed much of the manual labor that allowed the GI to devote most of his attention to the enemy. The KSC workers were really a mixed blessing. On the positive side, they performed much of the backbreaking labor required in maintaining a defensive line along a string of high mountains. They carried enormous loads on their backs using their A-frames. The laborers were mainly farm peasants. The KSC workers could be seen in caravans carrying such things as water cans, food containers, ammunition, and so forth up the steep winding hills. Without them, the war effort would have ground to a halt. They would dig trenches and construct bunkers along with the GIs and repair roadways washed out by spring rains.

There were clear disadvantages in our reliance upon the KSCs for manual labor. Having this unorganized and uncontrolled force of Koreans in our midst, many from the North Korean areas and so close to our vital rear areas, was a harbor for spies. More than a few times it was necessary to pull men from the lines to hunt down renegade or phony KSC workers. Some of the men in the KSC were infiltrators from the North and provided information to the enemy. In some situations, enemy soldiers were mistaken for KSC workers and vice versa. During one battle, two men believed to be KSC workers were instructed to carry one of our wounded men to the rear area. The fellow awakened only to find that they were carrying him toward the Chinese lines. Fortunately, he had a pistol and was able to provide them with new instructions.

The nearness of the KSC camps to our rear areas led to the development of a black market close to the front lines. The Korean black market was a vast enterprise, selling to both civilians and soldiers. The goods for the black market came from a number of sources including unprincipled ROK officers who apparently sold off materials that were supposed to be for the troops. Mac-Donald (1986) reported an incident in which the entire contents of a ship being off loaded in Pusan Harbor was hijacked and sold on the black market. While some GIs appreciated the ready access to black market goods, others bemoaned it as a detriment to an effective war operation. Even so, alcoholic beverages from North America like Canadian Club (CC) were popular with the GIs, especially compared to the Korean alternatives. In Chapter 8, I describe how we outfoxed some black marketers to obtain the prized CC.

LIFE UP FRONT

Darkness on the front lines added a mixed blessing to the routine of trench warfare. First, there was clear safety from not being seen and one could walk about the skyline without too much risk of drawing artillery or sniper fire. However, the night also provided good cover for enemy troop movements so the chances of small arms engagements increased after nightfall.

The front was, at times, a comfortable place. I enjoyed some aspects of being a front line infantryman. There was, occasionally, a feeling of contentment, a feeling that we were doing something important, something that few others could do. I felt that we were helping the South Korean people and at the same time, when things turned out as planned, gained satisfaction out of doing the job well.

Moreover, there was usually no official "harassment" on the front—no field grade, rear echelon, officers to enforce a rigid "spit and shine" code. There was no arbitrary police call to pick up litter and no KP duty as there was in every other duty station. One could generally live a pretty slovenly existence most of the time up front if so inclined, as long as they did not alienate their comrades. It could even at times be peaceful at the front. Sometimes at night there was a dead stillness with only the cold wind and the blackness of the night sky to occupy our thoughts.

The bunkers we slept in, or dove into to escape artillery barrages, and the command posts on the line, were usually only elaborate sections of trench. Although they could be made pretty comfortable they were usually small and cramped sleeping quarters that were simply widened sections of the trench over which a couple of logs or metal poles were laid. Then other metal posts, usually those provided for stretching barbed wire, were laid across the logs and then covered with a piece of canvas such as a shelter half or piece of plastic to hopefully keep out the rain and snow. Then the canvas would be covered with several layers of sandbags (the more bags the more protection from artillery shell fragments) and finally topped with a layer of rocks or logs for additional protection. Usually the area around the bunker was piled with a couple of rows of sandbags to keep out bits of shrapnel and the ever-biting wind and snow.

Later in the war we received some pre-fabricated "bunker kits" that we called Lincoln Log bunkers because the resembled the toy building set in they had pre-cut grooves that fit together. These bunkers were usually sturdy and easy to put together. Once a set of these logs was in place and several layers of sandbags deposited on top the infantryman had a fairly dry and relatively safe hangout.

The American GI usually carried along an air mattress to sleep on, which provided a bit of comfort and some protection from the cold ground. When we were in stable positions for a while it was customary for guys to make bunks out of commo wire. This was a skill that the older guys taught the new men. This was very useful information to have because the bunks worked like hammocks; it sure beat sleeping on the cold ground. There was an art to making a good commo wire bunk. It was easier if the bunker had firm posts holding up the ceiling, as there often were, because there needed to be substantial support to prop up the bunker roof because of the weight of the sandbags. With a couple of strong posts one could simply string communication wire between them, somewhat like the hammocks on the troop ship. Otherwise, the steel posts used for barbed wire also came in handy in constructing the common wire bunks. Blankets were stretched over the door to make the bunker "blacked out."

We usually were provided small charcoal stoves (sometimes heating oil stoves) that radiated some heat in the bunkers; every couple of days we received a new supply of charcoal to keep them fired. There was usually a chimney cut into the roof to let out the smoke from the fires. Even though the bunkers were pretty drafty, the stoves gave off enough heat to warm up frozen hands and feet a few degrees. One of the greatest inventions of all times, I came to discover, was the little Zippo hand warmer that most of us purchased from the PX rations. A fill of lighter fluid would burn these little marvels for hours, at least to warm up a frozen sleeping bag when off-guard time allowed a nap.

If we were going to be in a set of positions for a while we got a bit fancier with our preparations and even added some decorations—pinups of attractive women from magazines were popular. An interesting decoration that one of our guys, Frank Field, put up can be seen in the skull and crossbones as an ominous warning on the approach to the outpost!

One of our riflemen in one squad was handy at cutting hair using a pair of medic's scissors. (This fellow was well received as a comrade because the guy that had this duty before him nearly cut off one of our friend's ears.) Naturally, our new barber's bunker had to be decorated with a makeshift barber pole and a sign that read "Bear Ass Barber Shop." Another fellow, from Kentucky, decorated his bunker with a Confederate Flag that someone had given him before he left home. Interestingly, this flag probably caused a bit of a stir in the Chinese Intelligence Corp when a reinforced Chinese patrol attacked our line and overran this part of the hill for a time. When they were driven back, they took the Confederate flag with them, probably assuming that it was the standard for the unit they had over run. The Chinese Army intelligence staff may have had some difficulty in identifying the Army unit they were up against!

The front of our positions beneath the concertina wire that lay stretched across the length of trench and for several yards below were piles of refuse thrown there by several previous contingents of occupants over the past months. The tin cans accumulating under the wire had a useful function in that they served as warning devices. We often tied cans to the wire to rattle if anyone brushed again them. If an enemy soldier crept up to the positions the cans would serve as an audible warning. One great disadvantage of having the refuse piled in front of the positions was that it served as a home for rats.

FILTH BEGETS DISEASE: HEMORRHAGIC FEVER

A frightening disease lurked around the trenches in Korea—an incurable illness in which the victim hemorrhages internally in a manner similar to what hemophiliacs experience. This disease, a type of Ebola virus, is apparently similar to those making the news in recent times with several outbreaks in Asia and Africa. Sudden onset, fever, aching, and bleeding of the internal organs characterize the disease. Hemorrhagic fever was not a hereditary disorder, but one that was transmitted by parasites living on rats. We were informed that many of the Korean trench rats carried these tiny mites and that they would remain on the animal unless it died. When the host rat departed this world and "cooled off," then the mites would begin to look around for other warm-blooded animals to chew on. The only other animals around the trenches were the unsuspecting GIs. We were unsure as to where this medical information came from but none of us was willing to test out the theory with our own bodies.

This bit of news may well have been started by the rats themselves in order to assure them a longer life given all of the loaded weapons lying around. No infantryman in his right mind would kill a rat and run the risk of its mites then looking around for a new home. Actually, one of the men in our company came down with very suspicious symptoms that matched those of this blood disease. He was evacuated and never returned to the company.

In Korea, rats shared an important place with the infantryman. Both the dog soldier and the rodent seemed, at times, to be at the bottom rung of their respective societies, living in trenches often together, and often competing for the same space or morsel of food. Rats crawled brazenly through the barbed wire to the front of our positions, sought food in our refuse, and took shelter in our bunkers—searching our gear for whatever they might use. Rats were more valuable to us alive than dead it seemed. So our choice was to get along with them or else face the consequences of the fever. As long as the rat was crawling some distance away one felt safe enough to send him or her into eternity. Riflemen would often take practice shots at them; I have known times in which a hand grenade would be lobbed at them. But if the animal was moving in close proximity to the soldier then discretion tended to rule and, grudgingly, the varmint was allowed to pass unharmed. In these times it seemed as though the critter had a knowing smirk on its face.

One night, one of my new squad members, while sitting across the bunker from me, watched a large rat crawling on the planking over my head. He raised his carbine and fired two shots about four feet above my head while yelling,

"Duck!" I dived for the floor just as the now dead creature fell against the post that I had been leaning against. Needless to say I was not pleased by his action—because I could just imagine that the mites were looking at me as a potential new home. In my string of expletives afterward I did, however, acknowledge the accuracy of his shot.

One of the most emotionally charged circumstances that I encountered during my stay in Korea occurred one night as I slept. During the night, a slight movement on top of me awakened me and I lay motionless in the low candle lit bunker until I got my bearings. As I lay peering into the dimly lit room, my eyes fixed something unusual on the top of my sleeping bag. I moved slightly and so did it! I began to make out the form of an extremely large bunker rat with its whiskers moving rhythmically up and down a few inches from my face! I felt a moment of terror thinking about those mites and I jumped, as best I could, yelling "AAAGH" in a strange voice that seemed unlike my own. The surprised creature was flung against the sandbag wall. He then scampered out of sight.

Of all of the troublesome memories I had to follow me after the Korean War, this one was the most powerful. After I returned from Korea, I re-experienced that situation two times. At some point during the night I turned over and somehow brushed the sheet against my face. I awakened with the intense feeling of anxiety, as though there was a rat crawling on me. In each instance I awakened with a scream and found myself slapping my head and shoulders in an effort to "brush the rat off of me." This phobic experience was actually "cured" when I was a graduate student studying experimental psychology. My graduate assistantship required me to take care of the animal lab so I got a great deal of exposure to the rats, certainly a cleaner and nicer bunch of creatures than the Korean trench rat. In addition, I conducted my Masters thesis on rats and had to handle them every day. This exposure served to decondition my aversive reaction to them.

A CRAWLY VISITATION

Human beings can acclimate to a broad range of sanitary conditions if required. The Army has many ways of assuring that the troops keep clean and dispose of waste in an effective manner. But, under combat conditions these measures may get ignored or at least minimized in favor of simply keeping alive. One soon adopts a "two valued orientation to life"—staying out of harm's way and acquiring food. Everything else gets put on temporary hold at times. One common affliction that seemed to seek out soldiers under these conditions was a pack of little creatures called crabs that appeared to enjoy being around dirty soldiers. The actual dictionary definition of this insect is: "Crab or crab louse is a sucking louse that infests the pubic region of the human body." The "sucking" designation refers to blood sucking. In the past, lice and crab lice apparently traveled extensively with armies and have been known to carry diseases such as typhus that killed many soldiers. Because we were vaccinated against these major diseases, the crab louse in our Army served as merely a source of irritation

The crab enjoys inhabiting hairy parts of the human body where it apparently finds security and sustenance. They are, in some ways, harmless little fellows in that I have never heard of anyone dying from them. However, I have heard of many guys infected with them wishing they were dead! Crabs crawl about, digging their many legs into government issued flesh (usually at night) when all was quiet. Those infected with these tiny creatures usually spent much of their time scratching, groaning, and cursing.

During this time on the line I too fell victim to those little varmints. I noticed at first only an excessive scratching in vital areas, which soon increased to the requirement of sudden and aggressive digging to alleviate the painful, crawly feelings. The light and sporadic sleep we generally received on line became even more fitful and interrupted as my new guests boarded in for the duration, they hoped.

An oft quoted cure for these creatures was as follows: The cursed GI shaves a strip across the prominent infected area, usually the groin; next they rub their body with some type of strong alcohol which soon gets the little devils drunk; the soldier then carefully watches the shaven strip while holding a sharp instrument such as an ice pick or a bayonet; then as the little guys begin their drunken crawl, the soldier simply plunges the ice pick vigorously into them as they wander out into the open. I don't know of any soldier who actually attempted this treatment but I do know how it feels to want to do so!

Actually, the Army does have a quite effective treatment for crabs—a powdery substance that the GI pours all over himself. The ensuing night is horrendous because the crabs appear to have one last orgy on the soldiers flesh, but they are usually gone by the next day. We do not know whether the powder kills them off or simply encourages them to find other residence (such as the guy sharing the foxhole with you) but it was usually worth the horrendous sleepless night that accompanies the medicine just to have them gone for a while.

CUT-OFF FROM NEWS BACK HOME

It was usually a welcome relief to be assigned a section of the trench that had a steep hill or preferably a cliff in the front. This made the section easy to defend and one could sleep a bit easier. In early November we were on a portion of the line near Triangle Ridge when Old Joe began to act up a bit. His probes of our positions were ineffective but he overran some positions on our left and effectively cut off our communications and supplies for a few days.

It was during this time that the American presidential elections were held back in the States. The Korean War was the central issue in the 1952 presidential campaign. The war had dragged on for two years with no end in sight with the peace talks being stalled at Panmunjom. President Truman, with the lowest popularity of any president (23%) since such ratings were instituted, decided against running for re-election (Bernstein, 1989). Most of us, though some were unable to vote because of our age, were in favor of Ike Eisenhower rather than Adlai Stevenson. We felt that our fates would be better in Eisenhower's hands, given his interest in things military. We felt that he would get us out of this mess or else untie our hands and let us win the war militarily. Korean veterans often consider themselves to have been twice forgotten. The first time was during the war, when soldiers at the front often felt that we had been "written-off" by society; the second time came after the war, when society repressed all active memory of it.

November 5th, Election Day, came and went. We had no word on the outcome because we were busy fighting the Chinese. Unfortunately, our first word was that Ike had lost! We were very dejected.

It was a full three days later when we actually found out that Ike had won the election! When we heard the good news about Ike's election we felt that the war would now be settled one way or the other. All we had to do was wait and trust Ike. He would either get us out or else give us the resources to win the war. But to our chagrin, there was no simple solution to the war and it would be many months before most of us would be able to lay down our arms.

****

At some point during the "Battle for the Hills," while we were on one of the hills near Triangle Ridge, I turned nineteen. Birthdays were not significant events under these conditions and this day was not marked by any celebrations or even recognition that it was somehow different from yesterday or the day before. We were not receiving mail at that time, so there were no birthday greetings to mark the occasion. Given the fact that I was somewhat younger than the guys in my squad I always tried to minimize discussion and reference to age. I certainly was not going to call attention to it and run the risk of weakening the authority of my stripes. They all thought that I actually was older than I was and I was not going to weaken their confidence in me by acknowledging my real age. My nineteenth birthday was just another day in a far away place.

FREE CIGARETTES: THE DEVELOPMENT OF AN ADDICTION

All through my younger years, even in high school when a lot of my friends were smoking, I never used tobacco of any form. Some kids smoked because they were rebelling against their parents and asserting their independence. I did not need to do this. I was pretty independent of adult rule. I could do what I wanted. Perhaps the major reason that I did not smoke during these years was that I did not want to call attention to myself as being a "bad kid."

I did not begin smoking during my early days in the Army because of my desire to go into the airborne. I realized I needed all of the stamina I could muster just to pass the physical tests. I didn't think I could waste my breath on cigarettes because I could see that the heavy smokers had a tougher time making it through the long runs.

But it was very different on the front lines in Korea, and my attitudes began to change about smoking. I started smoking cigarettes for several reasons. The biggest was the abundance of cigarettes no matter where I was. Except for the two or three times when we were cut off and isolated from our company, I received a pack of cigarettes a day, free of charge. Cigarettes, unlike other necessary supplies like warm socks, always seemed to make it to us. At first I gave my packs to my buddies. But life on the front was boring and bleak with no opportunities for enjoyment. The guys that smoked appeared to obtain satisfaction from it and frequently invited me to join them. Friends were always handing me a cigarette saying, "This'll calm you down." I observed others using cigarettes as a tension reliever. More than once, someone would say, "I need a cigarette to calm my nerves." Many of us began to smoke when we developed a "live only for the moment" attitude on the front. Why worry about our future health—we may not have any future! Cigarettes provided us with a momentary pleasure—there was little else to look forward to during those long nights alone.

At the time, I did not question how the cigarettes affected me or understand how addictive they are. Now I know that nicotine addiction shares the same pharmacologic and behavioral processes as cocaine and heroin (President's Cancer Panel, 2007). Then, I had barely heard about heroin, knew nothing of cocaine, and certainly would not have experimented with such drugs. Soldiers like me did not hear of doctor's concerns like Ochsner (1954):

How many of our World War II and Korean War veterans will turn up sooner or later at veteran's hospitals as heart and lung-cancer patients?

We had heard the radio proclamations during World War II that Ochsner (1954) described, but had not made the connection that was why cigarettes were on the front:

I am convinced that hundreds of thousands of non-smokers were inducted into the cigarette habit by the generous cigarette makers who patriotically proclaimed on the air their free gifts of millions of cigarettes to our armed forces.

My buddies and I at the front were part of a longstanding "vital market" for the tobacco companies, made clear in marketing documents released to the public as part of litigation beginning in the 1990s. Military recruits tend to be members of some of the industry's prime targets: young adults, high school educated, lower income, and minorities (President's Cancer Panel, 2007). Smoking prevalence in the military (33.8% in 2002) is substantially higher than the civilian rate (20% in 2005), suggesting military service is a risk factor to tobacco use initiation and continued smoking. To many, tobacco use is seen as a "right" and, until recently, free cigarettes (now replaced with low prices at the exchange) a "benefit" (President's Cancer Panel, 2007). My nicotine addiction acquired on the front lines in Korea was persistent. It took twenty years, and many failed attempts, to free myself from nicotine's hold.

THANKSGIVING DAY UP FRONT

Traditions are important to Americans whether they are lounging in front of the TV viewing a football game, receiving family guests, or sitting in foxholes watching for Chinese patrols determined to end our stay on earth. Every year, toward the end of November, we have to have our turkey with all the trimmings regardless of where we are. The front line trenches of Korea in 1952 were no exception, and the rear echelon administrators pulled out all the stops to provide us with a hot traditional Thanksgiving dinner even though the food had to be cooked in the rear areas, transported in thermal containers, and hand carried up some rather steep slopes to reach our remote locations. The traditional dinner was then made available to hungry troops who were willing to risk leaving a deep, secure trench in order to partake of the feast. The plan, at least in the case of my squad, worked miraculously. We took our turn making our way back to the company chow bunker and filled up our mess kits until they were running over— even down to the apple pie (no ice cream, though). This was the most rewarding thing that had happened to us in a long while and we felt pretty good that people would go to all the trouble to give us this little touch of home. We thought that this kind of miracle could only happen in the American Army.

FREE AIR MAIL

One of the perks, if you want to call it that, of front line duty was that troops got to mail letters free. We simply had to write our letter, seal it in an envelope, put on an address, and write on the outside "FREE AIRMAIL" where stamps are usually affixed. The main problem that I had with this great opportunity was that I did not really have anyone that I could write to—no wife, no fiancée, not even a girlfriend. I occasionally wrote a letter home to my sister and told her what was happening, but this seemed like too good a deal to waste on an occasional letter. One night, with nothing else to do while all of my buddies were sitting around the bunker writing letters, I decided to write a letter home to a couple of former acquaintances, to my old pal Bob Baker and a young woman acquaintance from high school who happened to live on my old paper route (so I remembered her address). I couldn't really think of much to say after the greeting so I simply wrote several lines of phony oriental script, just pencil scratches that sort of resembled what Chinese or Korean words might look like. I thought this was a pretty funny joke and had a good time writing the notes, chuckling to myself about what the recipients would think of receiving such a strange piece of mail. I have no idea what they thought of it because I never received replies. So much for free air mail!

TOOTHACHE UP FRONT

As if the steadily increasing cold and constant danger from periodic 76 mm rounds wasn't enough misery to bear, one morning I woke up with a severe toothache. The tooth had been bothering me off and on for a while, usually when cold air rushed across it or if I drank something cold; but the pain usually lasted only a few sickening moments. This time it was different. The pain seemed to increase with intensity and after a couple of hours it became all but unbearable. The platoon leader, tiring of my grumbling, sent me and a buddy off the hill to the aid station to get the tooth pulled.

We walked back to Battalion Aid station arriving there about two hours later but there was no one available who could tend to the tooth, although a couple of the dental techs there jokingly volunteered to get out their pliers. I was not in good humor and they, noting my grisly appearance and the loaded rifle on my shoulder, thought better of further attempts at humor.

I was evacuated farther back to the rear, this time by jeep. We had not been all the way back to Division Headquarters before and had I not been experiencing the pain the brief trip to the rear might have been a lark. We found a "so called" dentist who solved the problem by pulling the offending tooth (he did not have the facilities to do much else with it). Once the tooth was out we returned to the line; all the way back to company rear by a relay of jeeps. The last leg of the trip was made courtesy of the U. S. mail delivery. It seemed weird but climbing back up the hill to our platoon's positions I felt the strange sense that I was returning home. I realized at the time that maybe I was finding home in the Army. It felt good.

THE LAND OF THE MORNING CALM

The nickname for Korea, the "Land of the Morning Calm," was clearly a misnomer much of the time that I was there. There were, however, many times when this historic description of the country applied. Breaking dawn after a quiet night on the front was sometimes accompanied by good feelings. Even though the guns were never really silent for long and the tracers from night-time harassing fire a constant reminder that the night was not perfect, when dawn broke absent any action in front of your position, it felt fairly peaceful. One could allow one's imagination to run and collect one's private thoughts about pleasant past events or people and could dream of better times to come. But as the first true light of dawn began to ooze up the hill, the sight of the concertina wire in front of our foxholes brought the stark reality of the situation into clearer focus. Another day up front was at hand!

MORE ABOUT GUYS IN THE PLATOON

Self reliance is an enviable quality and one that is important for young men to pursue in order to fit into American culture. It is a characteristic that we, as a society prize; our schools profess to teach it; the adults in our lives promote it. In short, it appears to be a major goal with which we, in our youth, must come to terms. In some ways, the military and its organization continues to require these qualities but, in addition, presents a powerful force aimed at reliance on others—a modification of the lone wolf philosophy and development of attitudes that instill teamwork and unit cohesion. Living under harsh conditions in combat and having to perform duties involving more than one person underscore the interdependence of infantry soldiers on each other. Most of us who have experienced the military recognize that friendships are never so close or as absolutely necessary as those formed under combat conditions.

An infantry soldier can consider himself fortunate indeed when he is thrown together with a true soul mate, someone who is steady, reliable, even tempered, and with a good sense of humor to help one get through the terrible times. These are qualities that help one make it through the harsh and boring climate and the hassles of every day duty in the Army. The combat infantry soldier is even more fortunate when his buddy's qualities are also laced with a good dose of courage and willingness to stick out his neck for the squad. Sullivan was one of those persons who was fun to be around and trustworthy when the chips were down.

Another such person was Pvt. Emmett "Dale" Moss, from Missouri, who was assigned to my squad shortly after we got off Jane Russell Hill and moved to reserve positions. Dale and I became fast and unwavering friends until his death on Pork Chop Hill just before the armistice was signed. The remainder of this book is as much about his experiences as mine, because we were near constant companions throughout these times—good and bad.

When Dale first joined our platoon he was initially a humble and concerned person—he was fearful, as he intimated to me (a nineteen year old with less than two months of combat experience himself), that he would not be able to handle combat situations and hoped that he would not let me down. Nothing could have been further from the truth. I quickly became so reliant on Dale that I asked him to be the BAR (Browning Automatic Rifleman) for the squad, tasked with providing cover for riflemen when they advanced. Moss was not a tall person, measuring only about 5' 7". He was somewhat mesomorphic in build and had short cropped sandy hair. When he first joined our outfit, he appeared to be unassuming at first, wanting to do what was asked and almost apologetic that he had not been with us on Russell. As he became more comfortable in the unit, we discovered an "extra" quality about him: usually cheery with funny remarks to lift everyone up when we were having a bad day. He was outgoing and talkative anytime he was awake and his distinctive "Southern style" Missouri twang could be heard above everyone else's voice, usually cracking everyone up.

Moss would be in the right place at the right time. He had a knack for knowing the right spot to set up automatic weapons to provide the maximum support for a particular patrol action. He was "Mr. Reliable" and always raised his hand to volunteer when we needed someone to pull a bit of dangerous duty. We ran many combat patrols together and I became so dependent upon his strengths that I felt tactically and personally vulnerable if he wasn't there for some reason.

One of the guys from the second squad that often hung around with our squad was Ray Millsap, originally from Wilderness, Missouri. Anytime there was something heavy to carry or work to be done he, being a rather large man over 6' 2" and muscular in build, was handy to have around. He always managed to carry the extra ammo or the five-gallon cans of water that needed to go up the hill. He never had to be asked, he always knew what needed to be hauled and saddled up with it. Ray also liked to sing along when it came time for Billy Marshall to get out the fiddle.

Clark Gable was one of the South Korean (ROK) soldiers assigned to our platoon shortly after we got off Jane Russell. Of course, that wasn't his real name—he received this "American" name because of his unattractive appearance. (I don't remember his real name because we always called him Clark.) He was a squat and extremely muscular man who had buckteeth that protruded in irregular lines. Clark Gable was a good natured, outgoing, and friendly fellow who was an excellent worker in our platoon. Everyone liked him very much. The first time that I saw Clark Gable (we almost always used both names, as did he) he was standing obtrusively on the top of a ridge line on the front in his white, long underwear, vigorously shaking the contents of a DDT powder can all over his body. Apparently, he like most of us at times in the trenches, had become the victim of parasites. What a marvelous target he must be presenting to the Chinese observers, I thought. I ran up to him and screamed, "Get down! Get off the ridge line, you'll get yourself shot!"

He did not have the slightest idea what I was saying because he couldn't speak or understand English. I motioned to him to look and I ran through a pantomime about the likely outcome of his behavior if the enemy saw him. He smiled at me, with teeth sticking out everywhere, pointing in all directions. He smiled, saying in his deep guttural voice, "*Kaw mahp SOOM nee dah! Kaw mahp SOOM nee dah!*" Which I took to mean some kind of acknowledgment or "thanks!"

Everyone came to love Clark Gable, both the Korean and the American soldiers. Built like a Sherman tank, he was popular when large heavy loads of equipment needed to be carried. He always did so with enthusiasm and pride. Clark Gable finally did learn a few words of English, for example, "Numba hucking ten!" was used for describing anything bad and "Numba hucking one!" to describe something good or to indicate pleasure about something. He, like the other ROK soldiers assigned to American infantry units, considered himself very lucky. The food in American units was much better and more plentiful than in the ROK units, where food was often scarce as a result of misappropriation of funds to purchase rations. In addition, the discipline in American units was much less severe than in the ROK army. The ROK officers had the reputation of being extremely harsh and could shoot or beat a soldier for minor infractions.

One day when we were in the rear in reserve a few of the Korean soldiers were wrestling, an activity in which the Korean men seemed to excel and have great fun in participating. They were laughing and trying to get the Americans engaged in their sport. When they noticed me watching they began to chide me into wrestling Clark Gable, which I quickly declined knowing that Clark would throw me to the ground immediately and twist my lifeless form into some odd, embarrassing shape.

Finally after their persistent banter, I gave in knowing full well the outcome. But, I had one trick up my sleeve that I had seen in a Western movie some years before, and I hoped that Clark Gable had not seen the same movie. We wrestled for a few seconds and he, as one would expect in a class wrestler, headed for the high ground. As he did, I immediately fell backwards on to the ground pulling him over my head; with my knee in his stomach he went flying through the air, landing in the rice paddy below. The crowd around us was in an uproar. He dusted himself off and within thirty seconds had me pinned to the ground, roughly in the shape of a badly misshapen pretzel. Clark Gable was in great spirits with his victory.

Later that evening when the beer rations were tapped and Billy Marshall got out his fiddle, we decided to teach Clark how to sing country western music. Being affable and outgoing he was a willing participant and his horrible singing was considered to be at least on par with my terrible wrestling. We did, however, teach him a few lines of Hank Williams' song "Your Cheating Heart," but he simply kept repeating a somewhat hoarse and quite off-key rendition throughout the sing along. "Yo ree chee ting hardt! Yo ree chee ting hardt!" and so on.

HOEDOWN IN THE RICE PADDY

Billy Marshall, originally from Hillsville, Virginia, brought his fiddle with him to Korea. He spent many evenings livening up of the platoon's mood by playing around the campfire. The music was a great treat for all of us and we kept Billy busy playing late into the night—often by the light of campfire. He played by ear and in our way of thinking it was the greatest music we had ever heard. Most of the tunes Billy knew were country songs that would be popular on the hillbilly radio stations in the Southern United States. But everyone, northerner and southerner alike, city dweller or rural bumpkin, was alive with enthusiasm for the fiddle tunes and would sing along.

Dale "Ziggy" Barnhardt, Carlos Coleman's ever present sidekick and ammo bearer (see photo on page 239), did not have a lot to say much of the time. He was usually quiet and timid and could often be found sitting by himself playing a harmonica. He was friendly and kind, that is, until death overtook him on Pork Chop like it did so many of our guys. Ziggy joined in some of the songs with his harmonica.

Even some of the Korean soldiers, who generally kept to themselves, began to join in the fun. Private Kon Do Baull, referred to as "Moosemaid" (an American rendering of the Korean name *musame,* for young girl), was one of the more outgoing ROK soldiers in our platoon. He was so nicknamed because of a somewhat feminine appearing face and so friendly. He particularly enjoyed sitting around with the music playing. A lot of the songs were happy refrains but with an occasional tearjerker thrown in, stimulating melancholia among the singers. The singing was loud if not professional and had the effect of bringing the guys closer together. There was not a man among us that wouldn't have elected Billy Marshall to the highest post in the land for his ef-forts with the fiddle.

In late November, we received word that our Division was being replaced on line by another unit and we were scheduled for a long rest. This was a timely announcement because the troops, now thinned in ranks because of casualties and rotations to the States, were not functioning up to the capacity of a first rate combat force. We were informed that we would be pulled off the line for about a month and would be going far back in the rear for a brief tour of duty to assist in guarding prisoners that had been accumulating for over two years. The Buffaloes of the Seventh Division were leaving the front for a time, bound for a place called Koje-do—an island in the Sea of Japan off the Korean coast south of Pusan.

6

Tour on Koje-do: A Rest or What?

OTHER THAN POTENTIALLY USEFUL BUT TEMPORARY tactical information that captured prisoners can provide they are usually considered to be unwanted by-products of war. Infantrymen generally tend to see them as a sometimes necessary burden to move back to the rear and out of the way as soon as possible. What happens to them when they are evacuated to the rear is of no interest to line soldiers. By the spring of 1952 there were more than 132,000 prisoners-of-war, both Chinese and Korean, who were being held by U. S. forces along the southern coast of Korea. The information about the actual number of POWs on both sides is somewhat confusing. The numbers employed in this chapter come from several sources: *Army Historical Series*, 1989; Fehrenbach, 1963; and Hastings, 1987. These POWs became a major problem for the governments of South Korea and the United States, which were considerably more preoccupied with the military defense of the country and not prepared for such a large number of prisoners, the available facilities for whom were makeshift and overcrowded.

Some of these prisoners were kept in compounds near the city of Pusan, at the southern tip of the Korean peninsula on the islands of Koje-do (about twenty miles south) and Cheju-do, around ninety-three miles farther south in the sea between Korea and Japan. Not all of the enemy POWs captured in Korea were alike by any means. The Chinese prisoners were largely military personnel who were being held on Cheju-do Island. However, the Koreans, who were being held in camps in Pusan (mostly on Koje-do Island), were the most mixed and the most problematic. The Korean prisoner-of-war compounds were highly volatile holding facilities. The prisoners were mostly military men and women; however, some were civilians. Some were enthusiastic communists while others were strong anti-communists and actually anti-North Korean. This latter group included many South Koreans drafted into the North Korean Army service against their will. In addition to the military prisoners, there were some who were simply civilians who happened to get caught up in the back and forth movement of the armies. There were also some who were actually "free loaders," that is, people who had no connection to the armies but who managed to get detained in POW camps because of the steady meals that were served.

During the early part of the war, the POWs were held in large, somewhat makeshift compounds, which were essentially temporary, pre-fabricated Quonset huts enclosed by barbed wire. They were largely guarded by MPs, who have been described by some as cruel, and by some men who were essentially rejects from front line units. The administrators of these compounds made no effort to classify and segregate the different factions but simply housed them all together.

The atmosphere of these POW compounds, particularly the North Korean camps, was tense and trouble-filled and the guards were often insufficiently trained in prison management procedures, generally operating under poor supervision. The Korean POWs were problematic from many perspectives. Simply the logistics of having such a large number of people living in crowded, uncomfortable compounds was mind-boggling. Feeding, guarding, and providing medical care for such a large number of people was an enormous job. McDonald (1986) pointed out that there were occasional food shortages that affected morale in the camps around Pusan.

More problematic, however, was the great turmoil in the camps that existed as a result of the political upheaval and agitation by some factions. Some North Korean political/military leaders allowed themselves to become POWs in order to create turmoil in the prison camps and potentially to break out of prison to create havoc behind the American lines. The political dissent among the prisoners, particularly the existence of "youth leagues" and paramilitary communist groups, made for violent confrontations among different factions. For example, in one Korean prison camp, a group of men from one faction held a kangaroo court to try POWs who did not want to return to North Korea if the peace talks ended the hostilities. They executed a large number of people they considered to be traitors.

The prisoners in the more extreme compounds became more aggressive toward their captors. In order to attempt to bring order to the camp, a battalion of the 27th Infantry deployed four companies of troops inside the barbed wire with fixed bayonets. The POWs were apparently not intimidated and attacked with more than 1,500 men carrying makeshift weapons, sticks, and rocks. Initially, the soldiers attempted to stop the mob with concussion grenades, but these had little effect. The soldiers then fired their weapons against the crowd. A total of seventy-seven prisoners were killed and 140 wounded; one American soldier was killed and 140 wounded (Hermes, 1966).

In addition to these logistical problems and political undercurrents the prisoners-of-war became a major bargaining chip in the peace negotiations. This issue itself became a political football that delayed the armistice between the North and South for the last two years of the war. The warring parties could not agree on how to exchange the prisoners. The Chinese and North Korean governments would not give an accurate accounting of the number of prisoners held. There were 11,500 American and other allied prisoners in addition to an unknown number of South Korean prisoners. The North Koreans and Chinese were reluctant to provide information or allow Red Cross supervision of the camps that held the Allied or UN Army prisoners. Regardless of the harshness of the U. N. Camps, those in the North were much more severe; for example, out of 7,140 Americans captured, 2,701 died in captivity. Furthermore, the Chinese and North Korean governments resented the fact that so many of the POWs in American camps did not want to go back to these totalitarian regimes—more than 60,000 prisoners wanted to stay in the South or go to Taiwan.

This prisoner exchange issue held up the armistice negotiations for many months while wave after wave of Chinese and American infantry units assaulted each other along the MLR. In June of 1952, apparently under great instigation from the Kremlin, prison riots broke out on the island of Koje-do where the largest number of North Korean prisoners was kept. The prisoners lured the camp commander, an American general named Francis Dodd, into the camp. He was captured and held prisoner for several days. This provided them the opportunity to make great demands on U. S. negotiators and call international attention to the prisoner issue. In order to free General Dodd, the replacement commander, General Charles Colson, made a number of concessions to the prisoners and admitted some "guilt" about prisoner mistreatment at the camps that proved to be an embarrassment to the American military command.

By this time, General Mark Clark replaced General Ridgeway as the UN commander. MacDonald (1986) pointed out that Clark was a vehement anti-communist who was "convinced that communists only understood force" (p. 160). Clark initiated policies to bring order into the camps by segregating the various elements—placing those not seeking to be repatriated in different quarters and sending the hardcore Koreans to Koje-do and the Chinese POWs to Cheju-do.

General Haydon Boatner was placed in command of the camp at Koje-do. He was determined to restore order and to clean up the compounds. The new POW administration, tired of the problems that the poorly run camps created, established a firmer program of control. Discipline would be implemented by a "shoot to kill policy" (if necessary). For example, the Eighth Army Commander, Van Fleet, pointed out to his men, "I will be much more critical of your using less force than necessary than too much." (MacDonald, 1986, p. 160). In this effort, front line combat troops were used to restore order.

At this point, the military had the support of the government to reinstate control over the POW camps and a sufficient amount of money and military strength was applied to break up the camps and segregate those POWs who were making trouble. In developing a strong hand, General Boatner had called in the 187th Airborne to assure that the prisoners got the message that the camps were going to be controlled. The U. S. military's orders in clearing up problems in camps were more clearly oriented toward maintaining discipline and assuring the safety of our own troops than making the experience a positive one for the POWs. The reshuffling and better screening of POWs would go a long way toward establishing order in the camps. In addition, moving the civilian refugee communities back away from the compounds deterred communications between the people in the camps and sympathizers in the refugee camps. In all likelihood, this was how communications between the Soviets and Chinese officials were influencing those in the prison camps.

Although order was restored to the POW camps fairly quickly, the Chinese and Russians employed the incidents at Koje-do, particularly the concession statements made by the American commander, to create great international embarrassment. This was a real public relations victory for the communists in that the Americans were made to look sinister and cruel—analogous to the Nazis just a few short years before. Needless to say, Koje-do was not seen by any self-respecting infantryman as a great place to be stationed after all this turmoil and political fallout.

USE OF FRONT LINE TROOPS TO ASSERT DOMINANCE

In order to maintain stability and reduce the aggression against camp administrators by the North Korean prisoners, General Boatner made the decision to continue to employ combat tested infantry troops to quiet the compounds and prevent the recurrence of riots. Initially the duty at the prison compounds was presented to the infantry troops as well deserved rest because they would be at least out of the range of artillery fire. However, over the nearly four weeks that units were assigned to prison duty, the troops came to dislike the tasks they were involved in such duty as guarding military installations and work details, inspecting (raiding) compounds, and walking guard along the enclosures. Many GIs looked forward to a return to the front after their sojourn to Koje-do or Cheju-do.

As far as this sort of duty goes, American infantrymen were not very well prepared for it and many of them came to prefer front line combat duty to the "softer" duty on Koje-do, particularly because they got more points to count toward their rotation home. Techniques of assuring camp security, crowd control procedures, policies of prisoner treatment under the Geneva Conventions, military law and justice pertaining to human rights, the role of the Red Cross inspectors in maintenance of responsibility, and so forth were not a part of the typical infantryman's training or experience. In short, most soldiers did not know anything about running or guarding prisoners. Infantry soldiers assigned to guard prisoners were usually given some brief guidance and warnings not to fraternize with the prisoners. Soldiers were especially warned to keep a good distance from them because they could be very dangerous indeed. Guards had been killed or injured by prisoners who appeared to be very effective at smuggling in or manufacturing weapons.

MORE RIOTS IN DECEMBER OF 1952

The 7th Infantry Division was replaced in their positions on the MLR by a "fresh" division and was ordered to Koje-do and Cheju-do to restore order. This duty was considered to be a "prize" because the 7th Division had been engaged in a very difficult war zone for a long time and had served with distinction. Our unit pulled back from the MLR to a reserve position for a few days of rest, a welcome clean up, and refitting with new uniforms and equipment. Preparations were being made to move our Regiment to the southern tip of Korea and new duty for a month.

Along with my new sergeant's stripes came some different responsibilities that I had not counted on and for which I was generally ill prepared—teaching classes to the troops. The instructional role of the NCO's duty was new to me but I was assigned the task of providing some lectures and practical training on several topics relevant to our duties.

The first lecture I was assigned to deliver for the new troops, who were streaming in to our company to replace those we had lost, was "How to conduct night patrols." This was a very practically oriented talk on a subject with which I had, by now, become quite familiar. I simply talked (not in a school bookish fashion) but in a one-on-one manner as if I was going out in the valley with them that night. Because there were no manuals available on the topic, I tried to provide a clear image of what they needed to do to stay alive on combat patrols. This was a topic for which they showed a lot of interest. They were given tips on how to get ready for a patrol, how to dress, what to take, what not to take, how to conduct one's self in the valley to avoid danger, and so forth. There were also a lot of questions that fleshed out my outline. This "lecture" was actually fun and I thought it provided some useful information to the new men; they wanted to hear specifics about what would be expected of them when the unit returned to the front in a few weeks.

When we were given our orders to prepare to leave for Koje-do, we had a week's time to prepare the troops for the duties they would be expected to fulfill. The new CO, Lieutenant Brandenberg, called me into his tent and handed me a couple of small Army technical pamphlets. One dealt with bayonet drill and the other with crowd control techniques. He put me in charge of training the company on these procedures. This was not something that I had been exposed to in my training, so in order to get up to speed on the procedures, I had to stay one jump ahead by reading the Army technical tracts and preparing for the topics by walking through the drills in my tent until I had them perfected. I believe it was something like learning dance steps—an activity that I had never attempted before, being somewhat cloddish as a youth. These written materials were actually quite graphic in that their drawings clearly spelled out the maneuvers and tactics.

In getting ourselves ready for Koje-do and our unknown tasks, we were determined that the communist belligerents were not going to take any of our guys prisoner nor were they going to hurt anyone from the 7th Infantry. We considered ourselves a tough bunch of guys, capable of taking care of ourselves. Frontline soldiers usually develop a somewhat cynical and defiant attitude—an unwillingness to take much nonsense from anyone. This attitude can be summarized as "I don't much care about this crap! What are they going to do to me—send me to Korea?"

TRAVEL TO KOJE-DO: A BIT OF LUCK AT CARDS

Army transportation is seemingly planned by the military to be sluggish, inefficient, and exceedingly boring in order to prepare soldiers to be happy and enthusiastic with the crappy tasks that they have in store for them when they arrive. There are, however, many ways that troops develop to try and foil the Army's plan to bore them into despair and dint their future enthusiasm by actually having fun during transport. There was a lot of time to pass because the train and ship trip to Koje-do would take three days.

Life on a troop transport, especially one that was as crowded as this one was, definitely met the Army's criteria of dull, boring, and unpleasant. In order to cope, playing cards became our number one preoccupation. The game of hearts was for those without money; poker and black jack for the rest. I had a few dollars to start the trip and found myself with a bit of luck at the blackjack games along the way. I wound up with several hundred extra bucks and a nice pair of Japanese made 10 x 50 binoculars. This seemed to me to be a good way to start our temporary duty assignment.

The peaceful sleep we were beginning to receive at night was a novel experience for us. It had been some time since most of us had known uninterrupted sleep—sleep without incoming "mail" (as exploding artillery shells were often called) or the chatter of a machine gun jarring us into the stark recognition of war. Front line duty makes light sleepers of everyone. In a few days, the hollow, sunken expressions (often referred to as "thousand-yard stares") that seem to characterize front line troops had given away to lighter and more pleasant countenances. The grim looks were beginning to fade.

DUTY ON KOJE-DO

Koje-do, a large island located about twenty miles south of Pusan in the Sea of Japan is described in travel brochures as one of the loveliest garden spots in South Korea. Before the war it had been a fishing community; since the end of the Korean War it has become the center of the giant ship building industry in Korea. Historically, the island had always had a nautical theme. It had been the site of a naval base for centuries, and since 1905 until the end of the Second World War the island had been a base for the Japanese Imperial Navy.

Koje-do was relatively untouched by the Korean War that had been raging on the mainland. It experienced little of the bombing and foreign troop movement through it as had the northern parts of South Korea. However, the people in the small civilian communities, refugee camps, or towns located around the island suffered a great deal from various shortages that accompany large-scale wars.

All of our briefings on the kinds of situations we would likely find on Koje-do rang pretty true. As noted by their press coverage some of the prisoners were indeed a very difficult lot to deal with. Although there had been some efforts to break up the most troublesome factions into smaller compound units this was only partly successful. Of several smaller compounds that our men were assigned to guard two of the buildings were particularly difficult. Even the women prisoners were considered unruly and dangerous. Among our charges was one compound of women prisoners. There had been a number of reported incidents in which women had stabbed American guards after having lured them to the fence with an offer of sexual favors. Our guys guarding the women's compound experienced hostile jeering and taunts on a daily basis. On one occasion, one women in the compound lured a GI close to the wire and threw a batch of feces at him. Such gross activity on their part did not promote much in the way of amorous interest in them from our guys.

Our units were required to supply manpower for several types of guard duty in the management of the compounds on Koje-do. The enlisted men below the rank of corporal were required to pull regular guard duty around the camps in several capacities. This involved walking posts, standing guard tower duty along the barbed wire enclosures, and guarding work details. NCOs did not pull guard detail in the same way as the privates, but managed and supervised guard details, a clear advantage of having made sergeant! Being now a tech sergeant, I was assigned to such duties as Sergeant of the Day, manning guard post phones, and inspecting guards at the various compounds. For this latter duty, the sergeants usually were assigned a jeep driver and they made their rounds several times a shift. Some of these duties required hanging around the Company Command Post during my hours. Being a fairly new NCO I had not gotten accustomed to post type duty and administration details although the officers in the company were pretty supportive of my rough spots. One duty outside the company area that was usually more interesting was the work detail. On these assignments the NCO would be in charge of a squad of armed GIs assigned to guard work details, often about thirty prisoners who would off-load freighters in the harbor, much as we had seen as we entered Koje-do port.

There were some unpleasant duties that GIs did not particularly like. One involved supervising the emptying of the "honeybuckets." Each morning a prisoner detail would line up with their famous Korean honeybuckets, which were large pots of human waste that accumulated in the compounds over the night. The honeybuckets were usually taken to local farms where the contents were used for fertilizer. Yes, Korean farmers used human excrement to fertilize their crops.

Another distasteful aspect of duty at Koje-do involved having to perform searches of the compounds at night. The idea here was to disrupt and defuse potential riots by eliminating weapons that kept showing up in the barracks. The patrol unit would usually operate somewhat as follows: Two armed men would stand guard by each of the two doors leading into the hootchie or sleeping quarters. Two men would enter the sleeping quarters, armed with their weapons in the ready position. One of the men also carried a high powered portable light that he would shine around the room to watch for any suspicious activity; that is, people not sleeping but engaging in meetings (such as kangaroo courts). This might seem to be an unnecessary show of force; however, it needs to be kept in mind that a number of guards had lost their lives and several officers had lost their careers in these camps so far. We did not want to have such outcomes in our unit. The compound raiding could be stressful at times even though we were always armed when we entered the fenced areas.

One night, because of suspicious activity in one of the compounds, we were ordered to conduct a raid after the prisoners had bedded down for the night. We went into the compound with six men, leaving Bill Estes with a machine gun mounted on a jeep outside the compound to provide support and cover for the raiding party. This night as we approached the barracks door that we planned to raid, one of the prisoners was seen milling around the shadows near the doorway. Suddenly he rushed at me yelling something loudly in Korean. He lunged at my weapon and I reacted quickly by hitting him across the face with the butt of the rifle and bringing the barrel to rest near his head as he fell to the ground. We held him in check while the raiding party entered the barracks—a long Quonset hut with a pathway down the center and elevated floors on either side for sleeping. We yelled (with the assistance of our ROK interpreter) for the men inside to "Move outside! Line up!" Our suspicions that there were problem activities in the compound were being confirmed.

The entire barracks emptied quickly; none of the Koreans seemed to be sleeping prior to our arrival. Once the sleeping billet was emptied, our search team conducted an extensive search of the quarters while the POWs were kept in a formation outside the barracks. The contraband that we discovered in the barracks was incredible. The raid turned up knives, sharpened sticks, scissors, long pieces of chain, ropes, even a partly manufactured hand gun—all implements that might be used in an escape or on assaults against other prisoners or guards.

As we were standing in front of the doorway packing up the contraband, one of the North Korean leaders, a very articulate and well-spoken man, came up to us from the formation and told us that the man who had rushed up to me or "scared" us would like to apologize for his actions. He reportedly was having a nightmare when he rushed at us!

****

In dealing with the prisoners in the camp, our rule was to try to be firm but fair. Never backing down but not making unreasonable demands on them. The Red Cross had surveillance teams posted at the camps to observe activities and oversee the maintenance of order, and to assure that the prisoners were well treated. This overseeing function had apparently increased since the riots in June and the toughening of discipline in the camps. We often felt that the Red Cross was hampering our performance in that we were limited in what we could do to defend ourselves. It was rather frightening going into the compounds and every time we went in we ran the risk of being overpowered and killed.

The situation that occurred in our compound on this evening was one that called for some prompt, aggressive action and an extensive search of the barracks. As required by international rules, Red Cross observers undertook an inquiry the next day into our actions. No violations were brought against our team or me. A Red Cross observer quietly cautioned us against the use of force on the prisoners in the future. We received a very different message—one of congratulations—from our company commander and the compound commander for our prompt and effective action.

Apart from the POW camp on Koje-do, the island itself was incredibly beautiful, with steep granite cliffs plunging into the sea and silent, scenic hills overlooking the beaches stretched below. A jeep ride to some remote parts of the island provided a grand perspective of the island's unique beauty—and a welcome respite from the front line action and aggravations of the POW camp. Even though we were well behind the Chinese and North Korean front line positions we still carried our weapons. We had been warned that there were likely enemy infiltrators living in the villages in a continuous effort to stir up trouble for the Americans over the prisoner issues that were being bandied about at the Panmunjom peace talks.

FRIVOLITY CAN BE DANGEROUS TOO

Apart from the raids that we were required to conduct into the compounds about every third night, Koje-do could be pleasant. It was particularly good not to have the incoming artillery and the night patrols into the frozen valley to contend with. It was also nice that we were getting three square meals a day and regular PX rations. We saved up our beer privileges for a few days and have ourselves a beer party when our squad and a few other close friends such as Ray Millsap, Bob Huggins, Ziggy Barnhardt, Charlie Otto, Don Zimdahl, and Ron Grasshold were off duty for the night. Several of the men, who had been detailed for a few days to guard a radar installation in the mountains, returned so it was considered to be a very good time for a party.

The night was as dark as anyone of us could remember. Moss and I were running from the PX tent back to our squad area where the friendly gathering was planned. We each were carrying a twenty-four can case of Blatz beer as we jogged quickly along the familiar path toward the squad tent. I was in front with Moss coming just behind me softly singing something about "Ninety-nine bottles of beer..." when I ran head long into one of the guys from the machine gun squad, Zimdahl (aka, Zimmy), who was running swiftly down the path from the other direction to get his mail. We hit head on with an enormous crash! My case of Blatz went flying over Zimdahl and down the incline

Left to right: The author, Dale Moss, and Ray Millsap on Koje-do Island, December, 1952.

of a small bank and Zimdahl crashed to the ground with me sprawled on top of him. Zimmy and I lay on the ground moaning, rubbing our heads vigorously while Moss was impatiently wanting to tap into the beer but rather much enjoying the crash scene. I had a headache for two days, not entirely from the beer, and Zimmy had a sore head, one black eye, and the distinct possibility of a broken jaw from the initial impact and the subsequent tumble to the ground. Sometimes it was more dangerous to party than to go out on combat patrols!

These evening blasts usually provided a lot of fun and more than their share of practical jokes. One evening, a couple of the guys decided to shave one of our Puerto Rican friends, a machine gunner named Munoz, when he passed out from drinking. The shaving was not, however, complete since they only cut off half of his full mustache. When he awakened to discover that half of his pride and joy had been removed he became angry and went looking for the fellows that did the evil deed. Even though Munoz was slight in build he was a tough case and no one was willing to own up to the deed. Later in the war Munoz demonstrated just how tough he could be when the chips were down. However, this time he had to limit his expression of displeasure to verbal complaints against unnamed offenders.

REINFORCEMENTS ARE NOT ALWAYS WELCOME: AN OFFICER WITH WEIRD HABITS

We received a new replacement officer in the company while we were on Koje-do who was assigned as the platoon leader for the third platoon. He was quite a colorful figure though not very popular with the troops because of his picky, unrealistic orders and his ready selfishness. Moreover, the men could see through his phony bravado and were worried about his behavior and what he would be like when our company returned to the front lines. (Overly zealous or reckless officers were very unwelcome on the front.) On the surface, he cut a dashing figure among the officers. He sported two very beautiful and flashy pearl handled revolvers, which gave him somewhat the outward appearance of a younger General Patton. These weapons, as beautiful as they were, were not government issue but rather a gift from someone before he left the States. They were also not very functional in that revolvers are a bit too slow and finicky for effective combat service.

The lieutenant also seemed odd in the way he talked about going into combat, often with a strange look in his eyes. He also had a bad nighttime habit. Late at night, when most people were sleeping, he could be heard playing with his pistols, aiming and clicking them incessantly. He talked a lot about going up to the front and expressed a good bit of bravado about seeing action. He really gave us the willies, and soon became the butt of jokes among the enlisted men.

The lieutenant also placed a great deal of distance between himself and the other officers who appeared to view his actions with a great deal of suspicion. He really had no friends in the unit, a difficult situation to be in given the nature of war and the basic need for men to rely upon others in such times.

A JOURNEY TO A REMOTE VILLAGE

One of the ROK soldiers in our platoon, a pleasant and hard working soldier named Lee, was originally from Koje-do and still had family living on the island. He came to me during our first few days on the island and asked if he might receive a pass to visit his family who lived in the interior. Lieutenant Brandenberg had mentioned in an earlier meeting that it might be possible for some of the men who lived there to get a pass to go home. I arranged the pass with the CO having confidence that Lee would return on time. I was not disappointed; Lee came back in a good mood and was very grateful for his pass.

A few days later Lee came back and said that he would like to have another visit but this time he would like to take me with him to the village as well. I thought about it for a few days and raised the question with our new platoon leader, Lieutenant Feiner. He did not hesitate but agreed to give me a pass because I had been pulling a lot of extra details lately. He cautioned me to be sure and go armed because there had likely been a number of escapes in the past and I needed to take precautions in the event we encountered escaped POWs.

The next afternoon Lee and I started our long walk into the mountains of Koje-do. We carried packs filled with rations, cigarettes, candy, and other supplies from the PX for his family in the village. The trail into the hills was winding and long, through ravines with flowing streams, and up steep inclines that appeared to be less well traveled footpaths. The journey inland made me think of the images conjured up in Hilton's novel The Lost Horizon, with scenes reminiscent of the mystical, remote, and beautiful Shangri-La.

Getting to the mountain village was no small task. I suppose this is what being remote means. I was enjoying the scenery en route even though we were now in the dead of winter. The air, even in the southern part of Korea, was cold and crisp. The countryside reminded me, in some respects, of my home state of West Virginia with its hills and valleys. We traveled mostly in silence, given Lee's limited English and my total lack of Korean language skills.

Our trek through the mountains was interrupted with occasional thoughts about possible enemies hiding in brush or crevices in the rocks that we passed along the way. We did not, however, go out of our way to explore these potential hideouts or seek danger. Our goals and mission at the moment were to avoid those unpleasant elements and go inland to a peaceful island hideaway. Though long and tiring, the journey was uninterrupted by any trouble of human making. I could tell that we were near our destination when Lee's pace quickened and his countenance changed to one of joy and anticipation. We were finally at Shangri-La.

Like the landscape I hiked, the village reminded me of West Virginia and the coal mining towns of my childhood. It was not really a town, but a collection of a few houses nestled into the hills. Most of the people living there were somehow related to each other, but I could not always understand the connection.

The houses were interesting in terms of their efficient construction. They were small homes with one or two rooms and a wooden floor over which a straw mat served as a carpet. For sleeping, blankets were then placed over the straw matting. Each house seemed as though it was built on top of a stone furnace. Actually, the houses were built so that a series of "ondols" or flues under the floor of the house, in the winter, could be fired up and the floor would become quite warm to the touch. I thought that this was an ingenious and highly efficient way to build and heat their homes.

Several friendly women and children came out of one of the houses into the yard to greet us. Lee's wife, an attractive woman who was holding on to a young boy about four years old, warmly embraced him. They talked for a while, almost oblivious to the tall American standing somewhat awkwardly off to the side. An elderly man, who had been squatting by the side of the road, in a fashion that was common for people in Korea, came over to Lee and made a greeting. Lee appeared to be very subservient to him, not because he was a relative (which he was not) but because of his age. He had passed his sixtieth birthday, called *hwan-gap*, an especially important milestone because it completes a traditional zodiac cycle.

Even though none of the villagers spoke English, it was clear that they were happy to meet an American soldier. The villagers were grateful for the presence of the American forces in their country. Lee introduced me to his cousin, Myon-Hee, a widow of an ROK soldier killed only three months after their marriage. She sat next to me at the large family dinner and showed me how to use chopsticks. There were about a dozen of us sitting on the floor. We sat for what seemed like hours—until my back nearly collapsed from sitting in this uncomfortable position. American backs, I became convinced, were not well suited for Korean ceremonial dinners.

The meal consisted of several courses including soup, rice, and many spicy dishes made from meat and vegetables. I was wary of some of the foods served, and not just because of my limited West Virginia tastes. I could hear the warnings from the Army's "while in Korea" lectures given during our layover in Japan. We were cautioned not to eat raw fruits and vegetables because they might contain germs. Even more troublesome were my memories of the smells from the "honeybuckets" carried by farmers on their A-frames—a most unpleasant reminder that Koreans use human excrement for fertilizer.

It was a balancing act—I didn't want to offend my new friends, but I needed to protect my stomach. I decided that no germs could possibly live in kimchi, a pungent, spicy relish that was available throughout the meal and a favorite of everyone but this West Virginian. I tried to like this dish, but it was pretty harsh on a palate that had grown very accustomed to C-rations such as canned hamburgers and pork and beans.

I could not make out anything about their conversation during dinner. It was difficult for anyone to explain. We just smiled a lot and acknowledged our good feelings about the company. Although I was totally in the dark about the topics of the evening I enjoyed myself.

My stay in the village was a pleasant break from the war. What I liked most about the two days that I spent there was the friendliness of Lee's family and friends. I regretted having to leave. This was the most peaceful time that I could remember in Korea.

CHRISTMAS ON KOJE-DO

It seems that everyone we knew in the States thought that GIs in Korea needed to have a fruitcake for the Christmas holidays. Someone in our group seemed to get one every day that mail came. We did our best to polish them off without complaint. One of the most favorite gifts that any of our guys received was the package that Grasshold occasionally received from home, which he always willingly shared with others though his judgment in this benevolent act could have been questioned. He always received several well-packed bottles of Maraschino cherries—not the usual sweet syrupy Maraschino cherries you can buy back home—but bottles in which the syrup had been poured out and replaced with good, tasty brandy. Now those were Maraschino cherries!

It seemed like the number of packages from home had quickened in pace toward the end of December, and we enjoyed them. Even I, with not much in the way of family back home, received a couple of packages at Christmas. My sister Joan had become adept at canning and tried her hand at canning a chicken. It turned out to be quite good, but the chocolate cake that she sent was an even bigger hit. It was a treat to get a cake that was not made of compressed fruit, as everything else seemed to be.

The guys in our squad tent were feeling very friendly at this point and the new men had blended well into our routine. We decided that we would try to bring some Christmas cheer to the platoon. We even put up something that looked like a Christmas tree and there were presents exchanged, mostly makeshift gag gifts.

The cuisine at this time of the year even took a sharp turn for the better. The Army usually did a pretty good job of handling holidays when guys are a long way from home, and Christmas on Koje-do in 1952 was no exception. We got a couple of days off from routine duty and on the Christmas Day, the Army provided a fantastic Christmas dinner, just as good as one could get back home. One of the officers, Lieutenant Barger, came by our tent after dinner and left a little present under our Christmas tree—a bottle of brandy. Billy Marshall and Ziggy, of course, provided music into the evening and a few Christmas carols were slaughtered. Most of us felt, by the end of the evening, that this was one of the most memorable Christmases that we had ever had.

JANUARY AND A RETURN TO THE FRONT

The return to the Korean mainland by troop transport was, as usual, long and boring, but at least highly profitable. It was shortly after payday, and this usually meant that everyone had some money to donate to poker and blackjack games. I had, by that time in my military career, become somewhat of an avid poker player and on this trip had some exceptional draws of the cards—

such a streak of good luck comes rarely in life. The great god of poker decided that it was my turn. One of the guys in the card game kept drawing "second best type hands." These are the worst kind of hands to get because they entice one into the challenge only to lose out after committing one's fortune. After each frustrating hand of cards that he lost, he muttered, "You dun went and dun it again...Remember, you bastaads! Lucky in kaads, unlucky in war!"

My good fortune, at least in cards, stayed with me throughout my return to the war zone. When I got off the boat and train rides I had over $2,000 in my pocket, nine wrist watches on my arms, and two hand guns—one an Italian Beretta (a derringer sized weapon) and the other a long barrel .45 Colt revolver, what used to be called a "hawg leg" back in the old cowboy shows. This was a good way to begin the new year. I sent the money back home for Joan and the boys to use as they saw fit. Actually, their financial situation had begun to improve substantially by this time and she was working as a telephone operator. She began to save some of the money from the Army allotments that I was sending every month. The poker money was a nice holiday bonus.

7

Return to the Frozen Front

OUR RETURN TO THE WINTER-CHILLED FRONT LINES came at a time that our division was seemingly gearing up for greater aggressive activity along its section of the front—near a place called "Spud Hill," a small potato-like knob adjacent to T-Bone Hill. T-Bone, named after its shape, became the object of a number of military adventures in January 1953. One of the most dramatic operations was known as Operation Smack—a somewhat ill-conceived adventure that received a great deal of media attention and brought substantial criticism for the military staff who engineered the attack against Chinese fortifications on the T-Bone. This military operation became more famous for its public criticism than for its success as a military mission—the newspapers apparently played it up back home as a "show" designed for the generals and news media.

The stated mission of Operation Smack included a number of simultaneous goals: The military objectives of the operation were ostensibly to create an aggressive military action against the Chinese, capture prisoners that might provide important military intelligence to determine what the Chinese plans were, and to better develop the air-ground coordination in a planned assault that would allow the military air wings, the Navy and Air Force, to have greater integration into the war effort. The military leaders also thought this operation might serve as a good bit of publicity if the news media could see an actual military action in operation.

Everything was well planned out in advance to maximize the benefits of the situation. The observers (news reporters and top brass) were housed in a nice safe bunker on the MLR that provided a good vantage point, what in the press was referred to as "heated box seats," on a high hill that over looked the terrain on which the raid was to occur. The invited guests were also given a printed program (printed in three colors) with a timetable so that they would be able to follow the operation as the various events in the scenario unfolded.

The air arm of Operation Smack, happy to be involved in an unusual combined air-ground action in order to show its flexibility and effectiveness, flew a number of "softening-up" missions against the tiny piece of real estate. Initially, the air strikes against Spud Hill proceeded effectively and in a classic manner. First the Air Force conducted about sixteen night bombing missions with B-26 aircraft dropping 500-pound bombs followed by over 100 daylight sorties against the tiny hill with Thunderjet fighter-bombers. Just before the assault, U. S. Marine F-4 Corsairs attempted to lay smoke in a strategic location to help the ground forces avoid direct detection and subsequent fire. The smoke screen was ineffectively placed and did little good.

Then on January 25, 1953 at 1:00 P.M. in the afternoon, the next phase of the show began with a combined armor and infantry assault on the hill by elements of the 31st Infantry Regiment. Two platoons of infantry accompanied a tank attack across the open valley. The Chinese were apparently not occupying Spud Hill at the time or else were buried very deep in tunnels on the hill and stayed out of harm's way.

The infantry and tanks came under intensive artillery fire and considerable heavy machine gun fire from strategically located Chinese positions on T-Bone Hill. The enemy fire against the attack force was quite effective at keeping the infantry force pinned down behind the tanks.

In terms of military value, Operation Smack was not successful. No prisoners were taken, no Chinese soldiers were confirmed killed, and the attack wound up getting three American infantrymen killed and sixty-one so severely wounded as to require evacuation. The stated accomplishments included the destruction of a tunnel on the hill that could have been used as a staging area by the Chinese troops. Nothing about this target was, however, ever confirmed.

There was considerable furor from Operation Smack, not from the Chinese army, but from the American press. Military leaders, particularly General Smith, the 7th Division Commander, were singled out and criticized for "staging" a show for the press. There were concerns that this operation was initiated simply in order to gain publicity and was launched without sufficient regard for the lives of the men involved. We do not know what the Chinese thought about the drama centered on Spud Hill. As we were to learn just two days later, however, the Chinese were well aware of our interest in the hill and planned accordingly.

A PATROL TO OBTAIN PRISONERS

Our Battalion Commander was interested in obtaining better information about the area around T-Bone and Spud Hill before our units returned to the sector of the MLR we were slated to occupy. Our company was ordered to provide a reconnaissance/ambush patrol to gain information about the Chinese forces on the day before our units were to return to the line. The Fox Company commander asked for volunteers for the patrol, and several members of our platoon volunteered to participate in the raid. The company officers did not tell us about the failed Spud Hill assault and we knew nothing of the fiasco until several days after we returned from our patrol to the same area and some of our guys received clippings from home about the controversy. We became curious about the timing of our patrol.

Our raid, as initially outlined, seemed simple to conceptualize but as we drew closer to actually implementing those plans it began to seem like a potential suicide mission. We were to crawl up to the Chinese positions on Spud Hill and either club a Chinese soldier over the head or use a concussion grenade to knock him out in order to bring him back to our lines for interrogation.

The plan seemed straightforward in the early planning stages. Our twenty-two-man patrol would, under the cover of darkness, make its way to the base

T-Bone Hill in winter, January 1953.

of Spud Hill. At this point on the valley floor, we would set up a covering force to provide support for the raiding team that would actually go up the hill to try and kidnap an enemy soldier. Frank "Vito" Field, Del Kenway, and I volunteered to try to capture the Chinese soldier. We would then return, hopefully with a prisoner in tow (or probably strapped to a stretcher), and rejoin the covering force for the return back to the MLR, which was to follow a different route than we followed on the way out. Vito, Kenway, and I were eager to go on this mission and we never questioned the sanity of it at the time. We were, in part, motivated by the bounty for capturing a prisoner that our Battalion CO had posted which was to be a nice rest leave in Japan. We were confident we would be going on this leave as soon as our patrol returned!

As planned, our patrol returned to the front one day prior to the time when the remainder of the company was scheduled to move into their position on the MLR. Our company was trucked to positions about twenty miles to the rear of the MLR to make preparations for the return. The remainder of the company had to march twenty miles up to the front. We viewed this as a slight consolation for the patrol—we were brought close up to the front by vehicle and did not have to make the long march.

FINAL PREPARATION AND RETURN TO THE FRONT

I went into the company command post to get a final briefing from our platoon leader and the company CO. Three other company officers, including the unpopular and odd lieutenant described in Chapter 6, attended the briefing. As we discussed the plans and the situations that could go array, the stated objective and the patrol's planned action began to seem pretty crazy to me (and dangerous). There seemed to be a lot of "ifs" tied to this raid. But, I felt committed to carry out my orders. When the company commander asked if I had any other questions or requests, I simply replied that everything was clear and I took my leave.

As I left the tent I passed by the peculiar lieutenant with his flashy pearl handled pistols gleaming at his side. He called me over to where he was standing and stared intently into my eyes. I was quite surprised and amazed by his odd and frozen expression. He appeared tense, saying, inquisitively, "Sergeant, are you really going to take that patrol out in the valley like that?"

A bit taken aback by his question after such a briefing, I confidently asserted, "Yes, we're on our way!"

He walked away muttering, "Oh my! Oh my!"

That was the last time that I saw him. He became agitated and upset shortly after our patrol left the area. I was later told that shortly after we left, he began to behave more and more bizarrely. When the rest of the company began to get their gear together to make the move back up to the front the lieutenant became extremely frightened and broke down under the pressure. He apparently became actively psychotic. He was crying and moaning and began, at one point, to fire his pistols in the air. Several people had to restrain him. Apparently he was experiencing delusional behavior and was hallucinating, that is, hearing voices. He was evacuated back to Japan for psychiatric treatment. A few years later, as a graduate student in psychology, I realized my observations of this lieutenant's behaviors fit the symptoms of schizophrenic disorder.

We finished our briefing and lined up to get our evening meal before the rest of the company was to chow-down. Just as we were finishing our meal, we noticed two jeeps pull up into the company area about fifty yards from where we were loading up ammunition and equipment for the patrol. Several women, dressed in Army fatigues, got out of the jeeps, including a strikingly beautiful blonde.

They were USO entertainers touring Korea. Our company was treated to a private performance! We could hear laughing, cheers, and music coming from the other guys. My men and I were preoccupied with getting ready for the patrol, and did not pay much attention to the show. As we were getting on the trucks, one of the men from the USO asked me to hold up our departure. The young blonde actress wanted to say goodbye to us. She had asked what we were doing at the trucks and was told that we were going up to the front on a dangerous mission.

When the show ended, the young woman came over to us and asked who was in charge. Everyone pointed to me and she walked over and asked my name. I was already on edge about the mission, but even more nervous when she focused her attention on me. She stood very close, saying that she wanted to sing a farewell song for us. She sang the "Tennessee Waltz" very softly and I was transfixed. I was taken by her beauty and her voice—singing on a very cold evening just for us. One of the guys from our outfit, who was wounded later and evacuated to Japan, happened to see this actress in a hospital there. She approached him because she recognized the 7th Division patch on his uniform. She asked him what happened to the patrol. I never learned for certain the identity of this kind, thoughtful, and talented woman. I wish I knew who she was.

A NIGHT VISIT TO SPUD HILL

The evening was not totally dark. The moonlit sky reflecting on the snow provided enough visibility to see eight or nine yards away as we made our way through the shadowy world. By about 10:00 P.M. we had crossed the valley and reached the old rice paddy where we planned to set up the fire support base. After we set up the automatic weapon gun teams in place to provide covering fire for our withdrawal, Frank Field, Del Kenway, and I moved forward for the final leg of the raid—the crawl up the hill.

The T-Bone loomed ominously over us as we slowly crawled away from the support team up toward the little potato shaped knoll. We took a long time crawling on our stomachs toward the ugly piece of terrain above us. We crawled about five feet apart, with Field on my left and Kenway on my right, because we did not want to get separated and have to make noise in order to find each other again. We crawled slowly through the night.

After about a half an hour of forward movement, we passed near a large wood and brush pile a few yards from Kenway. As we reached the base of the hill and started up the slight incline, Kenway excitedly got my attention and crawled over to where I was inching my way along. He was very concerned about something. By the time he reached me, Vito had also detected a problem and had crawled over to hear what Del had seen. Del whispered, "I saw several Chinks moving behind us near that woodpile that we passed."

The Chinese listening post had apparently waited until we had passed their positions and had moved troops in the vicinity of what was to be our withdrawal route. We decided that our situation was getting somewhat difficult and it might be us, rather than a Chinese soldier, who wound up being taken prisoner, so we decided to return to the firebase to further evaluate an impending attack by the Chinese.

Vito whispered, " I think we should return to the firebase and take 'em on there!"

"I agree," I said.

For a few minutes there was some jockeying around to return to our firebase to prevent the Chinese troops from getting into a position to bring us under attack. It had taken us almost forty minutes to crawl to our most forward position; it took less than fifteen minutes for us to make it back to the firebase. A person can certainly walk faster than they can crawl! We met up with the rest of the patrol at about the time that the first burp gun rounds were fired into our circle. Our patrol was set up into a defensive circle perimeter and could make a good stand against a ground attack. It was difficult to determine where the first rounds came from.

Red Chinese flares exploded in the night sky over our heads illuminating the landscape like atmosphere red-tinged lighting in some nightclubs I had seen. At that moment, as we were getting the patrol alerted for an attack, the enemy machine gun emplacements on the T-Bone came alive and quickly got our range and began to fire in our direction. We dived for the ground just as the bullets poured also from the hill above us, "kzing, kzing, kzing!"

The telltale path of machine gun bullets kicked up the frozen earth along the rice paddy wall two feet in front of my head. Our automatic weapons opened up return fire against their positions.

At that instant, one of the men yelled, "I'm hit! I'm hit!"

It was Ray Millsap. A Chinese burp gun bullet from the enemy in the valley had ripped through one of his arms and he lay on the ground, wrenching with great pain. In a matter of seconds, Vito and the medic pulled him on the stretcher that we carried with us while the area was being sprayed with bullets from both the hill and the valley floor. Vito assured Ray that we were going to get him back up the hill safely. Ray was in great pain and losing a lot of blood. The medic, hands shaking, plunged a hypodermic needle with morphine into his arm to help with the pain as he applied a tourniquet to try and stop the flow of blood.

Burp gun fire was coming from an area south of the woodpile and our patrol began to answer them from our defensive circle. We radioed our intentions to return back to the CP and indicated that we would need a medic on our immediate return. The impromptu firefight died away as rapidly as it began, and as the night sky once again became dark as the Chinese flares died out briefly, we began to think about our return trip to the MLR. With Vito leading the way and Moss following the column to engage the Chinese as a rear guard, if needed, the patrol headed back through the cold night.

The trek across the valley floor was a nightmare. Millsap weighed over 225 pounds, but with him and his BAR clips in his vest, the stretcher seemed to weigh a ton; it was a long way back to the MLR. We took turns carrying the stretcher across the frozen earth back toward our lines. Shifts of stretcher-bearers became shorter and shorter as we became more fatigued from carrying the lead weight across the rough terrain.

After we had moved some distance south and away from the rice paddy, the harassing fire from the Chinese machine guns was focusing on our previous location away from our current path of return. Each time a Chinese flare burst in a crimson light across the night sky, we remained motionless to avoid giving away our present position. Fortunately, the Chinese flares had a more limited range and time in the air than American flares so they were not as effective at locating our movements.

We inched our way across the frozen earth, stopping periodically to rest and change stretcher-bearers. At one time when I was taking a turn at carrying, I became so exhausted that I fell to my knees, barely catching Ray and keeping him from rolling off the stretcher—a situation that occurred several times on our return journey. After he nearly fell off the stretcher at one point Millsap awakened and in a drowsy tone of voice asked, "Am I going to make it?" Someone whispered back, "Millsap, you lucky son of a bitch. You've got a million dollar wound! You're going home!"

Ray said, "Damn. Damn." And then fell back into an unconscious state.

The journey back became more grueling as we left the relatively flat valley floor and started up the slippery hill toward our own lines. All the while we had to remain alert to the possibility that the Chinese force was following or had managed to get ahead of us. We had no idea how much damage our own return fire against the flashes of their weapons had done to their main body—we hoped that we had struck as painful a chord for them as their firing had caused us with the wounding of Ray.

Although extremely exhausted, we considered ourselves fortunate to have made the return with only one casualty. We had managed to make a pretty good accounting of ourselves in the firefight and we had crossed a very wide expanse of the valley on slippery ground with a heavy cargo. We were thankful that Ray survived the tortuous journey back. He lost a lot of blood and was unconscious when we handed him over to the waiting medics on the MLR at the top of the hill. Ray was evacuated to Japan and then back to the United

States for a considerable period of rehabilitation. The burp gun bullet had caused extensive damage to his arm. Ray died in 1978 of a coronary.

Unfortunately, dead Chinese on the valley floor would not bring a premium as far as the bounty was concerned. We had to go back without a prisoner—alas, no leave!

A COLD WINTER SET IN

After the raid to the base of T-Bone, we settled into our new positions on the MLR overlooking the ominous and unfriendly hill with the somewhat silly name in the distance. The section of the trench that we occupied already had established bunkers and firing positions. Our positions, however, needed extensive repair and reconstruction to accommodate our platoon's preferred ways of operating.

It was bitter cold at the front at this time and it was painful to inhale the cold air into our lungs. We never knew what the exact temperature was—no one really wanted to know. Officially, I think the Army kept this information from the GIs to prevent further demoralization, as if knowing the truth would really make much more difference. It was miserable regardless of whether we knew the actual numbers on the Fahrenheit scale! The cold wind blowing through the trench reaffirmed my belief that the little Zippo hand warmer was the greatest invention of all time, at least when we had the opportunity to squirrel ourselves away in our sleeping bags for a rest and a respite from the cold wind for a couple of hours at a time.

In order to protect ourselves from the winter nights, we dressed with as many layers of clothing as possible. We started with those ridiculous, itchy Army "Long Johns" and two pair of fatigue pants and shirts. On top of that we might also wear our field jacket with a wool winter lining and a muffler. This basic outfit was then topped with our Army flak jacket or armored vest to protect against shrapnel. The final outer garment, our cold weather parka, would be put on last with a muffler and then a furry cap under the parka hood. On cold nights we would wear two pairs of gloves. Some guys would cut the trigger fingers off the gloves to make it possible to actually fire one's weapon.

We were issued a very good winter boot that went by the name of "Mickey Mouse Boots" because of their resemblance to the Disney character's shoes.

These boots were both warm and water proof. When the GI wore two pairs of socks and the Mickey Mouse boots he could be assured of reasonable warmth—except, of course, if water some how got inside, say from crossing open water or deep snow. Then they might develop discomfort; the water inside the boot would not actually freeze but would warm up to body temperature.

With all of this clothing, we walked and looked like overstuffed sofas. All of this warm clothing only worked against the cold, winter Korean wind for a short period of time. On the coldest nights we shortened our outside guard shifts to allow more frequent warm-ups. This amount of clothing was too cumbersome to take out on patrol where one would have to walk several miles in deep snow, so the number of layers had to be reduced to allow the GI to move effectively. On several occasions, for patrols conducted under snow conditions, we were issued white "Outer parkas," or white garments that camouflaged us in the snow and served to provide some break from the harsh wind.

It was, however, impossible under combat conditions to completely insulate ourselves from the winter conditions. One of the most serious dangers from the cold was the ever-present danger of frostbite. Many of us experienced this nemesis and had a great deal of discomfort from the pain of frozen skin for some time. On the front, we treated mild frostbite simply by warming up the affected body parts. We tolerated the red inflammations on our skin. When frostbite became severe enough that it was considered "limb endangering," the GI would need to be evacuated to the rear area for treatment. Night patrols were particularly dangerous because we had to remain quite still, often for hours at a time, and the cold would soon make its presence known.

The cold weather was often problematic from the standpoint of any of our equipment that was made of metal; for example, the action of weapons was often sluggish in the cold air. However, one positive aspect of the winter climate (and there weren't many that I can think of) that should be noted is that the snow, which was generously available at times, when packed around the barrels of machine guns was an excellent coolant if they had to be fired continuously.

AN EXPERIMENT GONE AWRY

The winter of 1952-1953 was severe and the weather itself became as threatening to the infantryman's safety at times as was the Chinese gunfire. We often had visual images of the Chinese infantrymen sitting with their women in warm caves while we prowled the frozen valley below trying to harass them. Traversing the valley and icy slopes at night could be extremely difficult. One patrol that we took into the valley after a fresh snow found us sliding down the hillside plowing up the snow as we went. Once onto the valley floor we made a very tell tale track that the Chinese would likely to be able to follow, either with their trackers at night or, if we were still there in the daylight, their artillery observers could simply follow the nicely etched boot marks in the snow.

We were all shivering and wet from our frolic in the snow. Vito, serving as point man as usual, had crossed a partially frozen stream over which the ice gave way dropping him into the chilly water underneath. His wet frozen legs caused him to have an extreme shaking reaction that gave us all concern. It was necessary for us to cut short our patrol and get him back to the MLR to restore his circulation and prevent frostbite.

****

The Army, always trying to get more efficiency out of its troops with the latest in technology, developed a new set of underwear that was designed to solve the problem of the Korean winter. They provided us with snug, rubber-ized, air-tight underwear designed to keep the body warmth inside and cool air outside, thus keeping the GI nice and toasty while the rest of the world froze. This sounded like a wonderful invention so the Army, supposedly after perfecting this product in their laboratories, decided that it needed field test-ing under combat conditions—one of our patrols.

We were told that this undergarment would allow us to lie around the snow in just our fatigues, without a coat, even if our outer garment got soaking wet. This, of course, sounded just wonderful to us—like the best thing that we could imagine, not to be freezing while we were out on patrol. So we suited up with our new undergarments, without our heavy parkas, wearing only our fatigues and armored nylon vests for protection.

It was a bitter cold evening but all eighteen of us felt warm and secure in our new outfits. The men lined up in the trench and the NCO squad leaders made final equipment checks of each man's gear and weapon. As it began to get dark, we loaded up our gear and headed down the narrow trail toward the passageway through the barbed wire and between the minefields to the valley floor below.

Before I had walked ten minutes down the line I began to feel very warm, then hot, then extremely tired. I was sweating as though it was summertime. As I marched along in the center of the formation and I began to see a few of the men fall to the ground, exhausted and sweating profusely. I looked to my rear and observed a similar situation. What was happening? Why were the men dropping like flies? We had not even passed through our own positions on this freezing cold night, and we had already lost half of the patrol. Concerned over the mystery, and with the now decreased manpower of the patrol, I passed up the word for the patrol to return to the trench. There was something desperately wrong. The CO, complaining about why the patrol was returning, came running up to me.

"What's going on Sergeant? Why did you come back?"

I could hardly talk I was so weak. I said, "The men can't go on for some reason. Everyone is dropping out and can't go forward."

We were absolutely exhausted and perspiring much as one might find after vigorous exercise on a hot, humid day. We were all experiencing an affliction that we usually only encountered in mid-summer—heat exhaustion! The CO was angry over the use of our troops as guinea pigs in a quartermaster experiment and told off someone back at Battalion over the comm line.

Those damned rubber suits were not able to "breathe" and were retaining all of the heat to the point that we were experiencing an electrolyte imbalance that, in the summer, we usually counter by swallowing salt tablets and a lot of water. In just a short distance we had lost most of the patrol to a failure in the Army's research program. Needless to say we were absolutely disappointed about the rubber underwear. Apparently it had been designed for stationary action and not for any vigorous movement, but no one seemed to know that in advance. We sent the rubber suits back with some suggestions as to exactly where in their own posterior anatomy they might stick that junk!

THE PLATOON COMMAND POST

By January I had now moved up in responsibility, and was serving as the Assistant Platoon Sergeant. One of the most important duties of this job during the long cold winter nights, especially if we were in a relatively quiet sector, was to keep the platoon command post (usually a bunker that was large enough for four or five guys to sleep) as a warming hut with a charcoal stove going. We also tried to keep a pot of coffee brewing at all times during the night. Coffee was made according to the following trusted recipe: An ammo container, holding about a gallon of water, was filled about 2/3 and heated to boiling point; then coffee (a bunch) was dumped into the can and boiled until it became black; then the hot black liquid was dipped out as needed until there were only grounds left in the bottom of the can. When more coffee was needed, additional water would be added along with more grounds, all the while keeping the pot on the stove boiling. This pot would be kept going until it became too full of grounds to hold more water then it would be thrown out in front of our positions and a fresh ammo can started with boiling water. Coffee was plentiful, especially after the time that we relieved a platoon of Colombians (the Colombian Battalion was attached to the 7th Division) who moved out of positions that we took over leaving a bunker containing many tins of Colombian coffee. With coffee like we made in our platoon the wintry wind didn't have a chance to demoralize us.

A RISKY FIELD TEST FOR VIGILANCE

On the front lines it was crucial to have buddies that one could rely upon to hold up their end of the work, particularly when it came to standing duty watch. In the sector of the MLR to which we were assigned in February 1953, it was possible to operate with a half-on/half-off guard situation at night enabling one person to sleep while the other watched the approaches to our positions. This allowed the troops to get a bit of rest and to get warm for a while. Being able to fall asleep immediately was important because the two-to-four hour nap before the next stint of guard duty would end abruptly and one would be up peering over the valley floor in the cold night air while comrades slept.

Trust in one's companions was critical on the front. Falling asleep on post in a combat situation was a sufficient offense to warrant severe punishment such as a general court martial. But worse, this sort of sleep interruption, say a fragmentation grenade exploding next to one's head, would certainly ruin one's day. There had been a disturbing recent report about a tragic incident in one of the other regiments about an entire squad that had fallen asleep; sometime during the night they were visited by a Chinese raiding party that killed them all without anyone knowing what happened.

One of the men in our platoon, a fellow we called "Wally" because someone noted that he looked something like the cartoon character Wally the Walrus, had gotten the reputation of being somewhat of a laggard and we had some suspicions that he was not staying awake on his watches. I decided that I would run the supreme test on him one evening and informed his squad leader of my plan to test Wally's vigilance. This sort of test is risky and was probably not one of the wisest decisions that I ever made as a sergeant! But, I left the command post and rather stealthily made my way to Wally's foxhole. I crouched down very quietly in the shadows and observed his posture for a long time. He seemed to be almost like an inanimate object he was so still. I began to creep slowly up to his post, all the while listening for sound of movement from the foxhole. I was attending to the possibility that he might, as required, speak out the password, which in turn required a counter sign, or else he could, as sentry, begin firing at me. As it turned out I had nothing to fear from Wally's weapon because I soon discovered he was sound asleep. I stood for a time watching him enjoying his pleasant dreams of home then I quietly placed the business end of my M-2 carbine against his cheek and yelled out very loudly, "BANG! AAAAGH!"

Wally shrieked and fell back into his foxhole whimpering. I instructed him to get out of the foxhole and proceeded to give him a "chewing out" that he would not soon forget. I had no intention of turning him over to the company commander for his action, only to scare him into realizing the importance of staying awake. I also informed his squad leader about the results of Wally's failed test so that he could deal with the lack of vigilance at the squad level and arrange future watches in a way that we would not have to rely upon a weak link.

CLEANING UP AT THE FRONT

After a long period on the front line, troops get to smell pretty ripe. With no means of taking complete baths or changing clothes, personal hygiene became somewhat scarce or not at all. Some soldiers enjoy the front line atmosphere because it is away from the Army's customary "spit and shine" and, under some conditions, one might become quite accustomed to smelling like a mountain goat for weeks at a time. Most of us usually found that our scheduled visits to the shower point (roughly every week or so) were welcome indeed.

The scheduled shower for line troops normally worked as follows. On arriving at the shower point, the company of men would dismount their vehicles and line up in customary Army style in front of the first of a series of squad tents that had been rigged with makeshift plumbing and water tanks to feed the showers in some of the tents. The water source was several fifty-five-gallon drums lined up along the side of two of the tents. Adjacent to the line of tents was a deep trench with sandbags around it for protection in the event of an artillery barrage or in the unlikely event of an air raid. The tents were arranged like an assembly line in a factory. Soldiers walked through the line of tents participating in the various stages of clean up as they went.

Approximately ten soldiers would enter the sequence of tents en masse after first removing their outerwear and piling it outside. The parkas, flak vests, and field jackets were keepers—they would be retrieved at the end of the process.

When the GIs entered tent # 1 (Disrobing Tent) they took off all of their dirty clothes and piled them in containers along the wall. These dirty clothes would be later cleaned and issued to a future batch of troops. The small bevy of naked soldiers next entered Tent # 2 (Soaping Tent) and stood under the showers (cold of course) and tried to get off the layers of accumulated dirt. Still soapy, and by now shivering, the GIs next walked over to tent # 3 (Rinsing Tent) where the GI soap could be removed, leaving a head-to-toe clean infantryman. After drying off, of course on a government issued brown towel, the next stop was tent # 4 (New Clothes Tent). Actually, the now clean GI would be given recycled clothing from bags of clean fatigue (work) uniforms that had been washed from soldiers who had gone through the same procedures a day or two before. This was truly a communal army! With luck, the clothes that were obtained from the Quartermaster bag would fit; if not, the various articles of clothing would simply be traded around until the recipients came close to having an acceptable outfit.

The shower program was not designed for comfort but efficiency; it was not designed to provide long relaxing baths but simply dirt dissolving experiences that left the soldier a little cleaner than before. Neither was stylish or nice fitting clothing a priority; but no one complained much about a visit to the shower point.

On this particular day in February 1953, the shower point provided some additional entertainment to fun-starved GIs just out of the trenches. About halfway through the soaping routine, I had soap all over my head and upper body and couldn't see much, but I was startled by a terrible, piercing scream coming from one of the squad leaders at the end of the line of showers, "AACH, you dirty son of a bitch! What are you doing? Stop that!"

One of the Korean soldiers that was new to the company, trying to be helpful to his sergeant (who was busy soaping his head and face), had simply begun to lather up his leader's genital area for him. The sergeant became so panicked over the extra hands covering his lower body parts that he half ran, half slid through the soapy water across the plank floor and into the next tent. His mad dash through the tent was accompanied by thunderous laughter from several bystanders who witnessed the event with curiosity. Perhaps the situation resulted from a clash of cultures; perhaps it resulted from different personality styles. Whatever the source of misunderstanding, the sergeant, unaccustomed to such assistance in washing his lower body parts, remained a bit miffed at the young Korean man who perhaps simply saw himself as trying to be helpful to his sergeant.

Our good clean fun came to an abrupt end a few minutes later. Just as my little group had finished donning our fresh outfits and stepped outdoors to make room for the next batch of lucky bathers to take their place in the system, we heard the all-too-familiar whistle of incoming artillery rounds. We dived unhaltingly into the safety of the trench near the shower tents as several incoming rounds began to explode about a hundred yards away and seemed to be walking their way toward the tent area. No sooner did we get into the safety of the trench than we were inundated with other bathers piling in on top of us from each of the respective tents; some soapy, some drenching wet, others in different stages of disrobement. In spite of the danger from the shelling, and in spite of the cold weather, there was an evident cascade of harassing shouts and laughter coming from the frozen trench.

OCCASIONAL SHORTAGE OF BASICS UP FRONT

There were occasional shortages at the front, and times in which we were told to conserve ammunition or not fire too many artillery rounds because the 8th Army was running low. In terms of the basics required for existence, at the front we usually had what we needed: clothing that was almost warm enough; rations that almost quelled our hunger pangs (though never fully satisfying the human longing for descent food); and water was usually available, though it sometimes had to be supplemented, for example by melting snow.

Water was occasionally available from natural sources. In one section of the line, for example, when the ice in a close-by mountain stream began to melt, we got plenty of cool and refreshing water that ran down the brook from the north by our rear area on the reverse slope of the hill. We drank freely from this stream (of course, with two of our government issued purification tablets) with a number of people commenting upon how fresh and good it tasted until someone discovered a problem with the creek—a deteriorating corpse was found lying in the stream about a mile up to the north or our positions. Suddenly, we lost our appetite for this cool mountain water. We waited for the KSC choggies (laborers) or our guys to get water cans up to the front.

At times we experienced unusual deficits. On one occasion one of the squad leaders and I were asked to go back to Battalion HQ for a de-briefing of a combat patrol that we had run the night before out into the valley. After we were finished with our description of the patrol's action and the situation on the Chinese hill as we observed it, Major Noble from Battalion (a very well liked officer) asked us if there was anything he could do for us.

"Do you fellows need anything up there?" he said.

"A sock, sir," I said, hesitatingly

He seemed puzzled. "A what? What are you saying?"

I said, even more hesitatingly, "A sock sir. I only have one sock to wear and my boot that is rubbing against my bare foot is very uncomfortable." I explained further: "I try to change the sock each day from one foot to the other but I am experiencing some irritation from the boot. A sock for the other foot would help."

Surprised at what I had revealed, Major Noble asked if I would have the Battalion Aid medics look at my feet to determine if I had any medical problems then, without saying another word, he went into his tent and brought back a clean pair of his own socks and handed them to me saying, "Sergeant, I am going to see to it that this sort of shortage does not happen again."

Our supply situation improved significantly...for a while.

ARTILLERY FORWARD OBSERVER TRAINING

A novel experience happened in late February 1953. I was sent back to school for a week for a quick lesson in military science. I was one of five NCOs from our Battalion selected to receive a quick course in artillery observation. We were given a crash course into techniques designed to make us more effective in tracing incoming shells and in zeroing artillery barrages against enemy targets.

We learned, for example, how to perform a diagnostic evaluation of shell craters to determine the likely direction from which the round came. After an incoming shell blasted a crater, we were taught to go immediately (we also were told that we shouldn't fear because lightening does not strike twice in the same place!) to the hole and make some measurements as to the shape and scatter of the hole and shrapnel, likely type of shell, and the likely azimuth of the shells track toward the earth. This information was not of much use to us on the line but the artillery officers in the Command Headquarters could put these soundings into an informative pattern by getting readings from different locations. They could triangulate and pinpoint the location of the artillery piece from whence the shells came. I found this interesting and it gave us something to think about other than simply hiding from the incoming shells.

More than this sedentary diagnostic assessment of shell craters I was, at the time, more interested in some of the aggressive operations and wanted to learn how we could use the information to direct artillery assaults against enemy positions and troop concentrations. We were also trained in methods used in forward artillery observation. This procedure was straightforward—using rudimentary geometry (which, thanks to Mr. Hill back at Stonewall Jackson High, I understood), direct observation, compass headings, and radio communication with the artillery fire control center we could adjust artillery and produce interesting, effective results. We learned how to make range estimates to targets using our binoculars and then obtain coordinates for establishing an initial target range.

After establishing our range, we called for firing an initial round to zero in or "prove out" our estimated reading and then adjusted the estimate depending upon how far away the first round landed from our estimated coordinates. We then adjusted our coordinate and called for fire to the revised target reading and again observed the results. Once the next adjustment was made we then called for the artillery control center to fire the mission, which was referred to as "fire for effect."

This course provided some very helpful hints that we would find useful in coming engagements. In the ensuing months, we conducted several patrols for the purpose of firing artillery missions.

A GRUESOME FINDING

The section of the line we had recently moved into presented some interesting terrain problems. I did not like the placement of one of our .30 caliber machine guns because the field of fire was constricted and the gun team was somewhat vulnerable to an attack from behind a small knoll to their right. Reconnoitering the positions, I decided that the machine gun placement would likely be more effective and safer from attack if it were moved about thirty yards down the finger of the hill. We selected a new location which seemed ideal—it had an added benefit of having a large rock that could serve to offer some protection if the emplacement were dug in front and under the rock.

The machine gun crew began to excavate their new firing positions. Only a few inches down they uncovered a previous military emplacement and pulled out a broken M-1 rifle that had been buried there, probably for some months. They continued to dig around the area and then found a U.S. Army steel helmet containing the remnants of a skull, then other human remains, probably of at least two people. As they dug further, the stench from the hole became more unbearable and the ammo bearer who was digging at the time became nauseous, crawled a few feet away, and barfed noisily.

I suggested that the digging be stopped until we could get some body bags from the rear in which we could place the remains. We gave up on our new machine gun emplacement for the time being and waited for the Graves Registration unit to send up the bags. A couple of days later we received them and resumed the very unpleasant chore of retrieving the bodies. It looked as though the bunker containing the people had caved in after a shell had exploded on it. One of the two bodies we recovered was very clearly an American because of the steel helmet and the remnants of a dog tag; the other body was probably an American too, but the identification process was more difficult because of its condition. We threw everything we could find into the bags in hopes that Graves Registration would be able to make positive identifications.

In all probability the soldiers had been killed a year or so before when there had been extensive fighting in this vicinity. We found this operation very distasteful. At times the life of an infantryman in war is indeed terrible. This recovery process was the stuff nightmares are made of, but we were at least consoled by the fact that some families somewhere would have their anxious and frustrating wait for their missing soldier come to an end. It is probably better to know these truths, as horrible as they are, than to live with such painful uncertainty as accompanies the MIA designation. It's frustrating for veterans like me and family members of the missing to know that almost 8,000 Americans are still unaccounted for.

LUCKY SEVEN AND THE BLINDING OF A MOUNTAIN MAN

We were back in reserve for a few days. The platoon was very thirsty and some of the guys sent out a scouting party to go to the KSC camp down the road to look for some bootleg whisky. They found no Seagrams Seven, the usual liquor available, but the camp bootlegger had six bottles of "Lucky Seven"—a Korean concoction made from distilled rice wine, not generally developed according to the highest bottling standards and probably somewhat short of the standards followed the 1930's type gangster/bootlegger in the

United States. The milky, grey product tasted somewhat like moonshine liquor that was familiar to some of the Southern guys (actually resembling a taste that I recalled from my tour in North Carolina) but with somewhat more of a metallic taste. Our troops were certainly warned not to drink this Korean liquor.

I knew right away that I did not like this taste because it made me want to throw-up. Instead of swallowing the potent brew when it was passed my way I simply held my tongue in the neck of the bottle and stopped the flow. This strategy kept me safe from the horrible taste yet made it appear to my buddies as though I was participating in the fun-fest. As the evening progressed several of the guys got pretty sick and trips to the latrine or the bush outside the tent were common.

The evening wore on and the merriment got loud and a bit chaotic with a few fellows dropping out of the action. One of the BAR men, a corporal named Ken, who was a mountain man type of guy from Wyoming, suddenly became sick. A large fellow—6' 4" and muscular—he leapt up suddenly throwing his bulk against one of the main tent poles. He swayed awkwardly toward the tent flap seeking fresh air, falling en route over a bunk containing a half sleeping GI. He rolled on the floor groaning loudly in agony, "I'm blind! I can't see!! Oh God!"

He flailed about yelling obscenities for a few moments until some of the group reached him to try to restrain him in order to prevent him from hurting himself or, given his strength, maiming others. As he rolled on the ground of the tent groaning, "Shit, I can't see!" five of the squad members were able to hold him still for a bit until someone obtained a stretcher to try to remove him to Battalion Aid station to possibly receive some help.

As he was being lowered onto the stretcher, Ken swung his fists wildly, catching the canvas with great force and ripping a large hole near one of the handles. Ken was evacuated to a MASH unit. He never returned to our company and the only word we ever received about him was that he had not yet recovered his sight.

Nothing much was ever said about the incident, officially or otherwise. The next day the formation was silent, though many of the partakers of the merriment appeared to be at death's door. The unit attempted to restore its equilibrium and shortly afterward we returned to action in the Yokkokchon Valley.

BOOZE UP FRONT: AN ACCIDENTAL GUN SHOT

One other alcohol related incident that bears reporting, one that could have ended tragically, occurred on evening on the MLR, a rather quiet section of the line. Moss located a small, half-pint flask of liquor which he brought up to our positions. He had bought it from the mess sergeant who was known for having such things as alcohol and various exotic weapons for sale from time to time.

This was not enough liquor for anyone to get drunk on but just enough for a few sociable after dinner cocktails. Moss, Vito, and I sat for a while having a few drinks as we chowed down on our favorite C-ration meals. After the bottle was emptied, Vito left to go back to his bunker to go to sleep. Moss and I talked for a while longer about his suggestion that we go out on a two-man patrol over to the T-Bone, capture ourselves "a nice fat Chink," and win us a bounty to go to Japan. To the question of what weapons we might take with us on such a patrol Moss said,

"Just pistols!"

After a bit, Moss chided me by saying, "Show me your quick draw!"

Accommodating Moss's request to show him how fast I might draw this weapon from its holster, I quickly reached for the pistol. As I jerked the long .45 caliber Colt from my shoulder holster it discharged prematurely (a bad habit the weapon had) surprising both of us and sending a bullet into a water canteen hanging above and slightly to the right of Moss's head. After the bullet smashed into the canteen the water began to drip down his left shoulder and arm. Moss, without hesitation and in a soft and calm voice, said, "John, you missed!" (Because of all the unrealistic movie heroics they'd been exposed to, the guys in the platoon often used names like "John" or "John Wayne" to refer to someone who was acting gung ho.)

OBSERVATIONS ABOUT ARMY OFFICERS IN KOREA

Anyone spending time in the infantry, whether as an officer or as an enlisted soldier, becomes aware quickly that the unit runs effectively because of the NCOs—the non-commissioned officers. They are the backbone of the command structure. If the NCOs are ineffective so too will be the unit's performance. In some respects, the lowest non commissioned officers, the corporals, are the true commanding force in the infantry. They are the ones with the most direct responsibilities for getting the job done.

The Army officers in Korea were a mixed lot. Not all of them were as oriented toward the troops' wellbeing as were Major Noble, Captain Vaughn, Lt. Brandenberg, Captain King, and Lt. Barger. We always considered ourselves fortunate to have officers who were willing to take personal risks with the rest of us or were fair in what they asked us to do. I, on the other hand, encountered too many officers like "Whispering Smith," who refused to come out of his foxhole even while we were under attack on Jane Russell Hill (Chapter 3) and the lieutenant with the flashy pearl-handled pistols who had the psychotic breakdown (described earlier in this chapter and Chapter 6).

Often our platoon officers were recent graduates of ROTC or Officer Candidate School who were called "Ninety-day wonders" and "shavetails." Many were not career military, and had less experience at command than our least experienced corporals. They were placed in charge of men who knew a lot more about staying alive in combat and getting the job done. Adding to the problem, these officers tended to remain in an assignment for very brief periods—from a few weeks to no longer than three months—before being reassigned to the rear. Many never really stayed on the front lines long enough to get to know us or fully understand our operation. Not surprisingly, resentment towards the clearly inept officers was common.

An active rumor mill provided descriptions of hated lieutenants not making it back from an assault on a hill because of a vengeful grenade toss. However, these descriptions were always non-specific and I quickly saw them as tension-relievers, not based on actual events. There were many distasteful jokes about "hit lists" or as bounties on a given officer's head. A guy might say, "Lt. Jones is an SOB and he had better not be in front of me in the next attack!" Someone else might respond, "That'd be worth $200.00 bucks to me! Do I hear more?" Typically, these jokes were reserved for officers that had acted recklessly and gotten people hurt. "Chickenshit officers" (our technical term for those who liked to hear the sound of their voices ordering us to do unnecessary, irrelevant, or demeaning tasks) were also the butt of these jokes. I never had any reason to suspect that these statements were other than jokes. I witnessed nothing to suggest that they were expressions of intent to do actual harm. In the next chapter, we take a closer look at combat patrols. In any stabilized trench warfare like Korea, patrols are essential.

8

Patrols in Korea

IN THE 1980s, STATUES OF MEN ON A combat patrol were selected to be part of the design for the Korean War Memorial in DC. This was a fitting choice to represent many of our experiences during this war, given the predominant role of such engagements. Through rain or snow or throat-parching heat, regardless of the conditions, American and enemy patrols plodded through the Korean valleys and along the ridges to encounter their enemy. Combat patrols in Korea fell under two broad types: reconnaissance (recon) and contact. Recon patrols gathered information about the enemy. Contact patrols were varied and included raids, ambushes, artillery fire missions, or air strike coordination. Many of the patrols were conducted at night because the Allied Forces' air superiority meant the Chinese and North Korean forces were kept in their bunkers and caves during daylight.

EQUIPMENT AND PREPARATION FOR FOOT PATROLS

Some equipment was standard on any patrol: magnetic compass, flashlight, and map. The plastic ponchos, depicted in the Korean War Memorial, served two purposes. Not only did they provide protection against rain or snow, we also used them to huddle under at night to shield our flashlights for map reading. We always brought one grenade launcher on an M-1 rifle with a clip filled with crimped cartridges to use to launch grenades or flares. We usually made our own crimp cartridges with a pair of pliers to remove the slug from a cartridge.

Other equipment we took on patrols varied depending upon the mission. Those with the intent of aggressive actions against the enemy would be more laden with mission specific weaponry. For example, if the intent was to knock out a bunker, the patrol might carry along a bazooka or even a 57 mm recoilless rifle from the weapons platoon. If the intent were to go through barbed wire, we carried wire cutters, or even Bangalore torpedoes, to blow a path through barbed wire. If an ambush were intended then we would carry as much automatic weaponry as possible. We even had a couple of Thompson sub machine guns (like the gangsters in the movies used) and a cheaper version called a Grease gun that fired .45 caliber bullets. Having fast-firing weapons was important because many of the Chinese carried burp guns, a weapon that fired nine hundred fifty rounds per minute. In order to counter this type of firepower, my favorite weapon for patrols was the M-2 carbine that fired seven hundred fifty rounds per minute and was lighter than the M-1 or the BAR.

On patrols in which aggressive engagement was likely, we often carried a stretcher. Sometimes a medic might accompany contact patrols. We usually took a radioman that carried a PRC-10 radio. If the patrol was going to be out for a prolonged period of time, we also brought sufficient rations and water. Since all of this added weight it was only a necessity for long patrols. There was usually considerable preparation required prior to going out on patrol. In order to travel more quietly, we taped equipment that would rattle such as dog tags, canteens, and even the stocks of our rifles. Infantrymen would also blacken their faces, usually with a blackened cork, to prevent glare from lights or flares. If the patrol involved an unusual target, and if the opportunity was allowed, the patrol leader might actually "rehearse" the patrol by walking through the scenario at a location in the rear area before a patrol was sent out.

Aggressive patrol action, as was the style of warfare in the winter and spring of 1953, resulted in great losses on both sides. One rumor that sobered the lines in late May 1953 concerned the fate of a ten-man patrol from a company in the 31st Regiment in which all of the guys were killed during a recon patrol—the buzz had it that they fell asleep and they were all shot in the same way. This rumor turned out to be generally correct, however, the explanation for how they were all killed has not been resolved. Miller, Carroll, and Tackley (1982) pointed out:

Friendly and enemy patrols kept busy in the I Corps sector. The Chinese, apparently sensitive to the activities of the corps patrols and raiding parties, began to establish ambushes. One patrol of thirty-four men from the U. S. 7th Division fell into a trap set by the enemy on 9 March. Surrounded by some sixty Chinese the whole patrol became casualties: twenty men were killed, twelve wounded, and two missing. On another occasion a thirty-four man patrol from the U. S. 2nd Division ran head on into two Chinese companies. The patrol called for and received reinforcements, and the resulting engagement lasted until the next morning when the enemy broke contact and withdrew. The Americans suffered a total of sixty-three casualties in this fight, twelve of them killed, forty-three wounded, and five missing. Two platoons from the Columbian Battalion, raiding enemy positions on the morning of 10 March, engaged the Chinese in a short but intense fire fight. Forced to withdraw under heavy enemy artillery fire, the Colombians lost nineteen men killed, forty-four wounded, and eight missing (p. 279).

RECON PATROL ACTIONS

Ample and accurate military intelligence is essential to being properly prepared for defensive action and critical for developing offensive action plans. In Korea, one of the primary sources of military intelligence came from the direct observations of the GIs in close proximity to enemy forces. Although much can be learned from aerial reconnaissance and by a knowledgeable observer with a pair of binoculars scanning the enemy positions from a safe vantage point from our own lines, this approach seldom allowed the opportunity to obtain key information about enemy positions and activities, such as whether the Chinese were getting resupplied or whether any new weapons had been moved to the front. In order to obtain such crucial information, someone had to go close to those positions or even behind them to get a clearer look.

On one of our recon patrols we got close enough to the enemy positions to determine that there were women's voices coming from the Chinese line, laughing and talking. We were not able to get close enough to determine if the women were incorporated into their units as soldiers or whether they were there for other purposes.

In Korea, the reconnaissance patrol had as its mission the acquisition of pertinent current information. It was designed not to engage the enemy as this would jeopardize the mission of the patrol. These patrols often were conducted with relatively few persons (from two to twelve) to better avoid detection. The fewer heads bobbing through the valley, the less the enemy observers have to look at. Both contact and recon patrols had their risks. Anytime a patrol went out into the valley, regardless of initial purpose, one could expect the unexpected and to find danger coming from many possible sources. Sometimes, the danger came early in a patrol just as one left the MLR and at other times there could be danger encountered on the return. Vigilance was required at all times. A journey into no-man's-land produced feelings of nervous anticipation—a gnawing in the pit of one's stomach like those encountered on the first parachute jump or when enemy mortar shells were falling in our sector—that had to be ignored in order to go forward.

On patrol one snowy winter evening, as we were just leaving our positions on the MLR heading down an icy trail toward the valley below, we stopped for a breather. There was no place to sit comfortably, so I simply leaned my field pack, containing ammunition, against a snow bank and relaxed for a few seconds. One of the guys in the patrol shouted at me, "Don't move your foot!"

I looked down. My right boot was only an inch away from three small metal prongs sticking up through the snow. An anti-personnel mine. My heart skipped a couple of beats as I contemplated what would have happened if my boot had fallen just a fraction to the left!

Moss pulled me erect and I avoided tripping the mine plunger. We marked the spot so that later we could inform the officer in command of the section of the MLR positions from which we departed that the mine was there so he could have it mapped or moved to a new location. We usually had mines planted in front of our positions but they were always carefully mapped and marked so that they would not trap friendlies. Mines know neither enemy nor friend—and one of our own men could easily trip that mine because it was so close to the trail. As we went into the valley floor my mind toiled over the fact that so much in this business depended upon sheer luck. The space of an inch could mean either destruction or life.

A VERY COLD PAIR OF EARS

We were back up on the section of the MLR opposite the Chinese-held T-Bone Hill. Our hilltop positions ran almost parallel to T-Bone and trailed out into a pair of sloping "fingers." These slopes ran down toward the valley floor near two other hills called the "Alligator Jaws." Not far from the end of one of the Alligator Jaws was a frozen stream that, in warmer times, ran down into the valley below. We were close to the famed "Joe's Mail Box," where periodically the Chinese unloaded batches of propaganda leaflets, usually dropped in bundles, in hopes that the American troops would pick them up and distribute them to their friends.

The materials left by the Chinese propagandists were often rudimentary documents with stereotypic references, for example, referring to American businessmen as "Mr. Moneybags," and intimating that while we were freezing and dying in Korea Mr. Moneybags was off with our women in Florida. The text of one of the propaganda leaflets collected there is provided in Appendix A to give the reader an idea of the messages that were intended to discourage the American troops.

Sometimes the Chinese left "free passes" that promised the bearer safe passage through the Chinese lines and lots of money, good food, and a nice life just for throwing down our weapons and coming over to their side. Our brass considered possession of such a "free pass" as showing bad faith punishable by court martial. Nevertheless, some guys, even those with good old-fashioned American values, carried these passes with them as an "insurance policy," just in case of capture.

Close-up of the area known as Alligator Jaws.

The stream below the knoll was frozen solid and there were still snow drifts in places along the ridge. A George Company patrol reported that there was a body frozen in the stream at the eastern base of the knoll below the lower Alligator Jaw. Earlier that day my squad had volunteered for a recon patrol in the area. The CO told us to verify if there was a body, and to retrieve it, if possible. This area was under direct observation of the Chinese hill. We were advised to depart during the night and do our excavation while it was still dark. Having to dig up another body was not what I originally intended when I volunteered, especially after the gruesome experience described in Chapter 7. We did not know if the body was an American or Chinese soldier. Either way, we were to bring it back to the company area. Then it would be turned over to Graves Registration once we were back in the company. Graves Registration might bring in an intelligence specialist to determine if useful information, such as unit identification, was available from the body or its effects.

During my time in Korea I never witnessed body desecration by Americans, with two exceptions on the approaches to Outpost Yoke (see Chapter 12). On two different slopes, soldiers, likely Americans, had placed a human skull and cross bones along the trail, apparently as a warning to the Chinese. These bones likely came from unearthed old graves that overlooked the rice paddies, rather than our current enemies. They were in an area that was heavily shelled, and old bones were scattered everywhere. One member of our unit added his name to one of the skulls.

I did once see a gruesome example of body desecration around the neck of a soldier from the Turkish Brigade attached to our Division, right before this recon patrol. He had a string of ears around his neck. One of my buddies, when he learned that we were designated to go into the valley to retrieve the body, asked, "If you find a guy and he turns out to be a Chink, would you bring back his ears so I can make a necklace out of them?" We joked that we would try to accommodate his request, if he would really wear the necklace.

The proposed patrol action was pretty straightforward. Our task was to leave our positions on the MLR at 4:00 A.M. in order to take advantage of the cover of darkness and make it out to the tip of the lower Alligator Jaw before daylight. We would then be able to find the body frozen in the ice and break it out of there under the cover of darkness. This would allow us to get back to our own lines before full daylight and before Chinese artillery observers could get some shots off at us.

The walk out to the lower jaw was uneventful. I stopped the patrol a couple of hundred yards away from the knoll to enable Frank Field (Vito) and Del Kenway to scout out the area for possible enemy activity. They soon returned with the "all clear" and we moved into positions around the little knoll, setting up a fire support base to cover us in the event there were enemy soldiers further down the stream where the body was supposed to be in the ice.

Once the men were in place, Vito and I moved out along the ice covered stream searching for the body. It was still dark enough to provide protection from the hill but it was also difficult to make out forms in the ice. We had some difficulty detecting a frozen body as we moved along the bank. We waited until it got a little lighter and made another pass on the return back up stream. As we walked back up the stream, Vito stopped and said, "I see him! There he is. Right over there in the ice."

I moved up to where Vito was standing and squinted into the gray dawn, finally seeing the form of a man in the ice. His head, knees, and what looked like an arm were sticking out of the ice. I moved over toward the silent figure and reached for my sharp knife and the hatchet we had brought along to dig him out.

While Vito watched the front for any sign of enemy movement, I took my knife and began to dig around the head area. I cleared out the ice, removed my glove, and felt the head with my hand. As my hand ran along where the ears should be, I suddenly got a very cold chill up and down my spine. It was not a body, but simply a pile of rocks! I called Vito over to see my discovery, and we both began to laugh. Vito, almost uncontrollably laughing, said, "I thought you were cutting off his ears! Would you have cut a Chink's ears off, Butcher?"

All I could think of to say to him at the time was, "I don't think so, maybe." As I look back at this event, I am thankful it was a pile of rocks and not the body of a Chinese soldier. I hope that I would not have sunk so low as to take a trophy from another human being. Needless to say, we never did find a body.

CONTACT PATROLS

Unlike the information-gathering recon patrols, ambush patrols have war-like intent and motivation. The primary mission involves the goal of engaging the enemy in some manner and accomplishing a particular task, for example, to capture a prisoner, destroy emplacements, to interrupt enemy activity by calling in artillery on to their positions, and so forth.

About a month after the "ice man patrol" we ran one down to Alligator Jaws and Ole Joe's Mail Box to set up an ambush for the next evening in order to try and intercept any enemy "mailmen" en route to drop off propaganda. It seemed like a good plan given the fact that those propaganda leaflets had to get there somehow.

Our mission was to make our way to the hill undetected and find a hideout to quietly spend the day where we could observe the base of the hill from the

Recon patrol into the Alligator Jaws.

knoll and then get set up before the Chinese infantry started patrolling the valley at dusk. Everything went according to plan. At 4:00 A.M. we moved out of our positions and made our way quietly down the slope and across the valley toward the knoll that would be our residence for the day. Our plan was to get to our location, develop camouflaged quarters to avoid daytime detection, and catch up on our sleep in the warm sun while killing time until dark.

It was easy duty for the day at least! We scouted the slope of the knoll and gradually made our way to the top. Finding some comfortable hiding places among some large boulders along the military crest of the hill, we posted a guard and the remainder of the patrol began to accomplish the daytime chore of napping in the noonday sun. After two hours, we changed the sentinel and decided to place another guard down the hill a hundred yards to cover the approach more clearly.

The day-long wait on the knoll was boring and one of our corporals began to entertain himself by razzing a newcomer on his first patrol. He was from another squad, temporarily assigned to serve as our ammo bearer. The corporal was unmerciful in his mocking, and the newcomer was not assertive in defending himself. The taunts included: "You look like a girl! Are you a girl? Are you a fairy? What are you going to do on R&R in Japan...pick flowers? Go to Sunday school? How come you look like a girl?"

Such biased statements against women and gays were not uncommon among infantry soldiers in the 1950s. After awhile, I intervened, not because I saw the comments as offensive, which I now recognize they were, but because they were distracting from our mission.

Shortly after quieting down the heckling, we shifted our position. Soon we began to take some incoming rounds toward the base of the hill—not from the T-Bone, our usual gift giver—but from the valley east of the knoll. Vito and I crawled up the slope for a better look and saw an incredible sight: four tanks were approaching the knoll ahead of us with guns blazing. Our first concern was that we had been discovered and were under attack by a Chinese tank force.

Although we were operating according to a "radio silence" patrol police, we decided that it might be an opportunity to engage the tanks if they were enemy. Our radioman, Ray Daggett, contacted base but, as we were on the line reporting the tanks and getting division artillery alerted to the possibility of a tank shoot, we watched the tanks turn directly north and head for a knoll to the east of T-Bone. We now recognized them as American. They were heading around the T-Bone to do some shooting so we sat back to watch the show. Our CO also thought that it would be important to inform the tanks that our patrol was in their vicinity to prevent other rounds from coming our way.

The tanks fired a number of rounds against what appeared to be a trench line and a cave entrance at the base of the hill then turned tail and headed back to our the American lines to our right. Our next concern was whether our breaking radio silence to report the tanks had blown our own cover; however, it returned to quiet on our knoll for the next few hours. We decided that our plan for setting up the ambush was still viable.

As the sun began to disappear behind the hill to the west we moved the patrol down to the base of the slope to set up the ambush. Moss and the machine gun team set up on the high ground covering the approaches to the knoll as we planned while the remainder of the patrol found positions along the worn path that appeared to have been used by pedestrians in recent days. We settled in and waited for Ole Joe to come and make a mail delivery. Full darkness came, but no Chinese. It was evident that there was going to be no mailman that night.

The time to return approached and we packed up our gear and headed back to our lines. This turned out to be a patrol with no direct contact but certainly one that was far from routine.

IMMINENT DANGER FROM RETALIATORY ACTION

Patrols, especially when they have caused the enemy some inconvenience or damage, can result in retaliation in kind. One day my friend, Bill Estes from Belle, West Virginia, who was now in the mortar section of Fox company, and I had the task of going down the ridge on a two-man patrol only about 300 yards toward Hassakol to serve as forward observers on a fire mission against some suspected artillery observers that the Chinese had posted to fire against us.

The CO instructed us to fire only a couple of mortar rounds because he was afraid that we would be found out and would draw fire from the Chinese. He was right! In spite of the fact that we had found ourselves a pretty good position to avoid detection, as soon as we got off our rounds against the suspected targets, we came under searing machine gun fire from two different positions on the enemy hill. The Chinese also were zeroing in their mortars against our hideout. Bill and I decided that it was time to clear out. As we headed back along the trail back up to the MLR, the machine gun bullets were kicking up dirt around our feet. Our actions might have appeared humorous to someone observing because we were running clumsily at a crouch, stumbling, and falling here and there as we headed for safety. We, however, did not find it funny until we got back through our wire and into the safety of our emplacements. When we got back, we wondered out loud, "What are two peace-loving West Virginia boys doing playing such a dangerous game in this far away land?"

Trail marker for Outpost Yoke.

LOST IN NO-MAN'S-LAND

Patrols could encounter unexpected difficulties brought on by darkness or inclement weather, as well as enemy action. Navigating across unknown terrain at night without the benefit of light or recognizable landmarks was sometimes very frightening. One night we went on a large ambush patrol to a place on the valley floor that the Division Intelligence Corp had singled out as a likely heavy traffic area for Chinese patrols. An arrogant new lieutenant led the patrol. An artillery officer, brought along to handle the shell placement if we had to call in artillery fire for support, assisted him. The patrol also consisted of two machine gun teams, two BAR teams, and a dozen riflemen, most of whom were armed with automatic carbines. We were definitely a well-heeled group of men, in terms of weaponry and destructive potential. We were expected to make a good accounting of ourselves if the Chinese happened to visit our ambush site.

Unfortunately, no one, including the lieutenant, was familiar with the terrain in this area. We were departing from a different section of the line in order to approach our objective from a different direction. The patrol left our designated MLR departure point on time, just as the curtain of darkness was beginning to fall. As we proceeded slowly through the valley, the night sky became darker and then pitch black, and was indistinguishable from the dark earth stretching before us. The lieutenant was navigating only by compass headings, and every other man on the patrol was getting his bearings from the shadowy figure he was following a few steps in front of him. We had to stop the formation frequently to get our bearings. It was very difficult for us to make out anything other than the one person moving in directly in front of us. We had to be attentive to slight movements to keep from losing sight of each other.

We arrived at a location in the valley that the lieutenant thought should be our ambush point and he began to set up the automatic weapons teams in the desired line-up. One of the squad leaders, Moss, quietly raised a question as to our exact location. He did not believe the slight knoll that we were presently occupying was our designated location. The lieutenant insisted that we were in the right place and set up the patrol according to plan. After a while, further questions were raised about where we were. One of the BAR teams found itself occupying a position near a small stream—a stream that was not on the map we had studied earlier or that we had figured into our original game plan. It quickly became apparent to everyone in the patrol that we were not at the place we thought we were. "Where in the hell are we?" someone whispered. No one knew, exactly.

The lieutenant, with a flashlight, got under a tent made from his poncho to read the map. He finally concluded that we were in the wrong place but could not tell exactly where we were. We found out later that we had not made the progress that we assumed because we had to move so slowly in the darkness. In actuality, we had made it only half way to our objective.

We found ourselves in a difficult predicament. Not only did we fail our mission, we had difficulty returning to the MLR because we were given a designated position on the front line to which we could return. That is, we were expected to be at a particular sector of the line at a given time. No one else on the American lines expected a patrol to show up in front of their positions. If we tried to go back to our lines through any other point, we would likely draw fire from our own troops.

It was therefore necessary for us to remain in the valley through the night and move slowly up to the MLR without, of course, arousing the men on the line. It was also necessary for us to break radio silence to warn the line troops about this patrol that "did not know exactly where they were," since we could not determine exactly the location through which we were returning on the line. As we laid in front of the American positions we were nervous about the possibility that some machine gunner up there might detect movement on our part, and thinking we were Chinese, open fire. This was indeed a rather difficult circumstance!

Eventually, when we were able to get back through the lines, it was quite embarrassing for the patrol to return in this manner after such a showy send off. A couple of guys in the line company sector that we went back through noted that we sure had a lot of weapons and ammunition on us. They said, joshing us, "What a lot of nice guns you guys have! How many Chinks did you guys kill with that arsenal?" And, "Do you have silencers on those weapons? We didn't hear any of them go off!"

Things often do not work out as well as intended in wartime operations. It is always best for leaders to be open to information from everyone on patrol. Also, unexpected conditions in the environment often impede the best-laid plans of mice and men.

COMMUNICATIONS AND PATROL MISSION INTEGRITY

Crucial to the integrity of the patrol's mission, as well as to the feeling of security of the combatants on patrol, were clear and effective communications about what was happening. It was critical for the patrol to be well briefed in advance of the engagement and for the patrol leader to keep everyone informed as much as possible of the dangers we were facing or alterations in the plan of attack or objective. This was not always easy given the fact that usually both radio silence was observed and verbal communications between the men on patrol were kept to a minimum.

The most desirable forms of communication when troops were in no-man's-land were hand signals and whispers. The enemy patrols usually followed the same discipline as far as we could tell. One of our recon patrols once observed an interesting communication interchange in a much larger column of Chinese troops that moved quietly through the valley. At one point the first man in the Chinese formation stopped (possibly detecting our presence) and tried to get the rest of the group to stop with a hand signal. A man in the center of the formation, who likely was the patrol leader, signaled for the men to keep moving. When the point man went to the likely leader and spoke something to him, the leader aggressively kicked him then pushed him forward in apparent anger. Apparently clear communications were not the only factors being considered in this situation.

Patrols, whether recon or contact, required 360-degree observation and defense. Because we were running a large number of patrols into the valley, we developed an effective style of communication and patrol movement, using a point man (almost always Vito) and the remainder of the formation in a diamond-shaped formation with the patrol leader in the center of the formation. The men on the extreme points on the diamond were important lookouts in their respective directions and the last man in the formation was responsible for protecting the rear from attack.

The importance of clear communication was aptly demonstrated one night when we were taking out a large twenty-two man combat patrol deep into no-man's-land near the Chinese hill to interdict Chinese patrol actions. Our mission was to move out later in the evening and to try to catch Chinese patrols early in the morning when they were returning to their base along a suspected departure route. A lieutenant was leading this patrol from another platoon and I was second in command. We were also told that we would be taking with us on this patrol four soldiers, originally from a Spanish speaking battalion (recently disbanded), who had been reassigned to other units. These soldiers wanted to become an active part of the activities. When we pointed out to the CO that the four men (one a sergeant first class) could speak no English and that this situation might present some problems in communication on the patrol, we were told that we had to communicate with hand signals that the men could understand.

When the patrol passed through our own lines and formed into a diamond shaped unit to proceed into the valley we became aware that there was little light with which to guide our movement. It became clear that some modifications were going to have to be made in our marching formation because it turned out to be one of those inky nights that required a closer contact between men in order to avoid getting separated. As we proceeded through the valley on the way to our objective, the four new men missed the signal from the lieutenant that the formation was to stop to get our bearings and they simply kept moving through the darkness to who knows where. When we sent two men to find them they were nowhere to be found. They had simply marched off into the darkness.

We couldn't worry about them at this point but had to proceed to our objective with the force, now lessened by one fire team, that we now had. We located our proposed ambush site about an hour later and set up along the trail and waited. We were concerned that the four lost men would show up in our path at some point and engage in a firefight with us as identification would be very difficult in the dark, black night. We waited out our prescribed time for the ambush until about 4:30 A.M. and then headed back to the MLR arriving there just at the break of dawn. When we got safely within our own lines we began to inquire about the four men but nothing had been heard from them. Then, about an hour after daybreak, after we had gotten breakfast and were getting ready to sleep, we heard that the men had made it back through the lines. We were all relieved that none of the ugly possible outcomes had occurred and that they were safely back.

THE DANGERS OF BEING OVERLY ADVENTURESOME

The perilous nature of combat and the specific hazards of combat patrols were made apparent through the actions of one patrol that moved through our outpost positions one evening in the winter of 1953. A few weeks after our own misadventure on Spud Hill another patrol from a different company spent a few hours in our outpost positions awaiting darkness before they jumped off across the Yokkokchon Valley on a raid against the T-Bone, around Spud Hill.

The patrol leader, another arrogant lieutenant who was also overly confident, spent a few hours in our CP in preparation for his raiding patrol. Our company commander informed him about our patrol action against Spud Hill a few weeks before and suggested that he discuss with us the scenario he had planned. We tried to provide him a description of the terrain in the vicinity of his objective (we had already crawled much of the way across that valley floor!) He seemed to be hyped up and did not want to hear about possible problems that he might encounter. When Vito and I tried to point out where our patrol had been and what we encountered when the Chinese worked their way behind us he simply brushed us off saying, "We are not going to do that. We are going to do things my way!"

Some of the men in his patrol confided in our guys as they waited in our bunkers that they had reservations about the plan of action and felt that the lieutenant was "glory bound" and blinded by the enormous potential for medals and honor in the closing days of the Korean War. They thought he was from a prominent family back in the States and had political ambitions after the war and wanted to make a big splash in combat.

The patrol was a disaster. A few hours after they left our lines, there was a great deal of commotion on the valley floor—flares, artillery, and a lot of machine gun fire. The lieutenant and several of the men on the patrol were killed in action and several others were wounded as the Chinese pummeled them. One of the riflemen who returned from the raid indicated that the lieutenant had been impulsive in his launching the raid and had them assault the hill from too great a distance. They were exposed too long to Chinese fire and did not have a chance once the enemy knew of their presence in the valley. The intermixing of political ambition with military duty can be problematic when highly risky action and uncertain forces are involved. It is difficult to know what happened on that hill because the reporting was spotty. However, in trying to piece together the outcomes from the information we obtained, it appeared to many that the lieutenant had simply allowed his blind ambition to narrow his judgment and to make field decisions that did not reflect the reality of the situation.

Although it was extremely important for our forces to establish an aggressive presence through patrol activity it was indeed very difficult for patrol size forces to make the kind of splash that the lieutenant wanted. During the winter of 1953, there was heavy patrol activity in the Yokkokchon Valley, much of which had come up empty handed. Hermes (1966) pointed out that during February and March the Corps sent out 2,500 patrols to raid, ambush, or reconnoiter, and fewer than a hundred made any contact with the enemy. During March only one prisoner-of-war was captured (Hermes, 369-370).

A SUCCESSFUL PATROL AGAINST THE BLACK MARKETERS

Our skill at running night combat patrols came in handy in another sector of our lives—a raid on a KSC camp in order to obtain supplies for some planned festivities. One night, back in reserve, several guys in our platoon decided that we would have some fun, but for some reason there were no beer rations available. Moss, Vito, and I decided that we would surprise the guys in the platoon with some alcohol for a festive evening. There was a KSC camp close by with the usual contingent of black marketers at which we purchased some spirits to aid our celebration. Unfortunately, we could not muster enough money to buy even a single bottle of whiskey on the black market (fifths of Canadian Club or Seagrams sold for about $15 per bottle). We thus concocted a plan that would enable the black marketers to help us obtain alcohol that involved a little old-fashioned infantry ingenuity.

One of the new guys in the platoon had served in the military police for a brief stint before coming to Korea. He still had an armband with the often-dreaded initials "MP" on it and a police whistle that MPs usually carry. All we had to do was to improvise appropriate headgear for our deception. Using a helmet liner and some white tape from a first aid kit, we fashioned identification by taping the helmet to read in bold letters "MP." We were ready for our little visit to the KSC bootleggers.

The core of the plan was as follows: two of us would go to the KSC camp and locate the black marketer, which was not too difficult to do because they were quite prevalent. The third person (wearing the improvised MP paraphernalia) would wait in the wings until he saw a signal from us. We would bring the bootlegger close by, hopefully with a couple of bottles of booze in hand, and initiate a discussion about the price of the purchase. At the appropriate time, before we would be expected to hand over the money but after we got our hands on the bootie, we would light up a cigarette as a signal. Our phony police officer would then rush up, blowing his whistle, in a simulated effort to interrupt the illegal activity. The raid was slated to be at dusk in order to capitalize on the best lighting for the cigarette signal and for the MP lettering to be clearly visible for maximum effect. What a remarkable, yet simple, plan!

There has never been a patrol in the history of the U. S. Army that ran as smoothly as this one and had such tangible and refreshing results. Everything went as scheduled. We located our black marketer who happened to have several bottles of CC. He brought two of them to us where we waited in a stand of trees at the edge of a rice paddy. We insisted upon checking the tops and bottoms of the bottles to assure that they had not been tampered with (a trick they were known to do at times). When we were satisfied with the product, I lit up a cigarette, of course after first offering one to our black marketer friend. Just as I lit up my cigarette we heard a series of sharp whistles and the three of us looked to see our MP look-alike running swiftly toward us waving his pistol, yelling, "Halt, Halt! Stop right there. Police arrest!"

Our black marketer looked quickly at the "cop" and then headed as fast as he could through the brush in making his escape. We took his lead and headed back in our own direction with the MP chasing us—all three of us laughing gleefully. The fake MP chased us for some distance until we were all out of breath. We rolled on the ground laughing then opened the first bottle to toast our successful patrol. The campfire was indeed warm and the troops exceedingly happy upon our return.

A VISIT WITH THE ALLIES

Our compatriots in the British and Australian armies did not have to go to such extreme efforts to get a drink. They had NAAFI (Navy, Army, and Air Force Institutes) pubs, a source of envy for American troops. Our PX (Post Exchange) stores paled in comparison. My first, and unfortunately only, experience with a NAAFI happened one evening when we were in reserve. The NCOs of our company were invited to a NAAFI Sergeants Club. Stan Stinson and I caught a jeep and went over for a look-see.

We were bowled over by their highly civilized establishment. We were only three miles from the front lines and here was a very homey and quaint pub. It was a treat for a couple of grungy GIs just off the front to sit down, with music blaring from a jukebox, and have a few drinks. The other patrons in the establishment, mostly Aussies, wore headgear quite different from ours and carried strange looking weapons (Bren Guns). Otherwise, their circumstances and manner was interchangeable with ours. We had a most pleasant evening and wondered, as we left, why our country had broken away from such nice folks as the British so long ago.

9

Rotation Blues and R&R

AFTER MANY MONTHS, COUNTLESS PATROLS, mind numbing boredom, and not to forget the cold and darkness, I began to wonder what I was doing in Korea. During quiet times on patrol, but especially when in reserve, a hillbilly lament called "Rotation Blues," written by Lt. Stewart Powell and recorded by the likes of Elton Britt and Bill Monroe, repeated over and over in my mind:

I got the ro-oh-oh-ta-a-tion blu-ues.
I'm a lonely soldier sittin' in Korea...
I'm a lonely soldier sittin' in Ko-rea
But rotation's comin' so I shouldn't have no fear.

Just a few more weeks and rotation's gonna set me free
Just a few more weeks and rotation's gonna set me free
'Cause the F.E.C. is too far east fur me.

I'm gonna pack my bags and sail back over the sea
I'm gonna pack my bags and sail back over the sea
'Cause the A-frames in Korea just don't look good on me.
Rotation had better hurry up and set me free (I'm buggin' out)
Rotation had better hurry up and set me free (Section Eight's gonna get me)
'Cause the honey pots in Korea done started smellin' good to me.

Now that rain in Korea sure gets cold and wet
Now that rain in Korea sure gets cold and wet
And the rotation papers sure are hard to get.
(Reprinted by permission of Tannen Music, Inc., all rights reserved)

Lt. Powell's song captured our thoughts about going home and how difficult life in Korea became. We needed thirty-six points to earn the rotation home. Those of us on the front lines got four points a month, rear lines three points, and further back two points. The whole time I was in Korea I qualified for the four points per month.

My buddy Carlos Coleman's number for rotation home came up right before my departure to Japan for R&R. This seemed sudden to most of us, but Carlos accumulated something like sixty-four points during his two tours of duty. He had not been home in a year and a half. It was time, so Carlos packed his kit to head for the rear. The platoon would surely miss his contributions— good machine gunners were hard to find.

I would miss Carlos's cheerful greetings and his rough and ready attitude for any kind of action—whether it was for slipping off into a KSC camp in search of alcohol or for crawling through the night to make contact with the Chinese. He was a reliable volunteer to the end. Some of us wondered if he would have another change of heart when he got back to the rear and decide to sign up for another tour. After all, he did so last time. But, this time he never looked back.

He came by my bunker to say good-bye and I felt like I was losing more than a reliable trench comrade but also an irreplaceable friend. Carlos's last words to me echoed after his departure:

"Butch, take it easy and don't take any chances. You've gotta get out of this place in one piece! When you get back to the States we'll meet at the Old Pastime Bar back in Charleston and clean the place out!"

THE DIRECT OPPOSITE OF REST AND RELAXATION

After approximately six months in Korea GIs were automatically eligible for an R&R leave, usually in Japan. The military goal behind R&R for war-weary GIs was to provide a break from combat to enable soldiers to restore their fighting spirit. It evolved from efforts to lessen "shell shock" during World War I and "combat fatigue" in World War II. Today, the Army also uses the term "R&R" to identify "Resilience and Restoration" Centers. While sharing the same acronym, these R&R Centers, like the one at Ft. Hood, Texas, provide outpatient mental health services to active duty personnel. This type of R&R is not a leave for everyone in a combat zone, but is targeted for those suffering from "Post Traumatic Stress Disorder" or other mental health issues similar in nature to "shell shock" or "combat fatigue."

By the time my rotation for it came up, Rest and Relaxation was a misnomer. The troops, recognizing this, routinely referred to it as I&I (Intercourse and Intoxication) or A&A (Ass and Alcohol). Drinking to excess and military prostitution were the predominant features of many R&R breaks. Unlike my peaceful experiences at my ROK friend Lee's home village, there was nothing restful about the six days I spent in the Japanese cities of Osaka and Nara. I had been in Korea longer than my close buddies Vito Field and Dale Moss, so my number came up first. I was disappointed about not being able to share this much-anticipated adventure with them. Instead I was the only one from my company on the plane to Japan.

Notably, my R&R break had the exact opposite effect than that intended by the military. Six months on the front, Carlos's cautions when he left Korea and the glittering experiences of Japanese cities lessened my desire for further military combat. I began to see things very differently, more cautiously. The stark contrast between my enjoyable times in Japan with the reality of the day-to-day existence on the front was a real eye opener. I no longer wanted to be an infantry sergeant. I was a bit quicker on the jump response when incoming rounds whistled overhead. I wanted to live. Duty and three months to go until my rotation was up required me to return to the front lines. If the Army had known how deleterious R&R leaves could be to the combat readiness of soldiers like me, they would have, in all likelihood, discontinued the program immediately.

THE R&R DRILL AND ITS CONSEQUENCES

Before leaving for Japan, I learned the drill from those who had gone before. This information included:

- Bring $300 for expenses. (This money came from saving, borrowing, and lucky wins at poker.)
- What demands would be placed on you? NONE. "Eat, drink, and be merry for tomorrow we die!"
- How much alcohol would be consumed? Everything in sight.
- Find a Japanese woman companion for the week.

The last bit of information came from the expectations of my peers—late adolescent men who had been away from family and friends living in a violent and, what I now recognize (but did not then), misogynistic environment. During boot camp we trained with cadence calls on marches that objectified sex as recreational and rough; these offensive cadences are no longer allowed in today's Army (Lineberry, 2002). For us, they equated military strength with sexual prowess (Butler, 2000): "This is my weapon, this is my gun. One is for shooting, the other's for fun." This environment was intolerant of any individual who gave any sign that he might not enjoy an R&R experience like this—recall the corporal's taunts described in Chapter 8 in the section on Contact Patrols. Alexander (2004) suggested most GIs that chose not to have an "I&I" experience on leave would lie to their buddies that they did on return to the unit.

The only expectation or limitation I recall from the Army about behavior during R&R was to use condoms to prevent sexually transmitted diseases (STDs then referred to as VD). There were the basic training lectures stateside that we interpreted to mean, "Don't damage government property!" We endured periodic "short arm" inspections in the Army's attempts to prevent VD. Perhaps my oddest experience in Korea was standing in formation with 5,000 other men, pants down, penis ready for inspection by medical personnel walking through the long files. I also benefitted through observations of one of my buddies who returned to the front lines from R&R with Gonorrhea. No one in earshot of his agonizing moans during the long march to the company rear for treatment would want to follow those footsteps.

I don't recall any Army briefings about contraception. If it was considered at all, it was thought to be the woman's sole responsibility. Amerasian children in Japan, Korea, the Philippines, and Vietnam grew up without acknowledgement or support from their American servicemen fathers (Baker, 2004). They also were frequently ostracized, neglected, or abandoned by their mother's family and culture (Moon, 1997, 1999a).

No mention was made about the rights of the women we would encounter. There was never any suggestion that the women we met (or Japanese society at large) would be troubled by our I&I activities. We were ignorant about the likelihood that overwhelming poverty or violence, rather than free will, forced women into military prostitution. We didn't think about the recent past—when American soldiers like us were the enemy of these young women. We didn't consider how our differing racial backgrounds or larger sizes would be unpleasant or even frightening to young Japanese women. We didn't put two and two together—that some of these young women had lost all their family members to Allied bombing and had nowhere else to go when recruited in 1945 by Japanese police to service the occupying forces (Butler, 2000; Tanaka, 2002).

Professor Tanaka's (2002) extensive research into U.S., Australian, and Japanese archives revealed little concern for the women engaged in military-controlled prostitution at the time of occupation. Even a chaplains' report submitted to General MacArthur in 1946, condemning the widespread practice of prostitution in Japan, did not include any mention of violation of women's rights. Both chaplains and officers in the Public Health and Welfare (PHW) section of the General Headquarters (GHQ) of the Supreme Commander of the Allied Powers believed Japanese women, not clean and innocent American soldiers, were the source of the "evil VD." Chaplains concerned with the moral well being of the troops (and notably not the women) recommend the suppression of military-controlled prostitution. On the other hand, Professor Tanaka found that PHW officers' reports to GHQ recommended the opposite. Public health officers believed that VD could only be controlled by a system of military-controlled prostitution with rigorous VD exams and treatment of the women working in the sex industry.

When General MacArthur ordered with great fanfare the abolishment of "licensed prostitution" in 1946, it did not shut down a vast and profitable industry of unlicensed prostitutes and "comfort women" in restaurants, eating-

and-drinking houses and private houses of prostitution. This is what we saw on our arrival in Japan, about seven years after the so-called abolition of prostitution. It is only years later, through the efforts of scholars, feminists, human rights experts, and the testimony of surviving "comfort women" (e.g., Butler, 2000; Moon, 1999a, 1999b, 2009; Soh, 2008; Tanaka, 2002), that the R&R experiences described below are correctly understood to be sexual exploitation of women on both individual and institutional levels. My buddies and I were regrettably unaware of this at the time.

THE JOURNEY FROM WAR TO CITY

A cramped C-47 flew us from Kimpo Airfield near Seoul across the Sea of Japan to Osaka. This uncomfortable and rough ride was a Godsend for the couple dozen soldiers on it. None of us complained. We were too excited about our leave and what we would find. We came from different units so most of us did not know anyone on the flight. I ended up sitting next to Bill, a sergeant from the Second Division. We decided to stick together during our leave. I don't remember Bill's last name, but I recall he was from Michigan, didn't like college, and dropped out to join the Army. Like me, he had lost his dad when he was little. We got off the plane and boarded a truck to take us to the R&R Center.

As soon as we arrived at the R&R Center we knew we had stepped out of hell and right into the middle of heaven! So distant from the front and so strangely foreign in a positive way that it seemed like a dream for the entire time that I was there. The first stop was clean up. Even though we were in a military facility, the soap in the showers smelled like flowers. I experienced my first shave ever from a barber, who also trimmed my hair. The gracious Japanese barber did a much better job than one of the guys in the platoon using medic's scissors. After an invigorating massage, I was issued a new khaki dress uniform with my sergeant's stripes and the other paraphernalia—badges and ribbons—I had earned. I almost didn't recognize myself!

After getting outfitted, the R&R Center fed us a very uncharacteristic military meal: steaks grilled to order, apple pie, and real ice cream. I drank two chocolate milkshakes—the best tasting thing I had in months. We were clean, well dressed, and well fed. I'd never felt better in my life! There was nothing left for us to do in the R&R Center except leave and begin our five days in Japan. Bill and I walked out into the pleasant evening and the bright city lights of Osaka through a solid metal and wood frame door guarded by a single sentry. This friendly corporal checked our passes and wished us well.

When the door swung open, a sea of beautiful, smiling faces greeted us. Wow! We were dazzled and confused by the pleasant sounds and unremitting attention we received. Bill and I looked at each other and wondered if we had been killed in action and were now arriving in heaven! It felt as though we had been turned loose in a life-size doll factory with animated and stunningly beautiful creatures, some in Western dress, others in traditional Japanese kimonos.

THE DARKER SIDE OF R&R

We were experiencing, without any comprehension on our parts, what is now called the "commodification" and depersonalization of women and their bodies (Baker, 2004; Butler, 2000; Moon, 1997, 1999b; Soh, 2008; Tanaka, 2002). At age nineteen, and just off the front lines, I was blissfully oblivious to this dark side of the life soldiers like me encounter right outside the gates of so many U.S. military establishments around the world. During my short stay in Japan, I did not see any of the violence or other negative consequences (poverty, diseases, infertility, pregnancy, shunning) so common in these women's lives. Instead, I thought that Bill and I were having a good time with our new Japanese "friends" who were equally enjoying themselves.

This impression about being "friends" coexisted with our instructions from those who had been on R&R before. We were told not to worry about finding a woman companion for the week. All we had to do was walk out the R&R Center gate and we would be flooded with opportunities, as we discovered ourselves. For reasons I'm not sure why, I got multiple instructions not to accept the first fifty invitations made in the first thirty seconds at the R&R gate. The other GIs cautioned us to take our time, for there was no need to rush or expend any effort for the "commodity" was in ample supply.

We knew from our buddies ahead of time the cost for the services of our companion and how the financial transactions would be handled. The $300 we brought to Japan was to be handed over to the young woman selected. She would then handle all the costs for the five days (meals, hotel, transportation, and her fee). Switching escorts ("no changee changee") was discouraged for both health reasons and to simplify financial transactions.

These young women served many different functions during R&R breaks including tour organizer and interpreter. This made it easier to see them as friends instead of military prostitutes. We assumed any money they "saved" on our expenses went directly to them. We knew nothing of "debt bondage" (Butler, 2000; Moon, 1997, 1999a; Soh, 2008). Many women were kept in prostitution to pay off "liabilities" like exorbitant referral fees to "labor recruiters," usurious interest rates, kick-backs to the various establishments we frequented, medical care for STDs or pregnancies, or costs of their clothing and other such expenses.

OUR TIME WITH SUMIKO AND YOSHIKO

Bill and I, playing it cool, made our way through the sea of lovely, smiling women and into a nightclub. We decided to have a drink and to look over the scene. The bar was filled with a friendly gathering of GIs and Japanese civilians. In no time, all of our World War II stereotypes about the Japanese people faded. Those we met were not the hostile and inhumane "Japs" depicted in the old war movies I saw at the West End Theater in Charleston.

No sooner had we sat down and ordered a cocktail than two stunningly beautiful Japanese women came to our table. One of them greeted me in a warm friendly manner. "Hello, I'm Sumiko. Would you like to go with us to Nara—the most beautiful city in Japan?"

Bill and I looked at each other, than back at the two women. We were both ready to commit to them The financial hand-off was made expeditiously. Before we knew it, we were on our way to Nara. They took care of us for the rest of our time together. They were efficient tour escorts, navigating our way to the train station and purchasing tickets. We settled into the train ride and got to know each other.

Both women, perhaps as a testament to their survival skills and intellect, spoke enough English to converse with us. Bill was always cracking jokes, and they joined in our laughter. The two women looked to be in their mid-twenties and dressed in Western-style clothing when we first met. Sumiko was from Nara. Because the name of Bill's escort, like Bill's last name, has faded from my memory, I will call her "Yoshiko" here. "Yoshiko" was from just outside Hiroshima.

She had no scars that I could see, but Bill later told me about the burns over portions of her body. She told Bill that she got them from being near Hiroshima on the day the atomic bomb hit.

Yoshiko was likely in her mid-to-late teens when the atomic bombs were dropped on Hiroshima and Nagasaki right before the end of WW II. Tanaka (2002) provides vivid descriptions of how the police in the Hiroshima prefectural lured almost 500 women there to work in euphemistically called "comfort stations" for the soon to arrive U.S. occupying forces. While some of these women were prostitutes, others were young widows, orphans, or high school students working in munitions factories and living in dormitories. At a time when starvation was rampart, these young girls were guaranteed ample food. However, not surprisingly, almost all the women in the Hiroshima prefecture were extremely reluctant to work in comfort stations for Americans. Tanaka (2002) provides more details about the coercion used during the recruitment process.

I do not know what Sumiko or Yoshiko's past was like. They unquestionably were of the age and in the environment where these dreadful things routinely happened to young women. During the time we spent with them, they redirected any mention of World War II or their past to other topics. We would talk about the war in Korea, but most of our conversations were about our present activities and upcoming plans for the R&R. They did not share any possible ugly experiences.

As the fast train sped through the evening, we became lost in pleasant conversation. The spell was interrupted, however, when a train, going in the opposite direction, let out a very shrill whistle. "Screeech!" Both Bill and I immediately dived on the floor and covered our heads with our hands protecting ourselves against incoming shells while all of the Japanese commuters watched on, knowingly. After a few moments, we embarrassedly got back on our seats feeling somewhat stupid at our automatic reaction to "hit the dirt." Sumiko said to me, "Eets ok, GI. You're safe here in Japan. Don't worry any more." We rode silently for a while. Bill finally said to me, "You think we'll ever be normal again?" I replied, "I hope so. I hope so."

After a relatively short ride, we were completely away from the shadow of war. This was where we wanted to be. We stayed at a quaint Japanese hotel where we met a few guys from other outfits on R&R leave. There were four or five of us that hung around together.

Once a day we were taken to the community baths. At first we were taken aback by the public nudity. The Japanese baths were community events, open to all. We found old men and women, little children, whole families taking baths together. After awhile, we adapted to the nudity. However, Americans do not know what hot water is until they experience a Japanese bath. It seemed to us that the Japanese bathed in water Americans usually reserve for boiling lobsters. We all experienced these hot tubs as sheer misery and were happy when they ended.

We only had one uniform to last us for the five days, so each night all of our clothing was religiously taken away and cleaned, pressed, and made ready for the next day. In the hotels, all of us lived in kimonos. One evening Bill and I decided to look around town a bit, so we left the hotel dressed only in our slightly undersized kimonos. We became immediately lost in the confusion of the lights and signs (only in Japanese, of course). We wandered around somewhat conspicuously since we were a good two feet taller than everyone else. Fairly quickly, Sumiko and Yoshiko located us to our great relief. We were put in tow and mildly scolded for our escape into the night. Incidents like this made us feel like they were taking good care of us.

Indeed, we felt well treated, if not spoiled, by all we encountered. People at the hotel and in the streets appeared tolerant of the American soldiers in their midst. I remember joking with Bill that our biggest problem seemed to be dodging umbrellas when the rain came. We were so much taller than the fast walking Japanese that it was like being in a sea of black moving circles below our line of sight.

Alcohol was in abundant supply. Thanks to the Army and their Sergeant's Clubs, it was unbelievably cheap. We only had to spend $2 or $3 at "Nickel Night" to get so intoxicated that we blacked out. Unlike the Army's concerns about preventing VD, there were no attempts to prevent the negative consequences associated with excessive alcohol use by young men ages eighteen to twenty-four (e.g., violence, alcohol poisoning, development of addiction, etc.).

Like cigarettes, we saw the abundance and low cost of alcohol as a right we earned. I exercised that right at Nickel Night at the Sergeant's Club—I have no recollection of actually leaving the premises. I have some vague memory of our walking, stumbling, crawling, laughing, and barfing our way back to our hotel, with the assistance of Sumiko and Yoshiko. They always gave the appearance of joining in and enjoying our alcoholic revelries, but they were always ready to take care of us when we drank to excess.

Sumiko and Yoshiko tried to teach us something of their ways. They took us everywhere in two rickshaws. Particularly favorite places were the beautiful parks in Nara. We enjoyed walking among tame deer in one park and seeing the many ancient and picturesque temples in others. At one point during our visit our friends took us to a traditional Bunraku theater production. Bunraku is a high level of stage art using life-size puppets that has strong historical ties to Osaka.

Before we left the hotel for the theater, I recall filling our stomachs with Sukiyaki and drinking lots of booze. Several other GIs staying at the hotel joined us. I think we were the only Americans in the audience. About halfway through the performance we got restless. This form of entertainment did not provide enough action for a bunch of rough and tumble combat veterans; after all, "boys will be boys." At least that's how we characterized our behavior at the time. We were aware of embarrassing our Japanese escorts, but we were ignorant about how highly offensive and disruptive our behavior was in such a cultivated setting. We did not experience negative consequences for our behavior, but did Sumiko and Yoshiko? If so, it was hidden from us.

LEAVING R&R

Sumiko and Yoshiko accompanied us back to the R&R Center in Osaka, where we learned of the most marvelous SNAFU ever. Our flight back to Korea was delayed for a day! Even though our arrangements with Sumiko and Yoshiko were for a five, not six day break, they appeared as gleeful as we were. But, at that point, we were penniless, having turned over our funds to them at the start of the leave. They did not abandon us even though we could not give them additional funds for this extra day. Instead, they took us to a hotel in Osaka, accompanied us to dinner, and continued celebrating with us, as friends would do.

The next day it was over. All the pleasant parks, letting tame deer eat from our hands, even the steaming hot baths became fond memories too quickly.

The departure back to the war zone was difficult. Upon our return to the Army compound in Osaka, we were back in the hands of the military. Once inside, the Army knew what was needed—they took away our temporary khaki uniforms, issued us new fatigues and lined us up for breakfast before loading us on the C-47 transport to go back across the Sea of Japan to Kimpo Air Base in Korea. Most of us were still pretty drunk as we passed through the chow line for breakfast, which to us seemed like we were condemned men having our last meal before execution.

As I wandered through the chow line, I requested one of the bowls of apricots that I saw lined up in front of one of the cooks. He looked at me in a puzzled way and balked at my request. I became more insistent about getting the apricots and my friend, behind me in the line, began to tell the cook in a loud voice to give me what I wanted. The cook was uncooperative at first, but eventually handed me the bowl. After we got the rest of our food and sat down, I discovered that the "apricots" were actually uncooked eggs. Being a bit embarrassed, I tried to make the best of it and simply stirred up the eggs with salt and pepper and downed them as though I knew what I was doing all along. Admittedly, with my foggy mind, I was not ready to go back to combat.

THE DUAL WORLDS OF R&R

This is one of the most difficult chapters I had to write for this book. An early version of the material in this chapter was limited to my descriptions of the excitement and fun I experienced as a nineteen-year-old on a much-needed R&R leave from combat. It was similar to descriptions others, like Alexander (2004, p. 396), have written:

> Generally, Japanese girls and young women were not prostitutes in the traditional sense; rather they were working women who were attracted to the excitement and comparative high life that a man on R&R could offer.

My research for this chapter revealed a very different world for the young women caught up with military prostitution. I considered dropping any mention of I&I from the book, as others have done in their discussions about the Korean War. However, I concluded that would be dishonest and not in keeping with my goal of providing an honest accounting of my wartime experiences. Unlike some of the other chapters, I relied more heavily on writings by others to present the other side of military prostitution.

I hope that this chapter provides a more balanced description of R&R in Japan at the time of the Korean War. It is a legacy of the U.S. Armed Forces that went on for many years after the Korean War ended, even continuing today. However, the U.S. government—in a much-needed reversal—now recognizes military prostitution as a type of "human trafficking" and a form of modern-day slavery (Department of Defense, 2010). According to the DoD, human trafficking (prostitution is one form of trafficking) is tied with the illegal arms trade as the second largest criminal industry in the world. It is now DoD policy to oppose prostitution and other forms of forced labor. Even in cases where prostitution may be legal in a host nation, prostitution and patronizing a prostitute are in violation of chapter 47 of The Uniform Code of Military Justice and part IV of the Manual for Courts-Martial 2008. There is a command-wide program of "zero tolerance" to stop prostitution and human tracking in the United States Forces in Korea (Inspector General, 2006) that is being used as a model program in DoD law enforcement training programs (see Department of Defense, 2009).

This chapter demonstrates how much military prostitution was ingrained in the U.S. Armed Forces from the highest levels to the grunts like me. It will not go away easily. Fortunately, current efforts appear comprehensive. Laws have been changed, training of soldiers is ongoing, and law enforcement has better tools (Department of Defense, 2009, 2010; Inspector General, 2006).

The world we thought we were sharing with Sumiko and Yoshiko was an illusion. Had I known how destructive this system was to countless women, I would not have participated. I can't believe that any of my other close buddies would have either. I'm hoping that the comprehensive "zero tolerance" program being implemented by DoD will help today's soldiers see this previously hidden underworld of military prostitution and keep them from participating.

RETURN TO THE HELL OF WAR

On the plane ride back to Kimpo Airfield the crew chief from the Air Force told us that, based on the latest news reports about the prisoner exchange, the war was probably going to be over before our plane landed in Korea. The rumors had it that the Chinese had finally had their fill of the war and were in agreement to go along with the prisoner exchange plan that had been discussed for about two years. Even this news, however, did little to buoy the morale of the half sober, half dejected troops heading back to Korea. Some of us chose to sleep; others passed out. No one on the plane wanted to return.

Not long after I returned from R&R in early April, we received word of some important developments in the peace talks. There was actually some exchange of prisoners in a program that was referred to as "Little Switch." However, the cooperation was short lived and the Chinese launched a major offensive. Our Battalion was on the front lines, which resulted in the death and maiming of a large number of our troops—my buddies.

10

From Softball Field to the Gates of Hell: The First Battle for Pork Chop Hill

NATURE AND ARMY GENERALS ABHOR UNEVENNESS. In nature, the tides and flowing waters make jagged points smooth over time; the wind blows against desert sands making them even, undulating dunes. So too in trench warfare, Army generals, at least those in Korea in 1952 and 1953, preoccupied themselves with the task of straightening out a crooked system of trench line. If there was a jutting piece of real estate belonging to the communist Chinese Army that protruded unevenly into the flowing lines of the UN troops then the military leaders focused on "straightening." The Chinese generals likewise did not like to see American held positions, such as outposts like Pork Chop or Yoke, breaking up their smooth lines. These were clear invitations for them to attack us and try to occupy our hillocks of battered earth and bring them into their own sector.

Moreover, it appeared especially desirable to straighten out the MLR when it also served to increase the territory under one's control because of the "so called" peace talks that were taking place in Panmunjom. One of the most inconspicuous pieces of real estate that seemed to need straightening in April of 1953 involved the little knoll called Pork Chop Hill—so named because of its shape on a map. Retaking this hill that the Chinese had recently grabbed and possessing it for the peace talks would supposedly strengthen the hands of the negotiators. It was apparently important for each side to hold on to as much of the jagged pieces of real estate as possible because when (or if) a peace agreement was reached then the eventual pull back would be measured from the point of present occupation. Thus, the further up the peninsula our troops were situated the bigger the country of South Korea would be.

The politics that were influencing military actions at this time in Korea centered on the lack of progress in the peace negotiations in Panmunjom. The negotiators could not agree on issues of disengagement and the prisoner-of-war question that had played so large a role during 1952. To some people the war in Korea appeared to be like a chess game and we were the pieces to be moved about. The American chess pieces, especially the pawns—the lowly infantryman—would be moved to a particular spot. The Chinese generals and political officers would then move their pawns (similarly low infantry-men) into another square in a counter move. Our generals would then move knights, and so on. These grand schemes and strategies must have made great intellectual discussions at the respective War Colleges.

In the trenches of Korea, however, it was another matter—such movements resulted in human tragedy. When Ole Joe moved to a particular square and we moved to the same one to try and check him, it was done at the price of human blood—our blood and that of the Chinese. These chess moves were not fun, intellectual games; they involved the hopes, dreams, and lives of young men. Just a week before our leaving the line, the Chinese generals made a move that cost some human life, including that of our friend Zimdahl—he did not even get to know the outcome of that particular chess gambit!

We were moved in reserve behind the MLR across from a Chinese-held hill called Hassakol in the Yokkokchon valley. The hill of particular interest to the Chinese was the one we called Pork Chop Hill, a relatively small plot of real estate about 240 meters high. It possessed one singularly undesirable quality—it was located several thousand yards inside Chinese territory. Pork Chop was overshadowed by two other hills: the taller hill Hassakol and the larger but uglier hill Chink Baldy. The road leading out to the Pork Chop from beyond the American MLR was long and winding and was usually under constant observation by the Chinese artillery observers on Hassakol. It was a long walk out to Pork Chop, especially under the watchful eyes of the Chinese sharpshooters.

A DAY IN THE WARM SUN

Not long after we left the MLR, we moved to a blocking position near the Pork Chop. The squad tents we moved into were already in place when we arrived that night and we were assigned nice dry quarters. It was very hot since the rain had stopped and we rolled up the sides of the tent to get a breeze through our quarters. Although our platoon's tents were pitched in a wooded ravine with a small stream running nearby it was only a short down hill walk to the Company Headquarters tent. A brief period of relaxation in the warm Korean spring sun ensued. Everyone felt relieved to be away from the constant explosions of 76 mm shells, listening post duty, and the ritualized half-on, half-off sleep/guard watch that we were constantly observing at the front these days during this period of increased enemy probes.

One of the guys got the idea of having a softball game and the American contingent in our platoon challenged friends from another platoon to an old fashioned softball game; someone located a couple of gloves, a battered bat, and a softball. Bases were fashioned out of T-shirts which all seemed to have the same dirty grey colored appearance that the bases back home used to have.

For a time it seemed just like home—our cares were gone and the war was a distant thought in our minds. More important than the war was the fact that I didn't clutch up when it came my time at bat and got a hit, helped considerably by the bad bounce that the ball took in the rough infield which had been a rice paddy in its former life. Running the bases reminded me of playing baseball in the American Legion Junior Softball League back in Charleston only a couple of years before. Of course, a ball game in Charleston seemed like an eternity away now, or maybe it never really happened at all because it seemed so remote and so alien to our present situation.

A holiday atmosphere prevailed that day and the prospect looked merrier when we were informed that the beer rations that we had missed out on for the past weeks had finally been delivered. Army life could be fun, I thought. We were enjoying ourselves after a long time at the front. I felt pretty good about my place in the Army now as an assistant platoon sergeant—pretty good duty with a good bunch of guys. It was also reassuring to have a guy like Master Sergeant Rogers running the show. Rogers, a WWII veteran of the Italian campaign, was all business and garnered a great deal of respect. He was personable and knew what it took to be effective and to stay alive in combat. I had now been promoted to sergeant first class (a five striper) and enjoyed the responsibility of my new job, and the pay (as Army salary goes) was certainly very good for a nineteen year-old!

At 4:00 P.M., the NCOs were called to the company command tent. The CO was visibly upset. He had just received word that our company was going back up front at 8:30 that evening. Pork Chop Hill had fallen to the Chinese during the night and a counter attack, currently in progress, was faltering. Our company was needed to finish the job.

With the prospect of a potential disaster in the offing, our Company Commander, Captain King, was pretty sensitive to the ways GIs think and wanted to quell growing anxieties as much as possible. One problem situation that he was told about was that the menu for the evening called for our old nemesis, creamed chicken. He recognized right away that, superstitious or not, this particular meal would never do on the day of an attack, and he ordered the cooks to do something else—anything. Creamed chicken was considered to be a jinx for the company—this meal had been served when the company got clobbered on Outpost Charlie, before I arrived; it was also the meal served at the horrible blocking position shelling in which so many people were hit just before we went up on Jane Russell Hill. This meal was a bad omen indeed! No way was this stuff going to be served before the company went up on Pork Chop!

Many people had strong premonitions about the forthcoming battle. The tension was running high as we had our meal and went to the supply truck to get issued additional supplies an equipment—assault rations, hand grenades, extra bandoliers of ammunition. The atmosphere reeked of negative expectations and gallows humor. People were writing letters home as though these words to their families or girlfriends would be their last. Some guys had the habit of writing a "last letter" to be mailed only if they didn't make it back. If they did return they would retrieve the letter and tear it up until next time.

The chaplain came to the company about an hour before our departure time and provided services to those interested—and as it usually happened before a battle, there were numerous takers in. Not being the religious type I never participated in such services, but never joked about others feeling the need to do so. At the end of formal services, a few of the men asked for special individual meetings with him.

Three men from the company told the chaplain that they were afraid their number was up and asked him to intercede on their behalf with the captain to get them special dispensation—they did not want to go on this operation. The chaplain, seeing their sincerity and their obvious plight, interceded on their behalf with the CO and got them excused from the attack. One of these men, a friend in my platoon, came to me crying and feeling very guilty about letting the others down. He was shaking so much that he would not have been very effective on the hill if he even made it there. I told him that I understood his situation and that no apology was needed. He had to do what was in his conscience. Deep down no one blamed them or said anything negative as we were leaving because many people went up the hill resenting the fact that they had to place their lives in such jeopardy.

The three men who took leave from the engagement, however, were immediately distanced from the others. It was as though they had become lepers. The CO had also given orders that they should be transferred back to the rear and that they shouldn't be there when we came off the hill. He would see to their fate when he returned. Those of us who returned from Pork Chop Hill never saw them again. However, because of his wounds on the hill, the CO was unable to see their transfer situation to its conclusion.

MOVING UP TO THE PORK CHOP

Part of our journey to the MLR behind Pork Chop that evening was made in a column of eight Army deuce-and-a-half trucks (two and a half ton troop carrier trucks), each of which could hold about two squads of men with equipment. The officers and radiomen rode in jeeps to the drop off point. When we reached the point beyond which vehicles could not travel for safety reasons we dismounted and lined up our gear for a last minute check. We were told to fall out along side the road and have a break since there might be a further wait. We had a long march to reach our destination. One of the lieutenants said, "Maybe it's cooled off up there. Maybe we're not going up now."

After about an hour or so, we started wondering why the delay? We were told that we would be at the hill by 8:30 that night. Rumors were running rampant. Give an Army outfit an extra few minutes of waiting time, particularly when the orders are ambiguous, and a thousand rumors will appear to fill the information void. After a while, one of the officers came by and told us, "The operation was possibly called off because the company on the hill had withdrawn."

In a few minutes another person said, "We were going to make an attack— but at daybreak." No one really knew. We could see Captain King trying to get someone on the PRC-10 radio but did not seem to have much success. We waited and waited. Then the word came that we were moving out; we were going up the hill. There had been no cancellation, no further delay.

The hill was actually some distance away across the valley floor around the tip of the MLR hill. It was necessary to make our way through an initial valley then along a creek bed until we rounded a knoll and could see the outline of the Pork Chop in the distance. The column moved slowly along a small rocky trail, what had formerly been a stream, but was now dry. After about a half hour march along this trail the column came to a halt.

When the column stopped I sat on a rock listening for sounds of movement up ahead, a signal that we were moving on, for what seemed like an eternity in the fading light. As I waited I chanced to glimpse a beautiful wild, blue flower nearby. I touched it lightly to see if it was real or only in my imagination. It was real, but it seemed so fragile and out-of-place in this hellish scene. My thoughts were carried away to more pleasant times, to Japan where flowers were blooming everywhere near the little hotel in Nara.

As men and equipment shuffled ahead of me, my thoughts came back to the present and I realized where I was. I stood up and adjusted my equipment for the march ahead. For a fleeting moment my thoughts were on the little vulnerable flower alongside the trail. I worried that it would be trampled by the men who were following so I reached down and placed a few rocks in a sort of a wall to protect it against the war. It was now time to go.

A short distance down the road, marching in columns of two and maintaining the obligatory distance between men, I found myself at the tail end of our platoon's column, bringing up the rear just in front of the mortar platoon as we moved toward the shadowy uncertainty up ahead. My shoulders ached from the heavy pack crammed full of the necessities of combat including three days of assault rations, extra clips of M-2 ammunition, a couple of 60 mm mortar rounds, and some extra grenades. The evening sky was dimly illuminated but we could occasionally see the familiar tracer bullets making their colorful trails through the night sky hoping to find frail human bodies huddled somewhere in the shadow world. Skylines in pitched artillery wars are often highlighted with the bright red of flares interspersed with blue bursts of white phosphorus shells.

THE GATES OF HELL OPENED UP

The first incoming 76 mm shell, from somewhere on Hassakol or Chink Baldy, landed in the middle of the first platoon formation bursting and sending its deadly steel fragments into the frail forms marching through the shadowy night. Cries of "Medic, Oh my God, I'm hit!" pierced the night as the men in formation automatically dived to the ground. Flares now lit the night sky producing an eerie glow over our head. We were like a line of ducks in a shooting gallery as we moved along the approach road.

Someone yelled, "Go Forward! Quickly!" I don't know who yelled it—it could have been me. A second or so later, a third shell landed in the ranks dropping others in their tracks. Seeing that the possible slaughter of the entire company on that approach road was likely, the non-coms began to urge the line to hurry up the hill and into the safety of trenches some distance up the slope; their dark snake-like line could be seen now in the glow of the flares bursting overhead.

Bringing up the rear and feeling very exposed on the road I kept yelling for the troops in front to "Move it up! Get moving!"

As I moved forward at a faster pace, I noticed a crumpled form lying at the side of the road and went over to check it out. It was the ROK private we affectionately called Moosemaid; he was shaking and whimpering. I urged him to get moving up the hill.

He said, "*Aniyo, mianhamnida!*" (No, I'm sorry!) He then spoke almost in a whisper, "No Sajee (Sergeant). No, no I can't."

Knowing that it was sure death to remain on this path I gave him a gentle kick yelling, "Move, move to the top!" He half crawled to his feet and then moved haltingly toward the slope. The next series of shells burst in a synchronized line along our file dropping other forms violently to the ground. Moosemaid lay mortally wounded, breathing his last breath on earth just a few days before his eighteenth birthday.

S. L. A. Marshall (1956) wrote of Fox Company's entrance into the battle for Pork Chop Hill as follows:

> Fox's men started arriving on the hill at 21:30. One platoon was deployed into the Pork Chop trenches. Several of the officers rushed forward to talk to Denton and Clemons. Captain King, moving with the main body of the company, was still some distance down the rear slope. His radio had been jammed by the enemy as he began the approach, and he could get no idea of how his lead platoon was faring, nor could he talk to the commanders he was supposed to contact.
>
> At the same time, there was a sharp build-up of fire against the Love Company front and Denton could see a body of Chinese crossing the valley from Hassakkol. On the radio, he called on the artillery to fire "Flash Pork Chop" which would interdict the forward slope with killing fire. The barrage dropped quickly and it scattered the Chinese attack. Whether it was cause and effect, the Chinese loosed the heaviest concentration of artillery and mortar fire against Pork Chop that had hit the hill. (Denton believed that an enemy radio man hiding in one of the bunkers had called for the TOT). It dropped mainly on the trenches where Fox's lead squads were deploying and on the rear slope where the two platoons were still toiling upward. Before having any chance to engage, Fox Company lost nineteen men; and as the steel continued

to rain down, the entrenched men huddled and the columns broke and scattered. Such was the state of disorganization, that it took Fox another three hours to get the greater part of its force set on the hill, and the platoons never did get satisfactorily tied into one another. (Pp. 137-138).

The murderous fire on the road wasn't the last of our troubles; the shelling intensified as we moved up the slope toward the trenches. When the lead men in the company reached the trench line, the fire continued cutting deeper into the ranks. Evidently, there was a Chinese artillery observer somewhere to our rear handily placing the fire along our line as we proceeded up the slope. At this point, many of the remaining men had made it to the reverse slope and were dispersed along the hill jammed in little clumps like cars in a rush hour traffic jam. As shells continued to rain down, each man tried to dig his head and torso as close to the earth as possible to avoid the jagged shrapnel that violently erupted from each exploding shell. Almost everyone in the company experienced burning sensations from the shrapnel in some part of their anatomy.

"What's the hold up? Move into the trench!" someone yelled.

Captain King, Sergeant Robertson, and Sergeant Rogers were at the head of the column trying to gain a picture of what was happening on the hill and trying to locate the promised guide to find our positions. No one was there to provide directions to our movement. As we began to push the line forward to escape the inferno on the slope, we could hear Chinese voices shouting commands at the top of the hill and could hear small arms fire along the ridge.

"Some routine reinforcement!" someone muttered.

We pushed toward the closest section of trench, which was now crowded with bodies and GIs trying to make it to some defensible position. As I reached the trench I could see Rogers trying to get the newly arrived riflemen to disburse in an organized fashion. He said to me that he was taking the positions to the left and indicated that I should move any troops I could muster through the trench on the right. I could now see a trench line with a large bunker near the crest. This was the last time that I would see Sergeant Rogers until the next morning.

At that time, a tremendous shower of artillery shells burst along the top of the crest as I dived headlong into a bunker. The room was crowded with no place to sit, so I left the area and moved down toward the right to seek the next portion of covered trench. It was obviously going to be a very long night!

At the top of Pork Chop utter confusion reigned—both armies were disjointed with small bands of men roaming the trench line looking for comrades with like uniforms within the trench work; others finding a brief safety or rather the illusion of safety from the bursting shells in a sharp bend of a trench where one could cover both approaches.

One of our Puerto Rican soldiers, a machine gunner named Munoz, made his way above the trench slowly. As he passed a deep portion of the trench, he saw a Chinese soldier standing in the trench looking in the other direction. He leaped in on top of the man and quickly put an end to the fellow's misery on the Chop! This was the last I saw of Munoz who was seriously wounded on the hill.

Not finding a manned position on the right flank, I made my way back to the chow bunker where some of our men could now be found. We set up guards for the trench to watch for Chinese that might enter this section of the trench from either direction. Inside the bunker, we were using as an aid station were a number of wounded and displaced men from several units—some only recently making it up the hill from the fiery trail below. There was no communication between the hill and the Battalion Command post—all of the radios were jammed. Every once in a while you could hear, in the CP, a radioman trying to get through to no avail.

Bill Estes, my friend from Belle, West Virginia, had been knocked unconscious by the shelling on the road. When he made it up the hill about two hours later, he had a horrible shrapnel gash in his hand, a sliver of shrapnel still protruding. He stuck it in front of me and asked if I would try to fix it (there were no medics in the bunker but someone found a first aid kit). I pulled out the metal sliver and held a cloth over the hole in his hand. Not knowing anything about medical treatment, I filled up the hole with methylate and re-wrapped it. Though quite rudimentary in construction, the bandage appeared to work and Bill seemed happy with the outcome at the time. A few

The author (*left*) and Dale "Ziggy" Bernhardt, shortly before the battle for Pork Chop Hill, 1953.

years after the war ended, when we met back in Belle, Bill joked about the fantastic job I did on his hand that night.

It took another hour for the survivors from the approach road to make it to the top of the hill; most were wounded and couldn't walk the steep trail up the hill. From the trench near the chow bunker, we could see on top of the company command post where Captain King and the remnants of Love Company were holed up. For most of them this would be their last hour of life.

There were several Chinese soldiers crawling around on top of their bunker. I yelled for someone with an automatic weapon; Moss took a BAR and tried to clear the Chinese off the command bunker. The team fired about fifty rounds of ammunition at the rooftop and the vicinity. Moss and his ROK ammo bearer then moved the gun on top of the trench to find a better placement and continued to fire toward the CP. This was the last time that I saw

Dale on the Pork Chop until the next day when he, Vito, and I made it off the hill.

CLARK GABLE'S REVENGE

Two Chinese soldiers, apparently somewhat confused and separated from their main body of men, wandered into three men from one of our squads who were moving through the trench looking for others from the platoon. They surrendered to the Americans. A difficult predicament and complex decision ensued. What were the GIs going to do with prisoners? It was not even possible to evacuate our own wounded off the hill, let alone spare people to take prisoners back though the maelstrom we came up in. The squad leader left the two prisoners in the charge of one of the ROK soldiers, Clark Gable, who was seriously wounded and lying in the trench, unable to go anywhere. Clark had been hit by a large piece of shrapnel that severed one leg almost completely off and injured the other. Clark, barely conscious and articulate having been given morphine, acknowledged his willingness to guard the prisoners. No sooner had the corporal walked a few feet down the trench, in order to search for others in his squad, when he heard two shots ring out from the vicinity of Clark Gable's location.

The squad leader ran back to where he had left Clark Gable and the two prisoners to see what happened. He saw two crumpled, lifeless forms on the ground and Clark with his rifle still elevated was smiling a toothy grin. The squad leader was unsure as to what happened. He surmised, however, that the two Chinese soldiers could have decided to rush Clark and take away his weapon. Or, more likely, since Clark Gable did not like the Chinese for the things that happened to his family, he simply settled an old score. The true story of what happened here will likely never be known.

****

It is impossible to describe the artillery hell that was Pork Chop Hill. Through the night, American forces were firing shells with proximity fuses— that is, fuses that exploded about twenty feet in the air rather than on impact with the ground. These shells sprayed shrapnel downward and in a widespread direction as they exploded. The idea behind the tree top shell burst is that if the American troops can find cover in their bunkers then the proximity fuses exploding overhead would kill any thing walking around the hill and above the bunkers. Toward the end of the evening the American forces on Pork Chop Hill held two small enclaves and the Chinese occupied the remainder.

At one point during the night, with a lull in the shelling, I crept slowly down a trench looking to see if there were any more men in the gun emplacements to the north of the chow bunker. At a wide place in the trench, the depth became shallower because a large shell had apparently landed on the side and blew out a large crater on the edge of it. I peered through the shadows to look around the hill and saw three Chinese bodies in front of the trench fixed to the barbed wire, one of them absent the top of his head.

A bit further in, I ran into another GI making his way down the trench; he was from Love Company. He was trying to make his way back to the reverse slope of the hill and locate some troops from his unit. He mentioned that he had seen a couple of Chinese infantrymen a little ways down the trench. As we talked there in the night we decided to cause them some problems and throw a few grenades their way. We crawled down the trench line where it made a sharp turn to the left and lobbed several grenades in the trench in their direction. Afterward, with them taken out, we made our way back down the hill toward the CP and the temporary aid station.

The battle for Pork Chop Hill was the epitome of battlefield confusion. Incidents such as these were the rule rather than the exception. Everywhere on the hill, especially the high ground, there was in intermingling of Chinese and American troops throughout the night and neither side could get an organized force of more than a handful of troops to take command of the hill.

Without a sufficient force to sweep the hill, it simply became a matter of survival. Our goals became limited—to try and make it through that hell and gather enough forces at daybreak to claim the high ground. I had not seen any of the company officers or Sgt. Rogers for most of the evening, since we had parted ways at the top of the hill to set up in different directions. One report from the left flank indicated that all had been killed in a direct hit on a bunker. With all of the company officers gone I, being the senior NCO now on the hill, assumed command of what was remaining of the stragglers of Fox Company. We tried to organize the remaining troops so that we were still able to mount an effective defense around the makeshift CP.

THE LAST DITCH STAND

At around 2:30 in the morning the shellfire slackened a little, though the flares continued to light the sky as though it were daylight. One of the lookouts from the trench line running to the right of the bunker we had formed as a platoon CP and first aid station, yelled into the bunker that he saw a Chinese skirmish line moving slowly up the hill to our rear about 300 yards away. With the Chinese holding the high ground to our left, firing machine guns into our positions, we were afraid that we would be completely trapped between two bodies of enemy troops. We realized that we had to make a last ditch stand against the forces coming up the hill because we could at least see them.

Another NCO and I began to yell to our guys in the bunkers that were close: "Everyone out into the trench."

Someone else yelled, "Bring what weapons you can find. This is it! We're being over run!"

"Here they come," another cried. "I can see them about a hundred yards down the hill."

I moved through the trench whispering to each person, "Now, hold your fire till they get close on us. Make every shot count."

Our situation was desperate now; we could see a couple of hundred men moving up the hill in our front. We found ourselves effectively trapped between the two hostile forces. We assumed that this would be our last stand—a suicide stand—and we wanted to make the best of it. We now knew how Custer must have felt at the Battle of the Little Big Horn. Things were pretty grim.

We waited and watched as the shadowy figures crept toward us. Then one of the men to the left of me decided the approaching line of shadows was getting too close and so he tossed a hand grenade at the closest figures in the skirmish line. It burst a few yards in front of them and they began to speed up their charge at us—now yelling as they made their assault. We began to take aim at the advancing figures.

The first voice I heard coming from the advancing troops was in English. "Wait! Hold your fire!" Someone then yelled, "They're Americans!" The yelling got closer. Then one of the advancing troopers, a lieutenant from Easy Company nearly out of breath, recognized our helmets and called for his troops to hold fire and move into the trenches.

We were extremely relieved and elated over the turn of events. However, the Lieutenant was not. "Why did you throw that hand grenade at us?" he asked angrily. The soldier replied, "We thought you were Chinese! Why did all of you have your steel helmets off?" The lieutenant breathlessly pointed out that they removed their helmets because they thought it would enable them to move quieter! But, unfortunately it almost got them killed because in the darkness without the steel helmet they looked like Chinese.

They were lucky, it could have been even more of a disaster had we not recognized their true identity when we did.

Battalion Headquarters had informed the lieutenant before the assault that our company had been completely annihilated because they had not had any communications from us since last evening. Easy Company, as they attacked the hill, were operating under the belief that Fox Company had been destroyed and that the hill was completely in Chinese hands. So the Battalion commander called in artillery on our positions through the night. The brass at Battalion had simply written us off as dead and called for another counterattack!

All was well, though, and we considered ourselves fortunate. We had lived through the Chinese shelling as we approached the hill as well as "flashpoint" from our own artillery barrage as we tried to reform our platoons. Two separate armies had thrown their artillery at us incessantly throughout the evening and it had taken its toll.

In his book about Pork Chop Hill, Marshall noted:

During the first 24 hours the guns fired 37,655 rounds in defense of Arsenal, Dale, and the Pork Chop. The proportions were 9,823 rounds fired by the heavies and 27,832 by the light howitzers. On the second day after Arsenal and Dale had been saved and only Pork Chop was in jeopardy, the supporting fire built up to 77,349 rounds total.

Never at Verdun were guns worked at any such rate as this. The battle of Kwajalein, our most intense shoot during World War II, was still a lesser thing when measured in terms of artillery expenditure per hour, weight of metal against yards of earth and the grand output of the guns. It set the all time mark for artillery effort. Pork Chop when the fight was over was as clean picked as Old Baldy. And its cratered slopes will not soon bloom again, for they are too well planted with rusty shards and empty tins and bones. (p. 146)

Rogers returned to the trench line where we were located early in the morning, before daybreak. He had been pinned down most of the evening by Chinese on top of his bunker to our left. All of the officers in the company were either dead or severely wounded and the first sergeant was wounded and not able to command. Sergeant Rogers assumed command of the company, which was still out of radio communication with Battalion rear. He asked me to take charge of the platoon.

DEPARTURE FROM THE HILL

After the hill was secured, we rounded up the wounded and began the evacuation. The return trip was made a bit easier in that a couple of half-tracks, that is, armored personnel carriers, were brought forward to evacuate men back to the MLR area. A collection point for the wounded was established and we set about to determine what our casualty situation was.

Our unit was evacuated from the hill in the late morning. It was no longer an integrated, functioning unit. We were able to get all of the survivors from our company into only two trucks on our way back to the rear; we started out in eight trucks. It was a difficult ride to our new quarters. We had suffered nearly seventy percent casualties and in some platoons even higher. Over twenty percent of our company had become casualties before we got off the road to Pork Chop in our first few moments of the battle.

It was difficult to fathom the extent of our losses—the Chinese artillery had decimated our ranks. So many good men were gone now--Grasshold, Moosemaid, Lee, Zimdahl, and many, many others. The number of severely wounded from the artillery barrages was shocking, including Captain King and Lt. LaRoca. Many of us suffered shrapnel wounds that did not require us to leave the company.

WOUNDED EVERYWHERE

Even though Clark Gable was severely disabled from his wounds and obviously no longer suited for combat, the fight was not out of him. Moreover, he seemed drastically altered from the affable, fun-loving guy that we all loved. Another story was revealed about Clark Gable at the end of the battle of Pork Chop Hill when he was finally evacuated to the Battalion Aid Station in the rear area. Apparently Clark Gable had passed out for a while, probably from loss of blood, and when he awoke he was lying on a stretcher that had been placed among several rows of wounded men.

He awakened to find that he was lying next to a wounded Chinese soldier. Clark became enraged and crawled off his stretcher and over to the Chinese soldier. He placed his strong hands around the man's neck and strangled him to death before the medics could free his hands.

The ravages of war can take away from human beings the very dignity and humane spirit that our social orders instill in us from childhood. Clark Gable was not insane nor was he a cruel villain or a heinous criminal. He simply was a relatively uneducated farm boy who had been so violently jolted and misshapen by his circumstances in those hours on Pork Chop that he was no longer the person he started out to be. So go the horrendous tides of war as they break harshly over the hearts of men.

At one end of the company an area had been set up as an outdoor morgue by a team from Graves Registration. Row after row of corpses, in all imaginable shapes of mutilation; some without limbs, some smashed beyond recognition, others burned to a crisp from an enemy flamethrower, were laid out along the old rice paddy. This was a ghastly nightmarish sight, like something out of a macabre movie. With the heavy duties he had from his increased responsibility, Sgt. Rogers asked me if I would take on the gruesome task of identifying the dead from our outfit. Someone had to do it but as I proceeded through the heavy task, I was not handling this job particularly well. I moved zombie-like along the rows accompanied by the NCO from Graves Registration with my roster in hand trying to match up names with the dog tags and likenesses of the lifeless forms lying about. Some were easy, others not so.

The identification of the dead was one of the most unpleasant tasks that I had ever been given to do, and I was flooded with mixed feelings. I was angry, sad, and quite overwhelmed by the experience of seeing my friends who were now corpses—lying there mixed in with Chinese dead.

As we walked along the rows, as I was later told, I became so overwhelmed and frustrated by the sight of it all that I lost my composure for a moment and kicked the head of one of the Chinese dead lying on the ground. My foot struck this mangled head, that turned out not to be firmly attached to the body. I felt both surprised and a bit guilty about it, but I simply went on about the task at hand without comment. Without saying a word, the Graves Registration corporal quietly readjusted the head on the shoulders from which it came. We continued our silent walk through this macabre scene—stopping occasionally to check off a dog tag and check a name on the list.

The irritability I experienced and the anger that quickly surfaced during that walk was a common feeling that many of us possessed during the aftermath of Pork Chop. We were typically jumpy and on edge, especially with sudden or loud noises. Whistling sounds that mimicked incoming shells were particularly disturbing after our night in the shooting gallery. These mood alterations are symptomatic of PTSD.

The military historian General S. L. A. Marshall, who wrote the book Pork Chop Hill, had a team of interviewers conducting post engagement de-briefing interviews with each of us shortly after we returned from the action on the Pork Chop. Marshall's interview with me was poorly timed—following my return from Graves Registration site. The questions caught me in a pretty bad mood and I was not talkative. I simply cut the interview short, particularly when it appeared to me that the interviewer was simply fishing for sensationalistic and "quotable" stories. For example, he was particularly interested in a story that was going around that I had captured a Chinese hand grenade on Jane Russell and then threw it back at them on Pork Chop. This would of course had made interesting copy, but it was not true. The true story was that

I had obtained a Chinese "potato masher" type grenade on Jane Russell Hill and carried it around for a while. Actually, one of the guys would use it as a sort of a joke at times, particularly with new men. They would toss it with the pin still intact at someone. I do not know what happened to that grenade. The only grenades I threw on the Pork Chop were good old-fashioned American ones that I knew would work.

I believe this interview only added to my growing discontent with some aspects of the Army. I was already having great reservations, particularly some of the questionable command decisions that were being made. Why were we being sent into situations like Pork Chop Hill? Obviously, I thought, just for political reasons. By the end of the Pork Chop I began to feel pretty hopeless about the military situation. The tone of this after-action interview simply underscored my dysphoria. In addition, I think the duty of body identification that befell me as second-in-command of the company at that time added immeasurably to my low mood.

In spite of my beginning to question the meaning of the war and our leader's actions in sending us into hell pits like Pork Chop Hill, I moved up the chain of command and became a platoon sergeant. Sergeant Rogers indicated that he was taking over as the first sergeant and he wanted me to assume permanent command of the platoon. It wasn't much of a platoon at that point in terms of size. We had fewer than twenty-five percent complement at the time—less than a quarter of the men who originally went up the hill. It was indeed a meager, limping outfit that I inherited—barely what one would call a platoon.

Within a few days, however, we received a new batch of cannon fodder—enough men, both American and ROK, to bring up our strength to nearly a hundred percent. I stood with Lee Rogers as the new men dismounted from the vehicles and received their platoon assignments. My new batch of men fell into ranks and Rogers addressed them in a very emotional voice—saying words that made me feel uncomfortable, given my present state of mind after Pork Chop.

He told the formation in a shrill, cracking voice, "Men. You're now in the one of the best platoons in the Battalion. You are replacing a lot of good men who died on that hill yesterday! I want you to remember them."

He continued after a long pause: "This is your platoon sergeant. His name is Sgt. First Class Butcher—and that's what he is, too! You listen to him and you might have a chance to come back off the next hill. If you don't listen to him then I hope your affairs are in order. Now, I want you to go and mark your names clearly into your belts, your boots, and clothing so that we will be able to identify your corpses better! Fall out!"

Sergeant Rogers was sometimes viewed by the troops as a harsh ("Chickenshit" in Army terms) disciplinarian. At this point I was not sure what Rogers was trying to do with that introduction but it seemed to put a good bit of distance between me and the newcomers—setting a pretty frightening tone. He appeared to be as upset with the incredible losses we suffered on the hill. It seemed as though, in spite of his usual normally distant manner, he was as close to some of the men who died as I was.

As I moved to the head of the formation with Rogers to take command of the platoon I was initially hesitant—my voice was low and I searched for words. But, as I talked to them about my expectations of them in the field, I found myself sounding just like Old Scarface. A bit more hesitating perhaps, but it was almost like the words and ideas I was expressing were not my own. It was as though I was reading lines from a script prepared by a mean old sergeant somewhere, enunciating words that were handed down by some mysterious process from my NCO predecessors. It was frightening to my new charges to hear the things that needed to be said; it was even more frightening for me to have to tell them.

When the platoon was dismissed, I waited for a while then went to the command tent that had been set up for NCOs. There were a few new faces among them, but everyone was silent. I was quite shaken by all of the losses of close personal friends and I vowed to keep more emotional distance from this new group of men. I didn't even care to know their names. I needed to have insulation from emotional ties at that point. I did not want any more close attachments. A large piece of me died with those guys on the hill. Now I fell into the well-defined role of platoon sergeant and began to view these faces as nameless automatons, nothing more.

THE SACRIFICES OF FOX COMPANY ON PORK CHOP

Although Fox Company was devastated by the initial artillery attack and prevented from engaging in organized attacks, there was considerable hand-

Our Korean buddy "Moosemaid," Kon Do
Baull, killed on Pork Chop Hill, April 1953.

to hand and bunker-to-bunker fighting carried out by sections of our troops. These actions were often in concert with men from E or L Companies. Moreover, we held major sections of the trench on the hill throughout the night, preventing the Chinese from controlling strategic points of the trench line. Had these bastions along the trench line not been established then L Company's final early morning assault would likely have been a disaster—with Chinese waiting for them rather than our ragtag band. A large portion of the hill was actually held by elements of Fox Company when Easy Company arrived. Easy Company's arrival on the slopes gave us the fresh troops to gain the hill. When our tattered remnants left, there were American flags on the high ground.

After Pork Chop there were no oratories, no eulogies, no Gettysburg Address to honor those who struggled and lost their lives there. There was only the temporary silence of reserve positions for a few days to allow us to identify our fallen, indoctrinate newly assigned personnel to fill our depleted ranks, and to replenish our supplies of ammunition in preparation to return to the trenches.

There was the beer ration on our first night off Pork Chop—this time a very ample supply to go around because there were so few to join in. There was no music from Billy Marshall's fiddle. He, like so many others, was gone never to return to our now depleted ranks. He had been severely wounded and sent to Japan. During his long recovery in Japan he met and married a Japanese woman. They moved to Hillsville, Virginia and began a new life.

I had the opportunity to visit Billy Marshall a few years after the war at his home. We talked about the April battle for Pork Chop and the later one in July. After both battles, Pork Chop remained under U.N. control. However, we knew that the outcome of the sacrifices on Pork Chop was to blow up the mountain and hand it back to the Chinese. The hand-off to the Chinese occurred within weeks of the second hard fought battle, just before the Armistice was signed ending the fighting.

11

The Spring Rains

INFANTRY SOLDIERS LIVE MOST OF THEIR TIME OUTDOORS. Their mood and their morale, their physical wellbeing, indeed their very survival is tied to the natural phenomena we call weather conditions. Yet, it matters not whether the rain is falling in torrents or whether the sun is parching the earth like a brick oven, infantrymen must, in order to survive, do the following things:

• Live in holes in the ground or earthen shelters in order to gain a measure of protection from the merciless shelling. Artillery shells do not know or care what the weather is on a particular day, their only role is to explode and send shrapnel through the air—whether clear, wet, or snowy.

• Sleep on the ground or in makeshift bunks in the trenches. This often requires considerable ingenuity and luck just to get a brief rest in such close contact with nature.

• March along roads that are so dusty that the grime permeates your nostrils until you choke or gasp for air; or in the other extreme, when drenching rain transforms the road into a vast sea of mud, sliding you now to the left, then to the right, then down—taking human being, field packs, and precious weapons with them into the mud. The muddy spills and harsh elements leave the infantryman with enough earth caked to his clothing and body to form a new third Korean nation.

• Eat one's meals while sitting under a poncho, on top of a steel helmet, in dust storms or in rain showers that fill up one's mess kit turning an essentially unappetizing Army meal into a soupy, unappetizing Army meal.

The working environment of the infantryman can provide unremitting misery at times. Weather conditions always seem to color his mood and in some situations may actually impact his very existence. Sometimes, in order to escape from such harsh realities, if only for brief moments, the infantryman might attempt to, through mental operations, place psychological distance between himself and the ugliness of inclement weather. A brief sojourn into reverie could provide the only means of tolerating such climatic extremes. This mental distancing—the psychological defense mechanism called "denial"—provided a miserable GI brief respite from the harshness. It involved convincing oneself that all of this is not really happening. These, of course, are only temporary measures in a seemingly endless and bleak situation and are probably somewhat maladaptive, because you always have to return: there is no real escape.

BACK AT THE FRONT TO TRENCHES DEEP IN A RIVER OF MUD.

The environment changed drastically from the cold, frozen ground we had experienced during January through March into a warmer but much wetter habitat. Spring was here, along with ample rain. The spring thaw brought different miseries than the winter had delivered. No longer did the cold wind make us shiver deep in our bones and shake uncontrollably at times while peering through the night looking for shadows in the front. Rain, endless cold drizzle, poured from the skies in what some have referred to as Korea's "rainy season." This term seemed to me to be a clear understatement of reality because it implies that sometime, somehow, the rain will end at some point life will return to normal. The rain in Korea in the spring months provided no inkling of a cessation; even if it did stop, the roads and those brown treeless, trench-scarred hills could never dry out again because they were so saturated with water.

The profuse drizzle brought a number of different challenges—including marches under a constant, steady downpour and a wet cold; roads that disappeared under flowing streams that gushed from the hills.

Even though the threat of artillery shells persisted, no longer was it possible to seek refuge under the sandbag covered trenches—the trenches filled with water and the bunkers caved in, occasionally trapping people inside. On several occasions we had to dig out GIs who had fallen asleep in a nice dry place, only to awaken to a rumbling sound of wooden beams crashing to the ground trapping them inside. On one occasion a bunker cave-in resulted in the death of a soldier inside. Death up front is always tragic, but this mode of destruction seemed to us somehow to be worse than simply being shot.

Artillery shells bursting in rain- and mud-filled trenches present a different visual picture than those exploding on ice capped terrain or hard rock soil. But these appearances are misleading because the true business of these monsters of destruction remains the same and equally effective.

Our one consolation about the weather (and having to move outside the trenches) was the thought that the Chinese might be having it rougher. We didn't know this for sure, but we surmised that the gods of rain were dispassionate regarding our respective causes and would make the Chinese just as wet and miserable as they made us— perhaps even more so because the Chinese needed the protection of earthen caves more than we did. We had air superiority, that is, when weather allowed planes to fly and Joe Chink had to stay hidden. The caves they called home were likely to be just as susceptible to water problems as our bunkers, even more so.

At one point we conducted a reconnaissance patrol deep into the Yokkokchon Valley to get a look at what effect the rain was having on the Chinese positions. Were they showing a lot more surface trenches, fresh digging, and so forth? Had they evacuated to different positions? We could not determine much from the close inspection of the Chinese hills; however, we could see fresh digging and signs of activity around the hills. Ole Joe had apparently not evacuated as some had thought, although we could not determine much about his quality of life.

****

These days even moving back to a rear echelon job was no guarantee of an easy life. Our friend Watcott's new job as a rear echelon jeep driver proved to be nearly as dangerous under the new conditions as the shelling had been when he was up front. We heard that he had an accident in which his jeep had slid over a steep hill in the mud, rolling as gravity pulled the vehicle down the slope. Fortunately for him, his vehicle was equipped with a machine gun mount on the top that served to raise the jeep's roll, allowing him enough room to drop free from the vehicle. He escaped with only some broken bones from what could have been a fatal accident.

****

Troop movements during the rainy season proved challenging whether one moved by vehicle or by foot. The jeeps and two-and-a-half-ton trucks that occasionally served our movement along the front, often sat in quagmires along the roadways that at times appeared more like rivers. Men had to dismount, wade through the muck, and push the vehicles free of the newly formed swamps.

Marches through the drizzling rain were often more miserable. One would slip and slide, maybe crash up against one's comrades to the front or rear. It was always tougher to carry heavy equipment in the mud because of the need to slow periodically or stop to shift the equipment. Sudden movements, halts, or start-ups could cause a fall. Occasionally, when men shifted equipment between them in order to share the burden of carrying heavy weapons, they would both fall. Cursing of the gods of weather under such circumstances was generally approved and actually expected.

One of the most challenging motor skills that I learned to accomplish (albeit with some difficulty) during the rainy season was the ability to pry loose a cigarette from my dry pocket underneath my poncho, light it in the pouring rain, and then smoke it down to the stub without it getting wet. But, after a while I was able to do so with dexterity. I certainly was getting a lot of practice trying to learn it! The development of this skill bears witness to the fact that the nicotine addiction is a more powerful force than torrential rain.

****

The reader has likely gathered by now that Korea is an extremely hilly place. In order to get to some of our positions it was almost always necessary to climb a slope. Our trails always seemed to be steep and winding. This climb was often difficult but it was made especially so in winter snow or in rain.

In winter and spring, we were supplied ropes to affix on the trails to assist climbers. Of course, there were few trees to tie the ropes to on the barren hills so we had to pound iron posts into the ground. The rains and slippery hills did assure us somewhat that the Chinese were not likely going to make a major assault because they would have difficulty making it up the frontal slope.

Conducting combat patrols in the rain was somewhat of a mixed blessing. The expectations for covering great distances at night were lower and the missions more realistic; however, the ground was often very difficult to cover. An added problem was that the small streams that we negotiated during winter months over ice had now become seemingly as wide as the Mississippi and as deep as the Pacific Ocean. Traversing some of them was impossible if the goal was to maintain an integrated, effective fighting force.

VULNERABILITY TO SICKNESS UP FRONT

One dread medical problem that seemed to become more prominent in the spring in Korea was malaria. Several people in our company contracted the disorder and required treatment. Malaria is a parasitic disease that is spread by a mosquito that frequented the rice paddies of Korea. Once bitten by this creature the GI usually would become symptomatic in a week or two. The symptoms in themselves were quite disabling and recurring or appearing in stages. The symptoms of malaria included such things as a fever that can reach 105 degrees, uncontrollable shivering, profuse sweating, severe headache, general discomfort, and vomiting. The GI afflicted with malaria was usually evacuated for treatment by antimalarial drugs. After a period of time their symptoms would be under control and they would be returned to duty until they experienced a reoccurrence of the symptoms.

Another more common problem that seemed to hit us in the spring was an epidemic of flu-like symptoms. Whether or not this was related to the weather or simply an accidental association is not known—but our ranks were decimated by symptoms including high fever, diarrhea, vomiting, and fatigue. At one point nearly every one in the platoon had this malady. We should have all been evacuated for treatment but we tried to stick it out. Although I did not have the problem as severely as some in the platoon, I was out of action for several days. Several of the men did have to be evacuated to the Battalion Aid station because they simply could not function. During this period our line became extremely thin.

GETTING ACCLIMATED TO SOME NEW MEN UP FRONT

When I took over command of the platoon I was assigned a new assistant platoon sergeant who had no combat experience. This African-American staff sergeant, who I will call "Donaldson," was an "old soldier" having been in the Army for nearly fifteen years. His duty assignments had largely been in state-side training or quartermaster units. He was a very affable guy who seemed to know a lot of things by the book.

One of his jobs was to take care of the administrative details of the unit operation, such as developing duty rosters and other paper and pencil tasks. I noticed that when these had to be done he always took them back to his area, even if it was only a two-minute job. He would return in a few minutes with the paper work finished and neat. As I watched this happen over and over again, I finally asked him what was going on. He told me that he had never learned to read in school and that he was having one of the men in the platoon write the stuff out for him. I was amazed that he had gotten as far as he had in the Army without knowing how to read.

Working with Donaldson was not unlike having to accommodate ROK or Colombian soldiers who were assigned to my platoon despite not being able to speak English. As MacGregor (1981) noted, black recruits at the time had much more limited educational opportunities, which challenged the Army's ability to maintain a segregated system. My experiences with Donaldson revealed his many good qualities and I simply adjusted to his reading deficit and we went on about our business.

Another new man in the company, we will call "Dugan," was one of our more interesting new men in the platoon. Most people deplore war and do not take well to its fickle and cruel ways. Dugan was not of the majority—he thrived in combat, he tried to stir up action if the lines were quiet. Had Dugan lived in times past, previous wars would have lured him to action: his would have been a lead voice in Pickett's charge at Gettysburg; his weapon would have been the first to speak at the Normandy invasion because somehow he would have gotten himself in the first LST to hit the beach.

Before he joined our unit, he had already served two tours of duty in Korea and volunteered for the third. Although he had been a sergeant several times before, he entered our company with the rank of the lowest of privates, having been busted for some rule infraction in the rear area. Dugan was at the same time an outstanding soldier and a screw-up. He was usually quickly promoted when he was up front, and very promptly reduced in rank when he was not. He saw no value in rules and regulations. He did what he pleased. The latter part of the war in Korea, with its static line, was a rather tame place for Dugan—he sought the challenge of military combat, not to establish great causes, not to impress his fellow man, but simply because it was enjoyable to him.

Dugan was a gutsy infantryman. He thought nothing of running personal one-man patrols deep into enemy territory. He would wander out from our own positions and look for Chinese patrols. He was an outstanding fellow to have in a combat situation, although a bit hot-headed and prone to use his weapon against anyone who crossed him. One day in early May, only a couple of weeks after the battle for Pork Chop, we were sent back to the hill for a tour on that god-forsaken, devastated outpost—a pretty bleak environment still requiring a great deal of work rebuilding bunkers. Fortunately, we did not have to walk up our "road to hell" but rode APCs (Armored Personnel Carriers).

Shortly after arriving on the Chop, I was making some notes about the lines of fire when I heard noisy, fast-flying footsteps, accompanied by enormous laughter. Donaldson dived into my bunker just as a string of bullets from an M-2 carbine came rattling all along the trench after him, missing him only by inches.

Donaldson breathlessly held up a can of chicken and vegetables assault rations to show me as he laughed uncontrollably. He giggled, as he quickly applied his trusty can opener to get into the can. "I just stole Dugan's chicken and vegetables!" he said. (Dugan had made it known to everyone that the only canned rations that he could eat were the chicken and vegetables, and he traded everything else for them.)

I said, "Donaldson, you'll get us both killed here! Go straighten this out with Dugan!"

"Hell, I'm not going out there yet!" he said, as he attached an oily rifle cleaning cloth to his bayonet and held it out into the trench.

RRAATTATT, RRAATTATT—the bullets ripped through the filthy cleaning rag.

I said, "No, I guess I wouldn't either just yet till Dugan cools down a bit!"

FRIGHT AND FEAR UP FRONT

Another new man in the company, a somewhat inept private, presented a very different problem—one that caused us quite a bit of concern. He was absolutely frightened stiff about being on the front lines. It was not unusual for new troops to be afraid up front and most of us were pretty scared in the beginning; but this fellow was exceptionally scared and tended to freeze up with terror even when no danger was present.

For example, one night we were on the MLR and he was required to take a two-hour night watch (his first) by himself. His post was a relatively safe firing position in that out to his front there was a steep embankment lined with several rows of concertina wire. It would take an extraordinary effort for a Chinese raiding party to get to him.

After only a few minutes of watch he came on the intercom in a panic, "Sergeant! Sergeant! There's something out in front! Come quick!"

I hurried over to his firing position and asked, "What did you see there?"

Excitedly, he said, "I heard trucks over there!" He pointed in a direction of the steep embankment.

"Where?" I asked, trying to hide my dismay at his naiveté. The Chinese, of course, had no trucks within twenty miles and certainly could not drive a vehicle up the rugged slope below.

He pointed again in the direction of the embankment and said, "There! Listen!"

I listened for a while to try to make out what he was hearing. Soon I could tell that it was simply the wind blowing against a tin can that was out in front on the wire. After I reassured him that there was nothing out in front, I returned to the CP.

In a few more minutes he called again, this time in sheer panic. "Sergeant, I hear Chinks' voices! Come quick!" We went through the same routine and I tried to reassure him that there was nothing out in front. We relieved him early from his watch and let him get some sleep, which of course he was not able to do being so keyed up. The next night we replayed the same scenario. It was becoming apparent that he was not constitutionally suited for this line of work.

I felt that he would be dangerous to himself and to others if he remained on the front lines. The next day I told the company commander that I thought that the fellow should be sent back to the rear. I did not think he would ever be able to adapt to the circumstances of military combat. The CO agreed and gave him a job in company rear until he could be transferred back to division headquarters.

THE DEATH OF JANUS

One of my best and trusted friends in the platoon, Janus Krumins, was a Latvian-born soldier with great talents and common sense. He too was killed in the line of duty. This was one of the most tragic personal losses I experienced during the war.

Janus was Mr. Reliable—always ready to take that extra step and could handle any job, with any weapon we had on our side or any weapon the Chinese might have. Janus had emigrated to the United States and entered the military in order to facilitate his application for citizenship. He was one of the best soldiers we had on our side, and he died in service of a country in which he was not even a citizen.

The night he was killed we were on Outpost Uncle and he volunteered to go out on an armed listening post (LP). Often, the job of the observers on the LP was simply to detect the enemy's presence and then to hightail it back to the main position without engaging the enemy.

On this particular hill, due to the location of the main line in relation to the LP, it was not easy to effect an unobserved, speedy withdrawal. Moreover, the LP was really an advanced fighting position whose function was to fight the enemy as well as observe them. This particular LP was manned by two soldiers, usually with automatic weapons. Janus took with him a BAR and one ROK soldier to help with listening and carrying ammo; they set up their positions just before dark.

About an hour after dark, we heard the telltale whispers on the commline indicating that there was some movement in the front of the positions. This warning sound was made by blowing directly into the microphone a designated number of times. As soon as the warning came, we could hear the familiar sound of a burp gun followed immediately by the equally familiar music of the BAR rapidly firing. Then, more burp guns and several grenade explosions. Then silence.

In what seemed like ages, the BAR opened fire again in rapid succession. Then another pause—a few more rounds then silence again. No other sound was heard.

We waited in the main positions for a few moments, as standard operating procedures required, to see if they were going to return to the CP area. The LP team did not respond to a call up on the telephone. Then, we mounted a six-man patrol to go to the area of the LP to rescue the team if possible. When the relief patrol reached the LP they found both Janus and the ROK soldier dead. Janus was still clutching the BAR that was pointed downhill toward the finger of the hill below.

It was apparent from the area below the LP that the BAR team had effectively defended its position and had interrupted the Chinese raiding party. Although the Chinese, as they usually did, had taken away their dead and wounded, there was substantial evidence in the form of blood stains and discarded Chinese equipment that our guys had taken a major toll of life in their defense. It was estimated that Janus and the ROK had killed or wounded more than six or eight of the enemy.

ON THE EMOTIONAL DOWNSIDE OF COMMAND

There is an old adage among NCOs that reads: "Field officers send men to take obstacles; corporals send men to their deaths."

There is clearly no way of knowing in advance whether a particular order will result in a dire outcome such as the loss of troops in one's command. The effective NCO needs to make command decisions and issue orders without worrying about death. It may sound strange to say, but death may be the least of the NCOs worries in making decisions.

Most NCOs I knew in Korea were both competent and safety conscious; that is, they looked after the welfare of their troops with great regard. The system of promotion from lower ranks normally assured that these two qualifications were present. Errors do occur, however; exigency results in too rapid a promotion beyond competency in any field. But, most of our NCOs were conscious and respectful of the lives of their charges. None of us would have casually or willfully sent a soldier into certain death, although there were times in Korea that all of our activities carried with them a high potential for harm (like the time when Moosemaid was prodded up Pork Chop to his death). Everyone was in grave danger. Such actions cannot be faulted or regretted. We were all equally doomed.

There were times as an NCO in Korea when I had to select someone for hazardous duty, such as a listening post or a dangerous patrol. Volunteers were always welcome and the same guys would tend to step forward almost every time. It got to the point that a few men were carrying the biggest share of the hazardous duty. At times, if we had a dangerous project and there were not enough volunteers to do the job, we needed to assign personnel to the task. As noted earlier, when I became a non-com I vowed not to send anyone into a situation that I couldn't do or wouldn't do myself. It is very uncomfortable indeed to be instrumental in the death of one of your own through a command decision. Yet, command decisions sometimes had to be made that were followed by dire results.

Even though the demands of the situation were such that someone had to go, someone had to run the risks being faced, it nevertheless left a feeling of guilt and regret when something went wrong—which it could easily do in combat. The NCO making the decision may in times afterward "second guess" his decision or have remorse when something terrible happened, such as happened with Janus' death.

In order to be an effective combat leader one cannot dwell upon tragic consequences of command decisions when the duty awaits, though later doubts may haunt us terribly. In times like these it is important to keep in mind that one can never really be certain what the consequences of an order will be. That is, whether the order will result in anticipated doom. We had circumstances in Korea in which a unit leader sent out a contact patrol into the valley in a very likely hazardous mission. The outcome was enigmatic—the patrol returned unscathed only to learn that their commander, who sent them, had died when his relatively safe bunker took a direct hit shortly after the patrol departed.

The role of fate in molding our life circumstances is often underestimated. But its importance as an influence on human thought was well described by the Persian astronomer and poet Omar Khayyam in his *Rubaiyat*:

> *The Moving Finger writes, and having writ*
> *Moves on: nor all the Piety nor Wit*
> *Shall lure it back to cancel half a line*
> *Nor all thy Tears wash out a Word of it*

> *Tis all a Chequer-board of Nights and Days*
> *Where Destiny with Men for Pieces plays*
> *Hither and thither moves, and mates, and slays*
> *And one by one back in the Closet lays.*

Fate! Happenstance! The unpredictable! All of these things describe the feeling that men often have when facing capricious circumstance of combat. We are often at the hands of fate as Khayyam so aptly noted. The unknown hand may strike at any time. Take for example one of our men, a company clerk, who was transferred back to Division Headquarters. On his first day back in the safety of this distant rearward headquarters an object fell from a passing airplane hitting him on the head killing him instantly. Where is it safe from harm in a war zone?

Many men develop a way of thinking to help them deal with conditions of frequent danger such as combat. Combat troops often develop a fatalistic way of thinking—the protection that comes from thinking that one will go "when one's number is up." Combat troops get into the magical thinking that their "number is not up yet so they are safe." The NCO, in making command decisions, must assume that no one's number is up!

LOSS OF HEARING

I was hurrying along a six foot deep section of the trench heading back to the command bunker from a routine inspection of the trenches when I heard an extremely loud whistling sound. I started my automatic dive toward the relative safety of the earth at the same instant that the shell exploded on the rim of the trench sending an enormous, loud shock wave through the trench. The bursting shell exploded the shrapnel outward but threw a large wave of wet dirt all over me and the loud burst pounded my right ear. I lay motionless for a few seconds trying to determine if I had been hit by any of the shrapnel. I got up out of the mud and went into the bunker. The radioman spoke to me but I couldn't decipher what he was saying.

I sat stunned and somewhat confused for a while waiting for my hearing to return to normal. It did not. I couldn't hear anything out of my right ear. It was about three days before my hearing returned to normal. Even after I dug the wad of wet dirt that had been jammed into my ear by the explosion, my hearing improved but I continued to have hearing problems that lasted for some time.

GROWING INWARD DISCONTENT WITH THE WAR

In spite of my own low mood about some of the recent losses described earlier, the external situation with the war actually appeared good. We were winning the battles and holding on to the real estate. We were clearly maintaining our responsibilities on our section of the MLR; but why didn't we feel good about the war now?

Over the spring of 1953, I fell into a bad frame of mind in which the war began to seem a continuous, never-ending exercise in futility and unnecessary deaths. A lot of my daily thoughts dwelt upon the seeming endlessness of this war and the feeling that I was pretty much left alone here. Most of my close friends were either dead or had been evacuated with wounds to Japan or the States. It seemed to us that we were simply pawns on a broader political stage. It was just a game that the big shots were playing in Panmunjom while we were being sacrificed. I thought a lot about Grasshold and how he looked during the identification process and how excited he had been about returning to the States and getting married. I thought a lot about Sullivan and Krumins—guys that would likely have made great contributions to society had their lives not been snuffed out. Why was our government throwing away such great human resources? For what—a piece of trenched earth that we would soon see evacuated anyway?

There seemed to be very little escape, even in fantasy or socializing at a beer bust around a campfire. No more were we having any fun time to break the monotony of trench life or offset the horrors of combat. I certainly missed the happy tunes that Billy Marshall played on our beer drinking nights. The evening campfires, when we could have them, were less homey and often downright sad. The Chinese artillery and raids had devastated our ranks.

My own morale was at a low ebb following all of the personal losses that we had experienced on Pork Chop. Part of the problem came about, of course, from the fact that other guys in the platoon were not as friendly toward me—I was their platoon sergeant, no longer "one of the guys." There was clearly something to the old description of leadership as carrying with it a "loneliness of command." I was experiencing this isolation first hand. It was something that I had to get used to and had to learn to project a positive view in spite of my feeling of isolation.

12

Outpost Duty

ACCORDING TO THE PLAY BOOK OF TACTICS and strategy for infantry units in Korea, outposts carried a great deal of responsibility in the overall plan of defense along the stabilized front. The mission of an infantry unit assigned to outpost duty—to serve as the forward unit in order to gain information about any approaching enemy units and to deceive them as to the position of the main force—is simple in conception but often difficult in operation. The out posted unit's mission is also intended to disrupt the actions of the approaching enemy and to delay attackers that might be launching an offensive against the main body.

In some military situations the outpost is not expected to engage the enemy, only to warn of its presence. Many outposts in Korea during the latter part of the war, however, held a more strategic importance as a fighting force, not simply as observation posts. They were expected to put up an aggressive battle—often against great odds. Some of the bloodiest action of the latter part of the war took place on outposts like Pork Chop Hill and Yoke. These outposts, though small in terms of assigned unit strength (three or four squads), were heavily armed, self-contained fighting units. The old concept of circling the wagons in western movies, to hold off the attacking Indians who might come from any and all directions, aptly describes the mentality of the armed outpost. During the spring of 1953, our company was required to provide reinforced platoon size units to serve on Yoke, a remote outpost that lay well out into the valley. Usually the tour of duty on outpost was five to seven days. At night, Yoke was often visited by Chinese patrols and attacking forces. (See the photo of the marker on the slope of Outpost Yoke in April 1953 in Chapter 8).

The outpost usually contained eight or nine fighting positions placed in a circular position around the military crest of the hill. These emplacements were usually for protection from artillery and were often not the sleeping bunkers that would be near them, perhaps up the hill a few yards. These fighting emplacements were typically connected together by communication wire so that all of the men on the outpost knew what was happening anywhere on the hill. The armament on outposts consisted, as much as possible, of the automatic weapons variety—BARs, M-2 carbines, Thompson Sub Machine guns, light or .30 caliber machine guns, and even heavier .50 caliber machine guns.

Outposts were usually surrounded by a deep encirclement of barbed wire; in many cases there would be two or three separate barbed wire fences with triple strands of concertina wire strung between them. In order to provide friendly access to the hill, for example to bring in food, supplies, or particularly replacements, a series of gates would be provided through the sea of barbed wire.

Out in front, infantrymen would set up trip wires attached to warning flares or illumination grenades—hand thrown weapons that provided intense light instead of shrapnel fragments. (Although traditional high explosive hand grenades were also liberally employed as booby traps around the front of the outpost.) Enterprising GIs would also string booby traps at different locations around the hill. For example, one of my favorite defensive weapons was an ammunition can or a fifty-five-gallon drum filled with liquid napalm, a molasses-like substance that airplanes often dropped on entrenched hills and then ignited to burn deep into the tunnels. As a means of detonation, we would attach a white phosphorous or thermite hand grenade to the napalm can and string a wire from the loosened pin of the grenade, back to the bunker. If any enemy soldiers appeared in the front of our positions, the wire could be pulled exploding the grenade that ignited the napalm. Laid out in this way, the outpost could indeed be a formidable defensive position.

It was important to the security of the hill—as well to the platoon leader's peace of mind—to have close communications with all of the fighting positions in the perimeter of defense. There was usually a communication between the firing positions on the outpost, unless of course incoming artillery cut the wires. The CP was the control center—all of the status communications from the fighting positions were transmitted to it. Telephone checks were frequent, periodic, or as the situation required. If anything out of the ordinary happened at any point on the perimeter, it was a threat to the entire operation and was immediately dealt with.

EVER PRESENT DANGER ON OUTPOST DUTY

Outposts were also exceptionally dangerous places in that the Chinese usually had accurate coordinates for their mortars and artillery and would fire harassing rounds periodically just to keep us on edge. Since the outposts were often smaller knolls near larger, higher Chinese-held hills, they also employed snipers to restrict our movement in the daytime.

Fehrenbach (1963) pointed out the danger of outpost duty in a war that was all but forgotten back home:

One final bitterness, of all these people, was that much of the bitter struggle of the last spring went unreported. There were months when as many as 104 enemy attacks—from company to division strength—smashed against the U. N. Outpost line, and days when as many as 131,800 rounds of communist artillery fell on it within a twenty-four hour period. Few of these events, buried deep in newspapers, caused a stir (p. 426).

One afternoon I was sitting on a step that had been carved into the trench, eating my mid-day rations (a can of the delicious entree called hamburger and gravy), and looking down the dugout at one of the new riflemen in the platoon who was filling sandbags to strengthen the roof on a machine gun emplacement.

Suddenly, and without much audible warning, a sequence of mortar shells burst a few seconds apart along the trench line. One shell burst in the trench near the gun emplacement slightly beyond the rifleman, sending a shock wave and shrapnel down both directions in the line. I dived for the earth spilling the remaining juice from the rations beneath me as shards of shrapnel tore an ugly hole in the step on which I had been sitting but missing me by a couple of feet. The rifleman near me was not so fortunate; he was hit in both legs by shrapnel. He had to be evacuated from the outpost and carried back to the MLR where the helicopter could land.

CHEAP ENTERTAINMENT ON THE OUTPOST

The outpost near T-Bone was often the focus of Chinese entertainment—a frequent airing of propaganda through loud speakers on the hill. The Chinese placed these speakers in protected places so that they could keep the GIs on edge by broadcasting martial music interspersed with political commentary. Sometimes they even broadcast information about the units that were occupying the targeted outpost and were even known to mention the actual names of people in the units. Each succession of GIs going to the outpost tried to find where on the T-Bone the speakers were located in the hopes of firing rounds to eliminate them, but none succeeded. The recordings played on.

THE WILD, WILD WEST

Outpost duty was considered to be a riskier occupation than duty on the MLR, but it had its attractive side as well. One could usually ignore the spit-and-polish aspect of military life to some extent, although we were expected to shave every day regardless of circumstances. No one with any rank would show up at dangerous locations—like outposts such as Yoke, Eerie, or Arsenal—to check as to whether the men were actually complying with basic tasks. Outpost duty could be hazardous to your health—snipers, artillery rounds, and harassing attacks were par for the course. The job usually called for 100% alert. No one slept at night when Ole Joe prowled around the valley and nipped at our wire.

Seldom did the top brass visit us from Battalion or Regiment. Once during the winter when our platoon was serving a tour on Yoke, a colonel from reg-

Outpost Yoke, February 1953. *Left to right:* Franklin Brown, Charles Otto, the author, unknown.

imental headquarters conducted a so-called inspection tour of our positions. We were told that we would need to shave and clean up. When we inquired as to where we could obtain the water for such fancy activities, we were told to "melt snow!"

We were, fortunately, able to obtain an occasional hot meal on the outpost. The food was carried to the outpost (as was everything else) in a thermal container and served on a protected slope.

The colonel from regimental headquarters who visited the outpost for a few minutes, provided another bit of entertainment to the troops. The officer simply walked through the trench line for a brief spell looking at the enemy lines through a pair of binoculars, and then quickly returned to the main positions with the main company force. The outpost was quiet during the visit except at one time when a 76 mm round, simple not dangerous, dug up some rocks a distance away. A few weeks after the visit, the Army newspaper Stars and Stripes reported that the colonel received a Bronze Star for valor that day when he led troops on Yoke under enemy shelling. It was not uncommon for rear area brass to come up front (often at quieter times on the line) and wind up getting a decoration for valor.

PURIFICATION ON YOKE

The heavy weapons squad on Outpost Yoke had an interesting housekeeping strategy. Anytime they had a dud mortar round, that is a mortar shell that misfired, they would simply remove it from the mortar and dump it down one of the pipes that protruded from the earth making up the latrine system—an outhouse a few yards behind the bunker. Other guys in the 57 mm recoilless rifle squad dumped their defective shells down the hole as well. Other guys began to toss other types of unused or defective ammunition into the latrine such as bent machine gun cartridges that wouldn't feed or hand grenades that had gotten rusty or bent out of shape.

One morning on Yoke, Bill Estes came out of his bunker and found two medics carrying a gasoline can toward the latrine on a mission to clean up and sterilize the outhouse by fire—a common practice under such conditions. After dumping a gallon of gasoline down the hole they decided to ignite the petrol by firing a pistol down the hole. Estes, seeing that an exciting event was about to take place, yelled, "I wouldn't do that if I were you!"

One of the medics shouted back as they ignited the hole, "We have orders to purify this mess out here!"

Estes quickly headed for the bunker as he yelled advice to the medics to do likewise if they knew what was good for them. Within a few minutes, as the pit began to burn hotly (and, of course, reek more intensely) the .30 caliber ammunition began to pop off, followed by several large explosions of shells with the accumulated contents of the offensive pit.

As the medics wiped off the contents of the latrine from their clothes, Sgt. Estes thanked them warmly and enthusiastically for cleaning up the outhouse!

AN INCIDENT OF CIVILIAN "COOPERATION"

One night on Yoke, shortly after a KSC crew carried out rations and food, we began to receive intense shelling—more than the usual harassing fire—and we became alert to the possibility of an attack. One of our forward positions received a direct hit and two of the men inside were wounded. With an attack possible, we did not feel that we could spread our ranks thin by sending a full complement of stretcher-bearers back to the rear. Dugan (now operating as a medic in the platoon) and one of the ROK soldiers attempted to organize a stretcher bearing team to carry the wounded back using the KSC crew. The choggies were too scared of the incoming shells to help with the litter, they refused plaintively.

Dugan pointed his weapon at them yelling, "You commie bastards! We're taking these guys back!" The KSC crew had a change of heart and picked up the stretchers and began the journey back.

I did not quarrel with Dugan's handling of the situation, though it was a bit rough; everyone knew that he would likely have killed them had they not cooperated. One of the squad leaders on the outpost came to me afterward and was very critical of my not stopping Dugan's enthusiastic expressiveness toward the KSC workers and I thought he was justified to some extent.

However, I thought that Dugan's behavior, though extreme, was effective. Combat conditions, especially on outpost, tended to raise the level of emotions and a sense of exigency. I was inclined to agree with Dugan's efforts, but perhaps it was wrong to force these civilians at gunpoint to carry wounded back to the rear with the possibility of drawing artillery fire at them. I realized that in vociferously supporting Dugan, I had perhaps lost some of my previous composure and objectivity under these tight circumstances.

The means to the end was certainly harsh. Maybe my own judgment in this situation was impaired but I acted as I thought circumstances required, that is, holding the defense of the hill intact at all cost while getting our wounded and the KSC crew off the hill.

AT WAR WITH THE ETHIOPIANS

One night, after a week on outpost duty, we were being relieved by a pla-

Dale Moss (*left*) and the author on Outpost
Yoke, 1953.

toon from the Ethiopian battalion to return to the MLR. The Ethiopians were
delayed in their arrival at the outpost so I went inside the CP and fell asleep
on the top commo wire bunk to await their arrival. We had a lot of respect for
the "Epps." They had a reputation of being fearless and aggressive soldiers
who had a great prowess in night stealth. This was certainly true in this situation because they arrived at our positions in the valley almost undetected by
our sentinels until they reached the lowest strands of barbed wire strung
around the hill.

No one had come into the bunker to wake me up because they were all
getting their gear together to move back to the MLR. The first that I knew
that the Ethiopians had arrived was when I, still groggy from the nap, detected
some movement in the CP bunker near my bunk. I adjusted my eyes to see

where the noise was coming from when I was startled by a grinning black face about a foot away from my head. In an automatic reaction, I went for my weapon only to have him grab my hand. Laughing aloud, he seemed to be enjoying the fact that he had gotten so close to me without awakening me.

****

When I went outside the bunker to check to see if all of our guys were saddled up and ready to go, I heard some loud voices down the trench and went to investigate. There was an apparent disagreement over the ownership of one of the weapons. We had orders to take with us all of our own weapons and equipment including the heavy machine gun our weapons squad had recently acquired. The Ethiopian lieutenant had other plans for our heavy machine gun and began to insist that it was a sector weapon and was supposed to stay on Yoke. Dale Moss, our machine gun team leader, was equally assertive about keeping the gun because he had grown quite attached to it.

Moss, becoming angered over the lieutenant's insistence, settled the dispute by getting the drop on the officer. He quickly and adeptly drew his .45 caliber pistol from his holster and aimed it at the Ethiopian lieutenant's head, cocked it, and said, "We're taking our gun!" He instructed the ammo bearers to move it. That night the Ethiopians, who had a strong reputation for being fearless combat soldiers, discovered that the Americans could be a bit badassed too if pushed.

ON BECOMING A "SHORT TIMER": THE INCREASE OF MY ROTATION BLUES

The rotation system, described earlier, disadvantaged both the unit and the individual soldier. The units were disadvantaged in that the most experienced men were sent home and the unit morale and effectiveness often suffered from such departures. This also meant that the day-to-day functioning of the unit was conducted by men with more limited experience. The military became somewhat disenchanted with this rotation system after the Korean War and made modifications by rotating units rather than personnel.

Men were disadvantaged by the rotation system in several ways. Regardless of one's stamina and capability of handling increasing stress, all people fol-

On a break, May 1953. *Left to right:* Thorn, Daggett, the author, Schoen, Field, and Otto.

lowed the same system. It is well known that some individuals fare better under stress than do others. However, in Korea, the tour of duty was of the "one size fits all" variety. Men at the front often acted strangely as they reached the magic thirty-six point milestone. Fear of death or injury tended to increase; the "short timers" often became preoccupied with "not taking any unnecessary chances"—and for good reason. We all knew of guys that had made it through some pretty tough times and who had finally attained the required points for rotation only to be maimed or killed. Grasshold, who died on Pork Chop, was a good example. He had more than thirty-six points when he was killed. By the time I reached the magic point, I was unlike the seemingly invincible young man who marched blindly and carelessly into action on Jane Russell. I was becoming overly cautious and jittery about surviving. I was anticipating the worst at every turn. It seemed as if every incoming artillery round had my name on it. Every Chinese infantryman on the opposing strongholds knew my location and was out to do me harm.

I was now a short timer—ready for rotation. I had become one of the point counters, having been in Korea for more than nine months, and I too became more reluctant to take excessive risks. I began to eat my C-rations in my bunker rather than run the risk of being erased by a shell on my way to the chow bunker. I had transformed into a different soldier, especially after I returned from R&R in Japan where I came to realize that there was life and fun out there. I became more preoccupied with getting back home.

THE INTERNATIONAL INCIDENT AND SYNGMAN RHEE

We were on outpost duty when we received the news about an extremely unsettling political action by the South Korean government: a situation that threw us into a flurry of anger and concern over our own safety.

On June 18, 1953, without warning, South Korean President Syngman Rhee released 35,000 North Korean prisoners from the prison camps. We were absolutely astounded by the fact that all of a sudden we would have a large body of enemy soldiers to our rear—a situation we considered a traitorous act by the leader. We were here on the front lines keeping the enemy from South Korea's gate while their politicians made our lives difficult by turning a horde of the enemy loose at the rear. We became gravely concerned as to the security of our rear areas, and could visualize ourselves being attacked by guerilla forces from behind. After all, some of the men in our unit had been pulled off the line to chase infiltrators in our rear in the past.

Of course, we got no clarifying information from our own officers—most of whom were equally angered and puzzled over Rhee's actions. We were not the only Americans who had these concerns. Apparently the general staff and the president were infuriated by Rhee's brazen action. We were not told at the time that these POWs had opted not to return to the North.

Our anger at the politicians got expressed in an action that backfired and brought some "official" criticism of me at the time. One of the guys in the platoon happened to have a magazine picture of Syngman Rhee and set it up as a target on a bank near where we sometimes ate our lunch. Several of us let off steam by taking a few target practice shots at the picture after we heard the news of the prisoner release. A few days later, when we returned to the MLR, I was called on the carpet for creating an "international incident." It seemed that one of the ROK soldiers in the unit had complained that we were not showing sufficient respect for his leader. The CO seemed a bit exasperated at having to deal with our misbehavior. I, as the ranking perpetrator, was required to make a public apology to the ROK soldiers, many of whom I was to learn, held the same sense of outrage as we did about the prisoner release.

I don't think any of our generals or President Truman ever apologized for their angry expressions at Rhee. But then their anger was not expressed as openly as ours and, of course, we were at the bottom of the power hierarchy. Although this seemed like a crazy and traitorous situation to us at the time, many analysts have concluded that Rhee's releasing the prisoners actually had a positive impact on hastening the end of the war. This interpretation is based on the fact that the greatest stumbling block in the peace negotiations at Panmunjom was the prisoners. Now that these people were no longer in captivity, it took away one of the points of disagreement holding up the talks.

SKOSHIE R&R: A FORCED REST AT CAMP CASEY

In the late spring my time came due to participate in what was referred to as "Skoshie R&R." This was a planned leave to provide GIs who had been on the line a long time with a rest break to provide them a respite from the front and a brief period of relaxation at Division rear. I didn't want to take another leave and I protested that I needed to be here on the front because we were so thin in rank and with so many new men up front. But, the new CO ordered me to take a break. He said that it was mandatory for GIs with my time in the trenches.

The Army plan and the CO's implementation of it recognized that I was experiencing a bit of war weariness or operational ineffectiveness often referred to as "combat fatigue." Many GIs with my time on the line began to show that they were becoming a bit frayed and a felling a bit depressed. The GI often did not agree, as in my case, and considered it unnecessary. But the

On Outpost Yoke. *Left to right*: Vito Field, the author, and Don Schoen.

officers in Battalion and the Company insisted, so I got a break. It is interesting as I look back at this time that they were clearly right in insisting but I felt so strongly as though I needed a rationale or justification for not staying at the front with my men.

The goal of the Skoshie R&R was designed to give the GI a chance to clean up, get a couple of nights sleep, watch a movie or two, drink some beer, and basically interrupt the cycle of operational fatigue, a very visible condition shown by jumpiness, irritability, fatigue, and depression. All the others before me who were sent back for a rest enjoyed it. Just to be able to sleep without worrying about Old Joe slipping into your trench and cutting your throat was a pretty big relief.

Late one evening on my second night in the rear, after a bit of drinking at the Regimental NCO club, three other NCOs from another battalion and I decided to go into Ouijongbu, a town close by, to look for some excitement. One of the guys managed to acquire a jeep, unofficially of course, from a guy who used to be in his squad.

We were off. We drove around town for a while but everything was locked up and dark. We did not find much going on. After midnight, and a fruitless search for excitement, we decided to try and find our way back to camp before the jeep was counted among the missing. As we rounded a corner of one street, we chanced to see some lights and some people moving about in one of the houses. With lights on at that time of the evening we, of course, assumed that it was a nightclub of some sort and we stopped the jeep to have a look around.

The Koreans inside, mostly older men and women, were sitting around a room drinking a fermented, milky rice drink. They invited us to come inside and we took a seat on the floor. They offered us some of the wine and some dried squid to eat—a snack for which Americans do not gain a ready fondness due to the fishy smell. None of them could speak English and we, of course, knew little Korean. They were certainly friendly enough, but we felt uneasy with the situation. After a while one of the sergeants came to the realization that we were sitting there in the midst of a wake.

Apparently the deceased woman, an ole "mamasan," was to be buried the next morning. We felt a bit sheepish about our intrusion but we stayed there a while talking, or at least gesturing with the people, until we took our leave to return to camp, saying our friendly goodbyes. I have always wondered what the people at the funeral thought of four somewhat inebriated, heavily armed U.S. Army combat NCOs dropping in to pay our respects at the funeral of this old Korean woman.

INTO THE VALLEY OF DEATH

Our platoon was ordered to send an ambush patrol near Hassakol to interdict troop movements from the Chinese hill. The patrol leader was a capable lieutenant who was newly arrived in Korea and had no prior combat experience. Vito and I volunteered for the patrol, I might add with some reluctance because of my short time left on my tour of duty; however, there were few experienced men in the platoon at the time. In addition, it seemed like one more stroll through the valley wouldn't be too bad. Our preparations for the patrol were routine, except for large numbers of questions and what seemed like excessive worry among several new men we had to take along.

As we left the security of the barbed wire fences surrounding our lines and began to make our way down the outbound path, I heard the familiar sound of an M-2 carbine fire in short bursts. Initially, I thought that one of the new men had accidentally discharged his weapon—giving away our positions. I yelled out, "Who fired that weapon?"

No sooner did I ask than our ranks were littered with five or six exploding Chinese hand grenades. Several men in our ranks began to yell for a medic. We were ambushed at a vulnerable point in the patrol—while we were in single file and before we could get into our diamond shaped patrol formation. The Chinese, who were apparently well aware of the fact that our patrols always had to leave from this section of the line, had set up their ambush on this familiar trail. The Chinese had allowed our point man to pass; he did not detect their presence at this early stage in the patrol. The fact that their initial attack came from the ground off to the right of the trail, actually a minefield, suggested that they had successfully cleared a path on earlier patrols prior to that evening so they would not explode our mines in setting up this particular ambush.

As the firefight proceeded, some of the more experienced men returned fire—firing at shadows and flashes. From a crouched position, I emptied the clip from my M-2 carbine at the bright flashes coming from my right. Then I fell to the ground next to Jerry Manning, one of the new men who was walking in front of me, to insert a new magazine clip into my weapon.

As I lay there, I felt something warm on my leg. "What the hell?" I said.

Manning replied, "I think I pissed my pants!" His voice was pained. (Manning had actually taken a shell fragment in his bladder that promptly emptied it, filling up the slight depression in the earth in which we had fallen.)

Soaking wet with urine, I stood up and fired in the direction from which the flashes had come. It soon became quiet along the path that the patrol had followed. The intruders left as quickly and as stealthily as they came.

The action aftermath of the patrol was horrible, with almost everyone wounded and in a state of shock. The action was sudden, brief, and very destructive. Before we knew what happened, we had one man killed, one missing, and several severely wounded.

Sergeant Estes, leading another company patrol, arrived shortly as the remnants of our patrol was making its crippled way back to the MLR. We had the wounded lined up along a road and were calling for stretcher bearers to get them down toward the bottom of the hill where they could get picked up by an APC for the trip to the rear.

ASSUMPTION OF DUTIES AS FIELD FIRST SERGEANT

The Battalion Executive Officer asked me if I would like to take on a new position in another company—the job of Field First Sergeant in K Company—to replace a sergeant that had rotated back to the States. Although it involved a transfer to another company, I agreed to do so even though I only had a few days or weeks until I would be eligible for rotation myself. Although I would miss a few of the old-timers in the company, I decided that there were some things about the new look of Fox Company that I would not miss. I made the move in early July and we moved back on the line facing our old foe near the T-Bone. Although I was still only nineteen years old, the new situation as field first sergeant made me feel like an old soldier.

The move was a good one for me. My duties involved serving as the assistant to the first sergeant and involved command of the company troops in the field, including such things as combat preparations, weapons inspections, troop movements, and so forth. The company officers appeared to be clearly stronger than the ones that I had just left in Fox Company and were friendly. I liked the group of guys in the new company and settled in to complete my Korean tour.

THE SECOND BATTLE OF PORK CHOP

On July 8th, we received word that Pork Chop Hill was under major attack again and that our company was to be one of the units to be deployed in a counterattack if the hill was lost. We were instructed to prepare for a jump-off later that evening. The NCOs were called in to the CO's tent for a briefing just prior to the hour scheduled to load up the trucks for the ride up to the MLR behind Pork Chop. The CO indicated that the Battalion was being called in to put out the recent fires of the Chinese assault on Pork Chop and that evening our unit was moving up at 7:00 P.M.

After briefing the platoons, the CO told me that I was not going with the main unit, but that I was staying back with a contingent of men in the reserves in the event a counter attack was required. I was very surprised by the CO's decision to leave me behind, and I had a great deal of mixed feelings about his decision. I suggested that I knew the hill and might be of some help in the engagement. He firmly pointed out that I did not have direct command responsibility for a platoon in the company and that an "extra" NCO might actually be confusing to the command structure. In addition, he pointed out, "You have already done enough with the Pork Chop; and you are ready to rotate." With mixed feelings, I remained behind.

The Pork Chop again came to be a disastrous piece of real estate for our Battalion. Several companies were chewed-up in the seesaw battle that raged for two days. Many men in the company lost their lives on the hill that first night of the battle—including the company commander who had decided not to take me along—and most of the officers in the company. When the remnants of the company came off the hill the atmosphere was much the same as it had been back in April after the first Pork Chop.

After all of the troops were withdrawn from the Chop, I walked over to the Fox Company tents, which were pitched close by, a day after what was being referred to as the Second Battle of Pork Chop. I wanted to see if I could get word on what had happened to the unit during the foray and to see old friends Vito, Moss, and Estes.

Tragic news met me right away. Don Schoen, from my old squad, one of the few familiar faces around, told me that Moss had been killed. Dale and an ammo bearer, referred to only as "Doggie," had gone down on the point on Pork Chop to set up a machine gun to bear upon attacking Chinese coming up the ridge. Neither Moss nor his ammo bearer ever returned from the mission.

I couldn't believe that Moss was dead. This was an incredible revelation that I did not handle well at all. Sergeants are not supposed to cry but it was unavoidable. Moss the indestructible; Moss the happy dare devil; Moss the good friend was no more. This was the most unkind cut of the war. I felt numb from the shock and could not bear to hear more.

I cried all the way back to my own unit. The world had certainly lost one of the greatest humans ever to walk its face. This was not the only bad news from the Second Pork Chop. Vito had also been wounded and so had Bill Estes, who was the platoon sergeant for the mortar section. Bill took a bullet in his arm and was being evacuated to Japan. (Bill was among the many casualties evacuated to Japan after the Second Battle of Pork Chop, but his drama did not end when he left the hill. He told me some years after the war ended of a frightful experience he had during his evacuation. Estes and a number of other wounded men were loaded onto a C-47 hospital plane for the trip over to Japan. The plane was apparently overloaded and failed to clear the fence at the end of the runway. The plane crashed, spilling much of its already damaged cargo and killing the crew and several of the wounded. He reportedly was rather nervous getting on the second evacuation plane the next day to go to Japan).

It was a long and sorrowful walk back to my company.

FINAL DEMOLITION OF PORK CHOP

Hell's little outpost, that godforsaken knoll of death, was once again held by the American forces with the loss of many lives only to be given up when the politicians decided that this piece of real estate was not worth keeping.

On July 10th Pork Chop Hill was evacuated and left to the enemy (who probably really did not want it either). General Trudeau decided that the hill was not worth spilling any more blood over and decided to secretly evacuate the positions on the hill after they were laden with tons of explosives. Throughout the trench works booby traps, napalm, and dynamite charges were strategically placed to be ignited on command from the safety of the MLR.

An easy deception was then perpetrated. The troops holding the hill were simply taken off in secret. Then the hill would be returned to Chinese hands if they wanted it. The deception was made easy because the reinforcement of the hill was now being carried out with armored personnel carriers. The Chinese could not actually determine if the APCs traveling up the hill were loaded with men going up or coming off the hill. Over a period of several hours the Pork Chop was evacuated

After two days of relative silence the Chinese became aware of the lack of movement on the hill and decided to move up in force to reclaim it. Once they were on the hill the charges were blown at the same time that an intensive artillery barrage was leveled against the hill, and on the enemy approaches leading up to it. The emplacements on Pork Chop were soon only piles of rubble. The Chinese could now have this patch of real estate to occupy but they paid very dearly for the clear deed to it.

We watched the hill blow from our positions on the MLR. This was an incredible sight to behold. The hill's snake-like entrenchments were destroyed with an ear-bursting crescendo. Secondary explosions erupted and smoke billowed from the hill for several days after the detonation.

After all the lives that had been lost to gain and regain Pork Chop over the past several months, it was now removed from our list of real estate holdings above the 38th Parallel. Most of us concluded that it was "Good riddance!"

The ultimate irony is that this highly valued prize of the new type of "limited warfare" was now seen as a worthless relic—no longer did it hold the tactical value it had held for so many months during the later stages of peace talks. Such a conclusion was about four months late in coming.

13

Armistice: Return of the Morning Calm

FINALLY, AFTER TWO YEARS OF HAGGLING AT Panmunjom and tens of thousands of American lives expended along the front, a cease-fire agreement was signed. The designated time for the cease-fire was July 27, 1953 at 10:00 P.M. This was the time for all hostilities to cease.

We watched the clock intently. Would they actually stop fighting? Would the long bloody war finally end? Would we go home at last? We had our doubts, and for good reason because of the number of times that some last minute disagreement caused a walkout from the negotiations.

The companies on the front were ordered to send out listening posts and to run reconnaissance patrols into the valley as usual. However, we were ordered not to carry "live" ammunition. At our company level, however, we modified the instructions slightly and directed the troops to carry a magazine in their weapon but not to carry a round in the chamber. We did not trust the situation enough to send an unarmed patrol into the valley. We were instructed that we could fire only if the enemy directly fired us upon. There was to be no firing of weapons after 10:00 P.M., accidental or otherwise.

Early in the evening, a few guys in advanced positions down the finger of the hill fired off a few rounds. I went down the trench to see if there was anything happening. They were just "letting off steam" and loudly expressing their opinions about the war. The Chinese also expressed their view of us and the war by throwing a few token 76 mm rounds from the closest hill. As the clock ticked off the remaining minutes of the war, another sergeant and I climbed on the ridge line and watched the valley floor for activity. We drew our pistols and fired a ceremonial round at the dark, ominous Chinese hill to finish off the war.

The ceasefire began at 10:00 P.M. as planned. There was no more firing from either side. I believe that we, Americans and Chinese alike, all finally had our fill of war. All along the line that night there was total silence. The night sky was semi-darkened—bathed in natural summer moonlight and an unnatural low light glow projected out from the search light unit about a half-mile down the line near our positions. This was the most incredible silence I'd heard in my life. Not a tracer was seen dotting the sky, not an exploding round was heard. We marveled as we walked around our positions, unconcerned as to whether Ole Joe was going to test our resolve in some way during the night. We were ordered to pull our half-on, half-off watch as always, but seemingly no one minded being awake that night. No one felt much like sleeping; the excitement was too much. The evening passed without incident, the war was really over.

A poem by Oscar Williams (1945) entitled *One Morning the World Woke Up*, written for an earlier war, expressed the situation well:

> *No trucks climbed into the grooves of an endless road,*
> *No tanks were swaying drunken with death at the hilltop,*
> *No bombs were planting the bushes of blood and mud,*
> *And the aimless tides of unfortunates no longer flowed:*
> *a break in the action at last...*
> *All had come to a stop.*

****

Our orders for the pullback the next day were to saddle up and take all weapons, supplies, or anything of military worth. Nothing of value was to be left. The plan for the evacuation involved withdrawal back to a line two kilo-

The author, SFC Jim Butcher, age 19. March 1953.

meters to our rear where we would set up positions and hold them. This imaginary line would be established as a demilitarized zone that extended the length of the peninsula with no troops stationed or moving between the troop-free zone. All of the precious real estate that we had spent so long wrestling away from the Chinese and North Korean enemies, all of the concertina wire, all of the miles of our trench line and the network of mysterious Chinese caves would now become a part of the four kilometer demilitarized zone—the DMZ.

THE INFINITE LINE OF SHADOW FIGURES

Dawn broke on the morning of July 28, 1953 much like it had the many mornings I spent in Korea. I awakened from a short, light nap and felt stiff and numb from sleeping on the hard commo wire bunk. As I looked around at the grimy faces of the others in the trench we were stunned by the silence of the morning. This day was indeed different—there were no shells, no machine gun fire, and no yells for "medic." There was nothing but the stone silence—much like the sounds of a cemetery. All movement seemed to be in suspended animation as we walked around in disbelief.

Upon leaving the bunker, the first thing that I did was climb up on the ridge line, outside the trench, and scan the Chinese hill in the distance with my binoculars. I was expecting to see the usual barren hills devoid of vegetation and human life. I was astounded by the sight of movement across the valley. Instead of the bleak, naked hills that we had grown so accustomed to observing for so many months, we witnessed an incredible sight across no-mans-land toward the Chinese lines. There, as far as the human eye could see, were long lines of Chinese soldiers stretching from their forward caves and trenches all the way back to their rear echelon areas in the distance.

Thousands upon thousands of Chinese soldiers formed this anthill of activity, standing a few feet apart, passing supplies and equipment backward in an endless assembly line, looking like robots. We watched this mechanical procession for a long time, marveling at the immense number of enemy soldiers that were visible. Had we known the extent of their forces a few days before, had we known the locations from which these men moved out large guns and small, we would have not been so complacent and comfortable of our own strengths and capabilities. It appeared to us that everyone in China was here moving equipment back away from the now demilitarized zone.

Our own movements toward the rear were less spectacular. We half carried, half tumbled our way off the hill, moving what weapons, ammunition, and personal items we had with us. At the bottom were waiting trucks, moved up as close to the MLR as topography would allow.

We left a lot of things on the hill. All of the refuse that had accumulated, all of the spent cartridges that we had not policed up, all of the discarded, worn-out clothing. An extra steel helmet, the old blankets with holes in them, empty ammunition tins, a leaky water can, the miles of communication wire, the commo wire bunks, and a calendar circled with the date July 28, 1953— all were left behind. Along with the intentionally discarded items of war that we no longer needed were also some things left by accident, such as one corporal's harmonica, another's picture of his girl friend. Everything that was not taken was doomed to remain as it was, left for decades. The trenches and all that remained were turned over to the rats—the new owners of those digs.

Some guys wrote notes that they left tied to bunker posts for posterity to find. Some of the notes were simple statements, such as "Johnny slept here!" Others were more blunt and aggressive in explaining what the sender thought about the enemy with such statements as "Chinks stink!" Others, trying to be more philosophical, wrote what they thought about the war or the Chinese, but almost always these homilies were punctuated with clear, Army-styled four letter words.

****

The new DMZ, the buffer zone between North Korea and South Korea, was a strip of earth 249 miles long and four kilometers wide. It has been officially off limits to forces from either side except a few on some official duties, usually in the corridor between Panmunjom and Seoul. Some intruders have made their way into the DMZ from time to time; otherwise, things are pretty much as we left them except what time and the ever-present rodents have done to them. The North Korean military maintains a strong military presence, over a million men, around the Panmunjom area and periodically engages in violations of the DMZ by sending troops into the buffer area. In 1996, for example, the North Korean Army sent more than 300 soldiers in groups of ten to twenty into the DMZ to conduct maneuvers. The United States and South Korean forces have also had infractions of the buffer zone with people "wandering" into the DMZ on occasion. In 1977 an American helicopter was shot down, killing three people. In 1995 an American aircraft was shot down in North Korean territory, killing one of the airmen on board.

Tensions have erupted along the buffer zone on numerous occasions. For example, North Korean solders killed two American officers with axes when they were trimming trees near Panmunjom.

The South Koreans, for protection, have built a two-and-a-half story concrete wall running nearly the entire width of the peninsula (except the DMZ at Panmunjom). The North Korean Army has dug large tunnels under the

DMZ; tunnels that could be used to infiltrate or attack the South if they were so disposed. Four extremely large tunnels have been discovered thus far under the DMZ and it has been estimated that there are around twenty total.

In all likelihood, in the decades that have passed, the trench works have rotted away and collapsed. The hills that were once bald have likely been restored by nature as best as it can, with free ranging vegetation now covering the discarded shell fragments and bones that still lay littered about. Old Baldy probably even has a growth of brush covering the once barren slopes. The wounds to the hills have, in all likelihood, healed their scars of war far more efficiently than the people who fought on them. These scars still protrude from our consciousness—covered only by a superficial layer of civilization and more positive events that have come since the war.

LEFT IN LIMBO

About a week after the armistice agreement ended the fighting, our company was ordered to move farther back to an area a few miles north of Seoul, to Camp Casey, and the entire company except a guard detachment was moved out on trucks. I was left with three other men in charge of a "baggage detail" to guard the company supply and baggage until transportation could be sent back to pick us up in a couple of days. We were left with enough C-rations for the two-day period. Unfortunately, three days later, we were still waiting; with our food and water gone, no communications with the company, and no transportation. We had been deserted. We considered the various options and didn't find many available. We had plenty of weapons and ammunition so we decided, like our forefathers of old, to hunt ourselves some dinner.

Unfortunately, the Korean War, with all of its noise and destructiveness, had long since scared away most of the game from these hills. The only prospects for our hunt we saw were a few very high flying birds. So we tested our marksmanship, initially with M-1 rifles. After a few shots, we recognized that this would not accomplish much so we brought out one of the BARs and tried automatic weapons fire. Success! We hit one and it fell to the earth. It was a bit mangled and not worth making into a meal. More time passed and still no trucks. We opened a few of the duffle bags to look for food and found only a couple of candy bars. Finally, one afternoon a ragged truck came by with two Korean Service Corps civilians who were out scrounging around the countryside for what ever they could find. They were very surprised to find us there and came over to inquire about us. We told them the situation and they agreed (for a price) to sell us some food and water and help us locate our unit. They returned a few hours later with cooked rice, kimchi, and some other unrecognizable items for our empty mess kits. We ate whatever they provided. They also brought some whiskey that they were happy, by then, to sell for some of the company blankets and equipment (shovels) that we were happy to barter. We rationalized purchasing the whiskey as having a need for further sustenance.

The remainder of our wait for the company to retrieve us was more pleasant and our hunt for animals became a bit more aggressive as we staggered around firing uselessly at anything we thought might be edible. Some might have thought that we had restarted the war had they been close enough to hear the sounds of our hunt. After five days our company retrieved us, with an appropriate apology. Before I had time to register a complaint to the CO (my rotation date was long overdue now) he cheerily told me that I was leaving the next day for Inchon then home. I could hardly believe those words. Going home, at last.

A CUP OF COFFEE AND A DONUT, BUT NO PARADES

My return to the United States, originally scheduled by air transport, was changed because of congestion in the military transportation pipeline of rotation. I drew the short straw and was assigned to a troop ship that made me wait a few days for its arrival. When I finally boarded another Kaiser ship for the three-week return journey it seemed like a much longer voyage on the return because of the anticipation we were all experiencing.

In addition to the several hundred GIs in the rotation draft, our ship contained a contingent of about 200 released POWs who were kept completely segregated from the rest of the returning veterans. We were told that we were not to talk to them or to try to exchange any items with them. I was curious to learn about the treatment they had experienced at the hands of the North Koreans but had no opportunity to do so. There was some talk during the voyage about the POWs having thrown one of their group overboard because he had collaborated with the enemy but this could have been a rumor. There was always an abundance of rumors floating around the ship with so many idle soldiers sitting about.

As with the trip over on the troop ship, to pass away the time, I spent some profitable hours at playing poker, but much of my time on deck was spent just in reverie and anticipation of what the future might hold. This was not an unpleasant occupation and served to pass the time away. I wondered about what life would be like without having to face the ever-present danger of sudden death?

Finally, the troop ship passed beneath the Golden Gate Bridge, providing everyone with the most spectacular and memorable entry into the United States. The tug maneuvered our ship into the long concrete berth at Ft. Mason. Once the ship was secured and the customary wait time had dissipated, the long line of khaki figures, each with a similar, brown duffle bag, began its snail like pace in disembarkation. The facelessness of military transfer continued as we made our way onto the concrete pier. A five-piece military band struck up a military welcome; several civilians lined the wharf watching the column of troops in hopes of recognizing one of the uniformed figures proceeding down the gangway.

On the pier, at the bottom of the ship's gangway, stood a crew of Red Cross volunteers handing out coffee and a donut to anyone who stretched out his hand as we formed into a somewhat ragtag formation. Soon, we were herded into a large hall and informed of the processing procedures and plans for moving us out, hopefully to our homes, in short order. We were provided a very welcome diversion from the troop ship food with a steak dinner and a bunk for the first night on friendly shores. The next day, and without fanfare or celebration, we were cast into the four winds—to our respective corners of America. There were no parades, no grand speeches about a job well done, no waving ladies dressed in attractive clothing. There was only the grateful understanding existing among ourselves that we had been the lucky ones. We were home again.

****

After my post-Korea leave I was reassigned back in the 82nd Airborne Division, this time to the 505th Airborne Infantry Regiment. My status was different, with my rank of sergeant first class I was given a job as a platoon sergeant in an airborne infantry company. I was not just a paratrooper who had to knuckle under to the spit and polish of garrison duty, but now I was someone who had to inflict it upon others.

Having obtained all my rank under combat conditions, I was not fully up to speed on what was required of non-coms in garrison duty, so I was a bit awkward as to procedures. Moreover, I was young to be a platoon sergeant in the 82nd, only twenty years old, while most of the other non-commissioned officers were old timers who had been well schooled in the ins-and-outs of dress parades and general inspections. I was helped along a bit by a couple of squad leaders who had been in combat units and seemed to recognize and sympathize with my lack of facility with barracks routine. Needless to say, I felt somewhat of a misfit with the day-to-day routines of barracks life. I only felt at home during the occasional times when the unit went into the field, especially when it came to actually running simulated combat field problems.

When I first showed up at my new company, the first sergeant assumed that I would return to jump status now that I was back in the 82nd Airborne. I had not made that assumption at first but with nine months left on my enlistment, and considerable official harassment, I agreed to jump again (after he implied that not to do so would indicate that I was chicken). Sergeants have only a few limited ways to motivate their troops and some form of intimidation was usually successful!

So, it was once again jump time—but this time I did not have the opportunity for any training or even a brief refresher course. I was pretty rusty not having jumped in over a year and a half. Moreover, there was new equipment to get used to—a different plane (C-119) and a new type of chute (T-10).

The top sergeant, a very experienced jumper, appeared to want to "test out" my mettle so he decided that he would jump with me that day. All went as expected except that the sergeant (to see if I had the guts to follow) did not wait for the green light (the usual signal that the aircraft was over the drop zone). Instead, he jumped on the red light trying to jibe me into doing the same.

Not to be outdone by the top sergeant, I did likewise, all the while thinking that I was nuts leaping into the air over I knew not where. When our chutes opened, we found ourselves drifting down over the forest—tall North Carolina pine trees staring up at us some distance away from the drop zone. The sergeant, grinning widely as he descended, knew what he was doing and was steering his chute adeptly toward the sandy drop zone—he made the strip of soft sand handily. I, not so adept, landed in a tall tree. I was now back in the challenge of the airborne infantry!

As I settled into the routine, I came once again to enjoy some parts of the military duty. The Company Commander thought it would be desirable for me to increase my usefulness to the company and sent me off for a week-long training course called Heavy Drop School. This course taught NCOs how to rig heavy equipment such as jeeps, three-quarter-ton trucks, artillery pieces, and so forth for dropping from planes. This was an interesting experience and when the course was finished we had to make a practice jump along with some of the equipment that we rigged. I was on a team that rigged a three-quarter-ton truck for dropping. Fortunately, the rigging worked and did not crash to the earth embarrassing the riggers.

****

Toward the middle of 1954, my initial enlistment in the Army began to draw to a close and I was at a major crossroads in my life. As long as I could remember, I had wanted to be a career soldier. Now, I was in a position that these goals were being realized but I needed to decide what to do next. I considered several options.

For a time, I was tempted to re-enlist into a new unit that was just being formed called the Green Berets, an elite group that was being built around a corps of airborne troops, but I thought that this organization was going to be heavy into the training and dress rehearsal aspects of life, and might simply be more of the same only worse in terms of garrison duty.

For a while I also considered joining another Army (France)—one that was enmeshed in another Asian war—Vietnam. The French were about to be kicked out of their colony in Indochina and were holed up at a place called

Dien Bien Phu. Another Korean vet and I discussed the possibility of joining them, and learned that the Foreign Legion was seeking enlistments to fight in South East Asia. My friend and I spent a lot of time at the NCO club at Ft. Bragg during my final months, planning a new adventure. We looked into the possibility of going to France and joining in their fight. We even went so far as contacting the French embassy for information. The French were interested in the possibility of having some combat-tested recruits. However, they could not assure that we would get any rank based on our prior service. Not wishing to start another military career in a strange Army as lowly privates, we scrapped the idea.

Another possibility that I considered was to re-enlist in the American Army with the goal of going into training to fly helicopters. The Army was beginning to expand in the area of air cavalry, and this duty had an inherent appeal to me given the interest in aviation that I had since I was young. But there was no assurance that I would get such an assignment if I did re-enlist for six years. When I talked with the recruiter on base about the likelihood of getting assigned to helicopter school, he indicated that there was about a 50/50 chance. Then I inquired as to where I might be assigned if helicopter training was not available to me. The recruiter said in a very serious and quite enthusiastic voice, "You could always come back and be a platoon sergeant in the 82nd Airborne!" But in the end, I recognized that the fire in my belly for things military had diminished somewhat, and I decided to accept my discharge when my enlistment expired in May 1954.

So, at the age twenty, for better or worse, I left the home that I had found in the Army for an uncertain future as a civilian.

14

Questions That Endure

MORE THAN THIRTY-FIVE YEARS AFTER I LEFT Korea, my grandson, Nic Young-hans, asked, "Grandpa, the Korean War wasn't really a war, was it?" Somehow, while studying American history in high school, Nic questioned whether our fighting in Korea was a real war. Korean War vets have heard statements like that ever since their return in the 1950s. For those of us on the front lines, it is a painful question, given what we experienced and the friends we lost. On an intellectual level, I can reason that President Truman's decision to avoid going to Congress for a declaration of war resulted in this confusion about our actions. The Korean War was called a "police action" or "conflict" by the Truman administration for expedient political reasons (Hakim, 1995). Those labels, then and now, minimize the extent of the hard-fought battles and losses.

Ironically, Nic asked that question when he was about the same age I was when I volunteered to go to Korea. He was not that much younger than some of my close friends who died there. Among the thousands of young casualties, I lost many close friends. The battles on Pork Chop described in Chapters 10 and 12 included five close buddies among the many dead: Moss, Ziggy, Zimdahl, Grasshold, and Moosemaid. Sully died on Jane Russell (Chapter 4) and Krumins at Outpost Uncle (Chapter 11).

Nic's question brought intense nostalgia. My first thought, "just ask Moss," was left unsaid. Instead, I gave a very brief response, "Yes, it was a tragic war," and settled back into my usual mode of keeping the war to myself. For reasons that remain unfathomable, I was not ready to go into the details found in this book—even in a conversation initiated by my grandson.

It took almost another twenty-five years before I could complete this accounting I started so long ago. Unfinished business can gnaw away at one's inner peace. The impact and meaning of my experiences in Korea left me with a need for closure and a need to place those situations and circumstances in some perspective. Nic's question, and similar ones from others over the years, kept popping up:

- How did I end up in Korea in the first place?
- How did the decision to call war a police action affect GIs like me?
- How did Korea impact my feelings back home?
- What did I learn on my return visits to Korea?
- Were the sacrifices made offset by the accomplishments?

Here, then, are my answers:

HOW DID I END UP IN KOREA IN THE FIRST PLACE?

In June 1950, when the North Korean Army invaded South Korea, I was about to start my last year of high school. As I explained in Chapter 1, I immediately was ready to serve my country in this new war, but my country did not think I was old enough. My understanding of the Korean conflict was pretty basic. The communist North Koreans, by crossing the 38th Parallel into the democratic Republic of Korea in the south, were the aggressors; and our country, along with the United Nations, were the defenders of the South Korean's freedom.

While waiting to turn seventeen years old, my biggest fear was that the war would end before I was old enough to serve. Once the American and UN troops arrived in force overseas, they were able to overpower the North Korean forces, regaining South Korean territory that had been lost in the first weeks of fighting. I listened to the radio and read newspaper accounts of the triumphant UN forces. In the fall of my senior year, there was talk that the war would end by Christmas 1950. UN forces had driven so far into North Korea that they were at the Chinese border by October 1950. There was no reporting at the time about the responses of the Chinese Communist Forces (CCF), which were amassing along the Chinese-Korean border. The Chinese Army entered the war that fall and drove UN forces in mass back into South Korea.

The news from Korea during my last six months of high school was grim. We were retreating. In January, Seoul was once again under the control of communist forces. Fighting was intense. UN forces recaptured Seoul in mid-March. President Truman fired General MacArthur in April for failure to follow the policy of the U.S. In his speech about MacArthur's firing that I heard on the radio, Truman declared:

> In the simplest of terms, what we are doing in Korea is this: We are trying to prevent a third world war... I believe that we must try to limit the war in Korea for these vital reasons: to make sure that the precious lives of our fighting men are not wasted; to see that the security of our country and the free world is not jeopardized; and to prevent a third world war. (at http://teachingamericanhistory.org/library/index.asp?document=860).

As high school graduation approached, I was all the more convinced that I needed to volunteer. General MacArthur's military failures and humiliating retreat incensed me. I was not among the voices urging an end to the Korean War. I agreed with President Truman's policy of protecting South Korea from communist aggression. Our entry into the war, along with the other United Nations countries, provided a clear statement to the communist powers that the United States and the United Nations would not ignore violent take-overs of democratically elected governments.

World War II shaped me—there were good guys and there were bad guys (Chapter 1). And, it was my patriotic duty to serve on our side—either as a soldier or on the home front. I recall collecting scrap metal, planting victory gardens, and living through rationing as part of my home front service during WW II. My mother worked in a factory tied to the war effort until her death. I wanted a greater role in this new war effort. I was old enough to be a soldier. I was going to join another global effort to defeat the enemies of freedom. Those who remained on the home front during the Korean War would serve as well, like my family did in WWII. I did not, however, understand the impact of a "limited" war on the soldiers fighting it and how my expectations from childhood would not apply to this war.

HOW DID THE DECISION TO CALL WAR A POLICE ACTION AFFECT GIS LIKE ME?

The Korean War turned out to be vastly different than the war that preceded it by five years. At its start, President Truman called it a "police action" of the United Nations, not a war declared by Congress on behalf of the American people. Truman limited its goals to stopping the Communist aggression in Korea and avoiding a general war that would draw in mainland China and the Soviet Union on the other side. While we fought under the UN flag, the effort turned out to be not as global as Allied efforts during World War II.

The overwhelming burden of fighting fell primarily on the armed forces from two nations. More than 94% of the UN forces were American and Republic of Korea (ROK) military personnel. Hermes (1965) provided a breakdown of the nationalities of the forces serving in Korea that I include in Appendix B. During the first year of the war, Americans made up 45.6% of the ground forces, and by the last year of the war when I was there, we were down to 32%. The other UN troops hovered between 4-6% of the ground forces, with the ROK forces increasing dramatically each year. Commensurate with the overall level of commitment, the majority of the casualties were from the United States and South Korea.

Although the other nations made up such a small percentage of the forces, those of us on the ground in Korea appreciated their efforts. Several British Commonwealth nations (Australia, Canada, New Zealand, and United Kingdom) provided a substantial number of ground troops, averaging over 20,000 men for each year, to the war effort. Some of these units, particularly the Brits and Canadians, took heavy casualties and lost many men to captivity. Throughout the war Turkey provided a brigade of troops (roughly 5,500 men). This unit gained a worthy reputation for their fighting ability. We considered ourselves fortunate if the Turks were on our flank. (See Appendix B for a full description of the nations contributing troops to Korea.)

By the time I got to Korea, Truman had already firmly established, with the firing of MacArthur the previous year, our limited objectives. We were to defend the sovereignty of South Korea up to its border on the 38th Parallel. I did not pay much attention to the controversy and debates about limited war by the military brass and politicians. I did not realize I was in the middle of a major shift in American warfare: it was above my pay-grade. However, a number of generals and admirals were beginning to conclude that any future wars would likely be limited (Kaufman, 1986). General Ridgeway (1967) indicated that Korea taught us that all warfare from that time forth must be limited.

It certainly became obvious to anyone on the front lines that we were limited in the military actions we could take. Unfortunately, "limited" sometimes became synonymous with "limited resources," The shortages that began to affect our war effort in Korea actually became the subject of Congressional investigations in the last two years of the war (Hinton, 1953; Stevens, 1953). GIs like me suffered as a result of deficiencies in both supplies and manpower. Basic supplies like ammunition and warm clothing sometimes were too scarce. I would have gladly traded—at least before the addiction kicked in—the endless supply of cigarettes (see Chapter 5) for items that would keep me alive and comfortable like overhead flares and warm socks.

The new limited warfare did not mean limited casualties. Not enough American military personnel were sent to Korea to replenish our units given the number of casualties we suffered. Instead, as troop strength dwindled, we were forced to integrate non-English speaking personnel into our units. None of us had skills in these other languages. Yet we had to communicate tactical orders to those who did not speak English.

At one point my platoon had to function with soldiers speaking three different languages: Spanish, Korean, and English. We got by as best we could with pidgin English and physical gestures, as I described in Chapter 4. However, American

GIs and UN soldiers were often placed at risk by having to depend on others who could not communicate about dangers at hand. It is difficult enough to go into combat with full strength and with guys you know well. It is risky to do so with sometimes a quarter to a third of the guys in the unit not sharing a common language, as happened on the patrol described in Chapter 8.

In addition to the lack of a common language was the problem of differing training standards and operational effectiveness. On multiple occasions the company commanders would tell NCOs like me to retrain our replacement troops while we were on the front lines. We had to convey survival skills that we learned in basic training within a rifle shot away from the enemy. In too many instances, we had to fill vacancies in the American ranks with marginally trained replacements.

War-weary American civilians were not asked to make the sacrifices on the home front as they did during WWII. The prosperous 1950s were beginning, and I remember thinking that folks back home seem more interested in their new TV sets than what we were going through in Korea. Korea became a "Second Page War," and later was known as the "Forgotten War" (see Blair, 1987; Melady, 1983). The obituary section of the papers told a different story—with pictures of deceased Soldiers and Marines often being the only conspicuous reminder of the tragic events that were being played out so many thousands of miles away.

The around-the-clock celebrations and nonstop jubilation at the end of WW II were much more muted at the end of the Korean War. Victory did not come about with the signing of a peace treaty by the "winners" and "losers." Most of us quietly returned to civilian life without any fanfare. This was very different than what I witnessed just a few years before at the end of World War II. It contributed to feelings that the American people could easily ignore what we accomplished in Korea and its costs. The Korean War seemed to me to be much too easy to forget.

I feel empathy with today's soldiers fighting in the limited wars in Iraq and Afghanistan. Why are young Americans sent into combat sixty years after the lessons from Korea without adequate supplies like body and vehicle armor? I am greatly saddened when I see the faces and ages of those killed during the previous week in obituaries on the few television networks that carry this news. I note a similar lack of attention on the part of the public and media about our country's involvement in its current wars. Indeed, I recently saw a T-shirt online that said, "Afghanistan: The Forgotten War."

I imagine these young people feel the same disconnect from the civilian population back home that I did on those lonely, cold, and dangerous nights in Korea. That disconnect for veterans continues even back home and can pop up unexpectedly many years later. It is isolating and demoralizing, and probably was a contributing factor for my long silence about my time in Korea.

HOW DID KOREA IMPACT MY FEELINGS BACK HOME?

Rudyard Kipling wrote a poem called "Tommy" to call attention to how British soldiers in the 1890s were treated by civilians. It highlights how soldiers feel ostracized in the civilian world, at the same time they are called upon to defend it. Many times since my return from Korea, verses memorized long ago in high school come to mind:

> *While it's Tommy this, an' Tommy that, an` Tommy, fall be'ind,"*
> *But it's " Please to walk in front, sir," when there's trouble in the wind*
> *There's trouble in the wind, my boys, there's trouble in the wind,*
> *O it's " Please to walk in front, sir," when there's trouble in the wind.*

> *For it's Tommy this, an' Tommy that, an` Chuck him out, the brute!*
> *But it's " Saviour of 'is country " when the guns begin to shoot;*
> *An' it's Tommy this, an' Tommy that, an' anything you please;*
> *An 'Tommy ain't a bloomin' fool - you bet that Tommy sees!*

Kipling wrote "Tommy" to protest how British soldiers were treated in the 1890s. In anticipation of the end of World War II, Americans passed the Servicemen's Readjustment Act, commonly known as the GI Bill. This represents a major turnaround in how a country provided for its returning soldiers. Kipling surely would have approved. But even today, Kipling's "Tommy" is one of the most quoted and parodied of his poems. It still highlights the disconnect soldiers can feel with civilians (The Kipling Society, 2011):

Yes, it's Tommy this, an' Tommy that, an' spend less on defence,
But who walks the streets of Basra when the air is getting tense?
When the air is getting tense, boys, from Kabul to Kosovo
Who'll say goodbye to wife and kids, and shoulder pack and go?

Thanks to the G.I. Bill, I was able to build a new home in academia, after a few false starts. Although different in many ways, the rigors of my time in the military kept me determined and goal-oriented in college and graduate school. The Army and the GI Bill provided a way out of the coal mines of West Virginia to a professorship at the University of Minnesota.

I arrived at this large Midwest campus just as the tumultuous Vietnam War and the Anti-War Movement began to emerge. This was a confusing time, not only for me, but the country at large. Anti-war activists interrupted my classes at the university. I saw angry protests on campus and even tear gas being used against students and faculty protestors. I was confronted by students on a few occasions because I was a veteran, and therefore "pro-war." These experiences were very different than the discussions with fellow students at Guilford College about their pacifist beliefs (Chapter 4). I felt a great deal of intolerance and animosity directed towards me because of my military service ("For it's Tommy this, an' Tommy that, an' Chuck him out, the brute!"). It was hard to reconcile this rancor with the sacrifices we made in Korea; it seemed unpatriotic.

Some returning Vietnam veterans thought differently about the war they fought, and founded the Vietnam Veterans Against the War (Hunt, 1999). This group may be the first American Anti-War organization founded by veterans while the war they were protesting was ongoing. Some Korean War and World War II veterans also participated in demonstrations against the Vietnam War. These veterans described their activism as "the highest form of patriotism" (Hunt, 1999).

The social conflict grew and the unthinkable happened in 1970. The Ohio National Guard shot and killed unarmed student protestors at Kent State University. The world seemed out of control. At the same time I was in the early stages of a demanding research career. The only way for me to deal with the turmoil was to concentrate on my work. I learned this skill in combat: to focus single-mindedly on the mission ahead, rather than on the chaos surrounding you. I became apolitical. Korea was pushed to the recesses of my mind.

WHAT DID I LEARN ON MY RETURN VISITS TO KOREA?

By the 1990s, my career was established and much of my research was on a psychological test that was used around the world. I supervised many international graduate students studying at the University of Minnesota, including Korean, Chinese, Japanese, and Thai. I conducted workshops and symposia in thirty-three other countries. I basically remained mum with my students and colleagues about my time in Korea—I was living a very different and rewarding life.

The war came flooding back with an invitation I received in 1992 to speak at a conference in Seoul, sponsored by the Korean Psychological Association. I didn't hesitate to accept the invitation, but was surprised by some vivid flashbacks and a few nightmares about the war. Intrusive thoughts and feelings about the combat experiences and my lost friends were amplified during the months before the trip.

I was surprised by this reaction. I had already made trips to Hong Kong and China. My principal enemy during the war was the Chinese Army, not North Korean troops. I served side-by-side with South Koreans. Yet, going to China did not cause the same intensity of feelings as did returning to Korea. I even had an opportunity to discuss the war with a Chinese veteran from the Chinese Peoples Army. But, going back to Korea—I did not know what to expect. How would I react? What would the South Korean people be like?

Almost instantaneously on arrival, I re-experienced what I had known so well back in the '50s: I liked the South Koreans a lot. During dinners with colleagues in their homes, I was reminded of the very pleasant dinner I had on Koje-do (see Chapter 6). I re-experienced the same peace and warm feelings of family from long ago. Fortunately, my naïve palette, shaped by Army chow and cautions, had disappeared and I enjoyed the food shared with colleagues.

My most memorable experiences came when so many people expressed gratitude for what American GIs like me had done during the Korean War. I was treated like a victorious hero as soon as anyone learned I served in Korea after the North Korean invasion. My military experiences are hardly ever part of introductions at professional meetings. And, usually during breaks at these meetings, I'm asked questions about my lecture. This was not the case in Korea—I remember more expressions of appreciation for my service during the war, than I do content questions.

Author Jim Butcher posing with colleagues Kyunghee Han (*center*) and Jee Young Lim (*right*) at the Korean Psychological Association's conference, Seoul, Korea, 1992. The banner reads: "We welcome Professor James N. Butcher, a great scholar of the MMPI-2."

Other people I met on the streets were equally grateful. This happened even while shopping for souvenirs in the Myong-dong district of Seoul. As I was about to purchase a small trinket, a polite, elderly shopkeeper asked, "Have you been to Korea before?" I said, "Yes, in 1952 and 1953." He began to smile and nod his head. At the same time a saleswoman in the store, overhearing the comment, came up to me and said, "Thank you! Thank you very much for saving our country!" They would not accept payment for the souvenir I selected. Not only that, but the shopkeeper hurried back to a storeroom, returning with a little package. "Thank you very, very much," he said as he handed me the present. "We owe a great deal to Americans for what you did for our country. Please have this gift in appreciation."

Despite my misgivings about the trip, I had hoped to return to the Demilitarized Zone to see some of the places where I fought. One of my Korean graduate students contacted the Korean Veterans Association in Seoul (KVA-Seoul) to see if a tour of the DMZ was possible. At that time, tours were not allowed. However, I was invited to their offices to meet the staff of this veteran's group. My two students and I showed up at their office forty years to the day of the assault on Jane Russell Hill.

Retired Lt. Colonel Dong Koo Lee greeted us at the door. He treated me like an old friend. We talked about my unit and the places that I had served during the war. Colonel Lee explained that after the Korean War ended a group of the ROK veterans formed the Korean Veterans Association. They helped ROK veterans gain employment and provided advocacy for their needs. In 1975, on the 25th anniversary of the outbreak of the Korean War, they developed the KVA-Seoul Revisit Program as a way to express the gratitude of the Korean government for the veterans from all nations who served under the U.N. flag during June 25, 1950 to October 15, 1954.

In 1992, I had no expectations for what would follow this conversation with Colonel Lee at the KVA office. To my amazement, it was an award ceremony complete with an official proclamation:

> It is a great honor and pleasure to express the everlasting gratitude of the Republic of Korea and our people for the service you and your countrymen have performed in restoring and preserving our freedom and independence.
>
> We cherish in our hearts the memory of your boundless sacrifices in helping us re-establish our Free Nation.
>
> In grateful recognition of your dedicated contributions, it is my privilege to proclaim you an "Ambassador for Peace" with every good wish of the people of the Republic of Korea. Let each of us reaffirm our mutual respect and friendship that they may endure for generations to come.

***

My wife Carolyn and I participated in the KVA-Seoul 50th Anniversary

Revisit Program on July 24-27, 2003. We were there with 1,500 veterans from twenty-one different countries. During this visit, Carolyn and I were able to go to the DMZ. We attended the Armistice Signing Commemoration in the Joint Security Area. There were also numerous other ceremonies and tours, including a memorial service at the National Cemetery, a USO dinner where we met veterans from countries (particularly Belgium and Australia), and a World Peace Day Ceremony at the Korean War Memorial.

WERE THE SACRIFICES MADE OFFSET BY THE ACCOMPLISHMENTS?

The Korea I encountered on my return visits was vastly different than the one I left in the 1950s. Both North and South Korea were devastated by the war, but South Korea recovered to become a thriving democracy and North Korea remains under dictatorship and extreme economic hardships. It was heartwarming to see on my return visits how South Korea was able to rebuild and have such gratefulness for the American contributions to its freedom. It validated my beliefs:

- We won!
- The United Nations did not lose the war in Korea!
- The Korean War did not end in stalemate!
- We halted communist aggression!
- We dispelled the invading enemy!
- American soldier's lives were not wasted in a lost war!
- We won!

In some ways my return visits to Korea were like the celebrations held for the returning World War II GIs that made such a mark on me in childhood, albeit forty to fifty years after the fact. It was most gratifying to meet so many people in South Korea who shared my views. They provided some closure, but not enough. I still needed to finish this book and its last chapter.

One of the questions weighing on my mind is whether the Korean War was worth the cost in human lives and suffering wrought during the three-year conflict. The United Nations suffered around 37, 895 deaths. Of these, the United States had 33,686 combat deaths and an additional 2,830 other deaths. The United States lost 8,144 missing in action. The Republic of Korea Army reported over 47,000 dead (Bruce, 1993; Highsmith & Landphair, 1995; Langley, 1979; MacDonald, 1986). Accounts of North Korean and Chinese deaths are not as precise. Estimates suggest that over a million and a half were killed and captured during the war. According to MacDonald (1986), North Korea may have lost 12% to 15% of its population to the war. He also estimates that 25,000 Chinese were killed in the last month of the war alone as a result of extensive and costly offensives against American and ROK forces.

When I read accounts that suggest the outcome of the Korean War was other than a clear-cut victory, I have a visceral, negative reaction. I lose objectivity—such accounts mean to me that the tens of thousand who died did so for nothing. I cannot consider the Korean War as a "lost war" or even a "tie." If I did, I would be overwhelmed with bitterness. The United Nations forces won the major battles described in this book. The hills were taken, retaken, and eventually held under the rules of engagement that were imposed on us. Subsequent decisions by politicians and diplomats to give up territory we fought so hard to win, as what happened with Pork Chop Hill, are hard to accept given the massive losses in those battles. However, with the battles won, Truman's goals of stopping the communist take-over of South Korea, and preventing World War III, were accomplished. I think in my mind that will always be a win.

In early drafts of this chapter, I found myself writing a defense of my long held beliefs, and admonishing historians, political scientists, or others who wrote to the contrary. I felt that anyone who did not categorically recognize our victory in the Korean War demeaned the men whose lives were lost. These men deserved a better accounting and I would provide it! My beliefs provided me with a way of surmounting all the frozen fingers and toes, all the shivering nights in trenches, all the anxious moments on countless patrols, all the terror felt as artillery shells pounded our ranks, and all those buddies lost. They served as a wall of defense, protecting me from painful memories.

My wall of defense still exists, as this chapter attests. Nevertheless, I am trying to accept that my viewpoints do not trump those of others just because

I was there. My wife Carolyn helped me with the painstaking process of gaining some perspective. We talked about our 2003 visit to South Korea. The tributes were deeply moving to both of us. Like me, she saw the appreciation of so many South Korean people for the American contributions during the 1950s and later. Still, amidst all the celebrations, Carolyn recalls seeing small groups of South Korean protestors kept at a distance from us by police. I have no recollection of seeing them, another sign of a lack of objectivity that colors my observations about Korea.

Gradually I'm coming to the realization that my vantage point has been stuck in the trenches with the hellish experiences I had there. Through the process of writing this book, I am now able to consider some troubling repercussions of that war. Although South Korea grew into a thriving economic force over the last sixty years, the Korean peninsula remains divided. The Korean War did not end with the signing of a peace treaty, but a truce. Almost 30,000 U.S. military personnel remain in South Korea. The war could resume with devastating consequences for the two Koreas, the region, and the rest of the world.

Some South Koreans see the ongoing presence of American troops in their country as negative, and forget the accomplishments of the 1950s. Moreover, the U.S. military's complicity in the coercion of "comfort women" over many years is a legacy that contributes to anti-American sentiments in the region. Continuing historical and political analyses of the Korean War and its aftermath are necessary. Some are likely to differ from my conclusions about the accomplishment made and be more critical of the war effort. I recognize that I need to be more willing to listen and learn from them.

I left Korea in better shape that many of my buddies. I was alive. My hearing loss from a shell explosion and the shrapnel wounds from the battles on Jane Russell and Pork Chop seem so superficial compared to the battle scars of others. The nine months in Korea shaped who I am. Not even out of my teenage years, I learned how to work with others as a leader, developed a deep appreciation for other cultures, and learned to keep focused on important goals. The GI bill allowed me to use those qualities to build a successful academic career. After all these years of thinking about writing this book, I'm finally done. I have overcome my silence about the war and its life-altering experiences. This book is about shared sacrifices and accomplishments, as well as personal reflections. Many questions about that distant war will endure beyond the lives of those of us who served in Korea.

Appendix A

Propaganda leaflet obtained from Joe's Mailbox in the Alligator Jaws, Yokkokchon Valley, January, 1953 (reprinted here with typographical errors included):

(front cover of leaflet)

MERRY CHRISTMAS
AND
HAPPY NEW YEAR
FROM
THE KOREAN PEOPLES ARMY
THE CHINESE PEOPLE'S VOLUNTEERS
KOREA 1952-1953

WHERE THERE IS PEACE
THERE IS BLESSING

SEE INSIDE

(inside of leaflet)

American Soldiers

We are wishing you a Merry Christmas and a Happy New Year. We also have something to talk to you about.

Christmas is a day of peace and happiness. And a day for family reunions.

But this Christmas, for you, there is no peace. You are far away from those you love, in Korea, a country you never heard of three years ago--hundreds of thousands of casualties ago. Your family longs for you across the wide pacific. Will they ever see you again? Will you ever see them again?

You've been told you came here to stop "Communist Aggression." But what do your own eyes and head tell you? The Koreans are fighting in their own country. The Chinese are defending their own nearby borders. Neither of these people ever dreamed of invading the United States. It is U. S. Troops who have come here with bombs, napalm, +++ and other weapon of mass murder.

Bombs and guns can't break the spirit of the Koreans and Chinese because they are guarding their homes. What about you? Is there any reason why you should be here instead of home with your folks? You are risking death or crippling wounds to hold on to one or two bare Korean mountains. What for?

The heartless men who sent you here have sent American soldiers to Europe. These soldiers too are told that they must protect different countries from "Red Aggression." But everywhere they go they hear the people yelling, "Yanks, go home." This wasn't the way GI's were greeted everywhere in world War II when they were really fighting agains aggressors--the Nazis and Japanese warlords. Then they got flowers. So something is wrong. What is it?

The truth is that American soldiers today are helping oppressors, not fighting them. You know how the Koreans "love" Syngman Rhee! You know how the Chinese "loved" Chaing Kai-shek whom they kicked out in spite of $6 billion worth of U. S. aid. In Japan the U. S. is letting convicted war criminals out of jail and giving them a new army to play with. In Germany, it's the same. In France, in Italy, they back governments which have sold out their own peoples for dollars, governments which order the police out every time working people strike for a living wage. Isn't this true? You know it is.

Why are Americans sent abroad to do this kind of dirty work, the exact opposite of every fine thing America ever stood for, in a way that would make Washington, Jefferson, Lincoln turn over in their graves if they knew it? Because the American government has been stolen from the American people by greedy Big Business which cares nothing about your life or anyone else's but only for its lousy profits. The corporations have made more money since the Korean war than they ever did before, out of arms orders for which the American people are paying through higher taxes, higher prices in every grocery store and the lives of their sons--YOUR lives. That's why the Brass Hats are throwing monkey wrenches into the talks at Panmunjom which could have succeeded a year ago. That's why they want more war everywhere, not peace.

Every people on earth is getting wise to this new kind of business--Murder for Profit. Americans at home are getting wise to it too. Millions are asking for peace and getting fed up iwht the lies. American fathers and mothers have refused medals sent to them after their boys died in Korea. Hundreds of American pilots with decorations for courage in World War II have refused to fly in Korea. Tens of thousands of young men are dodging the draft. This is not because they are cowards. It is not because they aretn't ptriotic. It's because they are beginning to understand that they've been fooled.

The patriotic thing is to fight for peace! The patriotic thing is to fight for friendship, not war, between peoples! What harm can peace do to any country, to America? What good does war bring to any nation, Americans included? The real traitors, the real criminals, are the few who send troops, thousands of miles away so they can rake in dollars. They think they own America, and for that matter the world. They think they own you. Who gave them the right? What kind of free American citizen are you when they can shove you into uniform, pack you in a boat, and send yo to all end of the earth for no reason than this?

We the Chinese People's Volunteers, are writing you this letter, We came here because, after we cleaned out the dirty grafter Chaing Kai-shek, you stormed into the land of our neighbor and threatened the first chance we ever had to build up our country. We don't want to fight anyone. We want to build in peace. We are in favor of peaceful coexistence and trade for every people in the world.

Don't believe the Big Money boys and politicians at home. They are no different from Chaing Kai-shek whom we ran out of China. Don't do what they want. Do what the people want.

We offer you peace and friendship. America for Americans. Korea for the Koreans. China for the Chinese. Why should not we all, Korean soldiers, Chinese soldiers, American soldiers join our efforts for peace? Then we don't need to be soldiers any more. Then next Christmas, if not this one, can really be merry. Then we can have a really Happy New Year in 1953! Let's make it so!

— The Chinese People's Volunteers

Appendix B-1

Strength of the United Nations Ground Forces in Korea
(Source: Hermes, 1965)

Date	Total	United States[a]	Republic[b] of Korea	Other United Nations
30 June 1951	54,577	253,250	273,266	28,061
30 June 1952	678,051	265,864	376,418	35,769
31 July 1953	32,539	302,483	590,911	39,145

[a]Includes Marine and Navy personnel under operational control of the U.S. Army.
[b]Includes KATUSA, ROK marines under operational control of U.S. Army, and civilian trainees.
Source: Comptroller of the Army, ROK and U.N. Ground Forces Strength in Korea, 7 Oct 54, OCMH Files.

Appendix B-2

Distribution by Country

Country	30 June 1951	30 June 1953	1 July 1953
Total	28,061	35,769	39,145
British Commonwealth	15,723	21,429	24,085
United Kingdom	8,278	13,043	14,198
Australia	912	11,844	2,282
Canada	5,403	5,155	6,146
New Zealand	797	1,111	1,389
India[a]	333	276	70
Turkey	4,602	4,878	5,455
Belgium[a]	602	623	944
Colombia	1,050	1,007	1,068
Ethiopia	1,153	1,094	1,271
France	738	1,185	1,119
Greece	1,027	899	1,263
Netherlands	725	565	819
Philippines	1,143	1,494	1,496
Thailand	1,057	2,274	1,294
Italy[a]	0	64	72
Norway[a]	79	109	105
Sweden[a]	162	148	154

[a] Contribution consisted of noncombat medical units only.
Original Source: Comptroller of the Army, Summary RO.

References Cited

Baker, A. (2004). *American Soldiers Overseas*. Westport, CT: Praeger.

Bernstein, B. J. (1989). "The Truman administration and the Korean War." Chapter in M. J. Lacey (Ed). *The Truman Presidency*. Cambridge: Cambridge University Press.

Blair, C. (1987), *The Forgotten War: America in Korea 1950-1953*. New York: Times Book.

Bruce, F. H. (1993). *M.I.A., Or, Mythmaking in America*. Rutgers University Press

Butcher, J. N. (2005). "Return of morning calm." *Stars & Stripes*, 59, 44-45.

Butcher, J. N. (2000). "From softball field to the Gates of Hell: Fox Company on Pork Chop Hill." *Buffalo Bugle*, March, p 4.

Butcher, J. N. (2001). "A fateful ambush patrol." *Buffalo Bugle*, May, p 20-21.

Butcher, J. N. (2003). "Discontinuities, side steps, and finding a proper place: An autobiographical account." *Journal of Personality Assessment*. 80, 223-236.

Department of Defense (September 15, 2010). Instruction: Combatting Trafficking of Persons (CTIP). USD (P&R) Number 2200.01.

Department of Defense (October 15, 2009). Trafficking in Persons: Law Enforcement Intervention and Investigations Training Module. ctip.defense.gov/docs/training-TIP-LE.ppt

Fehrenbach, T. R. (1963). *This Kind of War* (1994 Reprinted by Brasseys). Washington, D. C.:MacMillan.

Hakim, J. (1995). *A History of Us: All the People*. New York: Oxford University Press.

Hastings, M. (1987). *The Korean War*. New York: Simon & Schuster.

Hermes, W. G. (1966) "Truce tent and fighting front: United States military in the Korean War." Washington, D. C.: United States Army.

Highsmith, C. M. & Landphair, T. (1995). Forgotten No More: The Korean War Veterans Memorial Story. Washington, D. C.: Chelsea Publishing.

Hilton, J. (1933) *Lost Horizon*. London: Summersdale Press.

Hinton, H. B. (1953). "Ammunition Short, Van Fleet Asserts," *The New York Times*, 6 March 1953, 1;

Hunt, A. E. (1999). *The Turning: A History of Vietnam Veterans Against the War*. New York: New York University Press.

Inspector General U.S. Department of Defense (November 21, 2006). "Evaluation of DoD Efforts to Combat Trafficking in Persons." Report No. IE-2007-002.

Kaufman, B. I. (1986). *The Korean War: Challenges in Crisis, Credibility, and Command.* New York: Alfred Knopf.

Khayyam, O. *The Rubaiyat of Hakim Omar Khayyam.* Translated by Fitzgerald in 1967. Teheran, Iran.

Langley, M. (1979). *Inchon Landing: MacArthur's Last Triumph.* New York: Times Books.

Lineberry, K. (2002). "Cadence Calls: Military Folklore in Motion." http://missourifolkloresociety.truman.edu/Missouri%20Folklore%20Studies/Cadence%20Calls.htm

Marshall, S. L. A. (1956). *Pork Chop Hill: The American Fighting Man in Action.* New York: Jove Books.

McGregor, M. J., Jr. (1981). *Integration of the Armed Forces, 1940-1965.* U. S. Government Bookstore.

McWilliams, B. (2004). *On Hallowed Ground: The Last Battle for Pork Chop Hill.* Naval Institute Press.

McDonald, C. A. (1986). *Korea: The War before Vietnam.* New York: The Free Press.

Melady, J. (1983). *Korea: Canada's Forgotten War.* Toronto: Macmillan of Canada.

Miller, J., Carroll, O. J., & Tackley, M. E. (1982). *Korea: 1951-1953.* Washington, D. C.: Department of the Army.

Moon, K. H. S. (2009). Military Prostitution and the U.S. Military in Asia. *The Asia-Pacific Journal:* Japan Focus, Vol. 3-6-09.

Moon, K. H. S. (1997). *Sex among Allies: Military-U.S. Prostitution in U.S.-Korea Relations.* New York: Columbia University Press.

Moon, K. H. S. (1999a). "South Korean Movements against Sexualized Military Labor." *Asian Survey,* 39, pp. 310-327.

Moon, K. H. S. (1999b). "Military Prostitutes and the Hypersexualization of Militarized Women." In F. D'Amico & L. Weinstein, *Gender Camouflage: Women and the U.S. Military.* New York: New York University Press.

Ochsner, A. (1954). "Smoking and Cancer: A Doctor's Report. http://tobaccodocuments.org/ness/4167.html

President's Cancer Panel (2007). "Promoting Healthy Lifestyles." Washington, D. C: U. S. Department of Health and Human Services.

Ridgeway, M. (1986). *The Korean War.* New York: De Capo Press.

Sobieski, A. J. (2005). *Fire for Effect: Artillery Forward Observers in Korea.* Bloomington, Indiana: Author House.

Soh, C. S. (2008). *The Comfort Women: Sexual Violence and Postcolonial Memory in Korea and Japan.* Chicago: University of Chicago Press.

Stevens, A. (1952). "Army Says Forces Lack Ammunition for a Korea Drive," *The New York Times,* 20 December 1952, 1.

Tanaka, Y. (2009). *Japan's Comfort Women: Sexual Slavery and Prostitution during World War II and the U. S. Occupation.* New York: Routledge Press.

The Kipling Society (2010). "Tommy" (The Queen's Uniform). www.kipling.org.uk/rg_tommy1.htm

Truman Library (2012). "Desegregation of the Armed Forces." http://www.trumanlibrary.org/whistlestop/study_collections/desegregation/large/index.php?action=chronology

Wheaton, J. K. (2010). *The Forgotten War: A Brief History of the Korean War.* Hustonville, Ky: Golgotha Press.

Williams, C.L., & Berry, J.W. (1991). "Primary prevention of acculturative stress in refugees: The application of psychological theory and practice." *American Psychologist,* 46, 632-641.

Williams, C.L. (Winter, 1991). "Mental health consequences of international policies: The case of the Khmer border camps in Thailand." *Newsletter of the APA Office of International Affairs,* Psychology International, Vol. 2.

Williams, O. (1945). *One Morning the World Woke Up.* New York: Creative Age Press.

General Readings

Anderson, W. E. (1960). *Banner Over Pusan*. New York: Evans.

Anderson, K. (1984). *U. S. Military Operations 1945-1985*. New York: The Military Press.

Appleman, R. E. (1961). *South to the Naktong, North to the Yalu*. Washington, D. C.: Office of the Chief of Military History, Department of the Army, United States Government Printing Office.

Army Historical Series (1989). *American Military History*. Washington, D. C.: Center for Military History.

Bartlett, N. (Ed) (1954). *With the Australians in Korea*. Australian War Memorial.

Baum, K. C. (1991). *The Truth about the Korean War*. Seoul: Eulyoo Publishing Co.

Bevin, A. (2004). *Korea: The First War We Lost* (Updated Illustrated Edition). New York: Hippocrene Books.

Blair, C. (1987). *The Forgotten War: America in Korea 1950-1953*. New York: Times Book.

Brady, J. (1990). *The Coldest War*. New York: Simon & Schuster.

Bradbury, W. C. Myers, S. M., & Biderman, A. D. (1968). *Mass Behavior in Battle and Captivity: The Communist Soldier in the Korean War*. Chicago: University of Chicago Press.

Brune, L. H., ed. (1986). *The Korean War: Handbook of the Literature and Research*. Westport, Conn.: Greenwood Press.

Cagle, M. C. & Manson, F. A. (1957). *The Sea War in Korea*. Annapolis, Md.: United States Naval Institute.

Chae, K. O. (1958). *Handbook of Korea*. New York: Pageant Press.

Chafe, W. H. (1985). *The Unfinished Journey*. New York: Oxford University Press.

Cheung, D. K. (1989). *The Three Day Promise: A Korean Soldier's Memoir*. Tallahassee, Florida: Father & Son.

Collins, L. J. (1969). *War in Peace*. New York: Houghton-Mifflin.

Congressional Record (1951). "Substance of statements made at Wake Island Conference: Washington, D. C.: Compiled by General Bradley." Prepared for the Senate Armed Services and Foreign Relations Committees, U.S.P.G.O.

Congressional Record (1951). *Military situation in the Far East: Hearings before the Joint Senate Committee on Armed Services and Foreign Relations 82nd Congress, 1st Session*. Washington, D. C.: Compiled by General Bradley. Prepared for the Senate Armed Services and Foreign Relations Committees, U.S.P.G.O.

Cowart, G. C. (1992). *The Miracle in Korea*. University of South Carolina Press.

Cummings, B. (1981). *Origins of the Korean War*. New Jersey: Princeton University Press.

Curtov, H. B. (1956). *China Under Threat*. Berkeley: University of California Press.

Cutforth, R (1951). *Korean Reporter*. New York: Heineman.

Davies, S. J. (1955). *In Spite of Dungeons*. Chicago: Hodder & Stoughton.

Dean, W. F. (1954). *General Dean's Story*. New York: Viking.

Dorman, J. E. & de Lee, N. (1979). *The Chinese War Machines*. NY.: Crescent Books.

Drury, B. & Clavin, T. (2009). *The Last Stand of Fox Company*. NY: Grove Press.

Edwards, P. M., (1998). *The Korean War: An Annotated Bibliography*. Westport, Conn.: Greenwood Press.

Felton, M. (1953). *That's Why I Went*. New York: Lawrence & Wishart.

Fehrenbach, T. R. (1963). *This Kind of War* (1994 Reprinted by Brasseys). Washington, D. C.:MacMillan.

Field, J. A. (1962). *A History of U. S. Naval Operations in the Korean War*. Washington, D. C.: Naval History Division.

Forty, George (1985). *At War in Korea*. New York: Bonanza Books.

Futrell, R. F. (1961). *The United States Air Force in Korea 1950-1953*. New York: Duvell, Sloan, & Pearce.

George, A. L. (1967). *The Chinese Communists Army in Action*. New York: Columbia University Press.

Giesler, P. (1982). *Valour Remembered: Canadians in Korea*. Ottawa: Department of Veteran's Affairs.

Gittings, J. (1967). *The Role of the Chinese Army*. New York: Oxford University Press.

Gughler, R. A. (1970). *Combat Actions in Korea*. Washington, D. C. : Office of the Chief of Military History.

Goulden, J. C. (1982). *Korea: The Untold Story*. New York: McGraw-Hill.

Griffith, S. B. (1968). *The Chinese People's Liberation Army*. New York: Weidenfeld & Nicholson.

Grist, D. (1976). *Remembered with Advantage*. New York: Barton Press.

Hackworth, D. (1989). *About Face*. New York: Simon & Schuster.

Halliday, J. & Cummings, B. (1988). *Korea: The Unknown War*. Pantheon Books.

Hastings, M. (1987). *The Korean War*. New York: Simon & Schuster.

Heini, R. D. (1968). *Victory at High Tide*. Philadelphia: J. B. Lippincott.

Hermes, W. G. (1966) *Truce Tent and Fighting Front: United States Military in the Korean War*. Washington, D. C.: United States Army.

Highsmith, C. M. & Landphair, T. (1995). *Forgotten No More: The Korean War Veterans Memorial Story*. Washington, D. C.: Chelsea Publishing.

Higgins, M. (1952). *War in Korea*. New York: Lion Books.

Higgins, T. (1960). *Korea and the Fall of MacArthur*. Oxford Press.

Hinshaw, A. (1989). *Heartbreak Ridge: Korea, 1951*. New York: Praeger.

Hoyt, E. P. (1983). *The Pusan Perimeter.* New York: Stein & Day.

Hoyt, E. P. (1984). *On to the Yalu.* New York: Stein & Day.

Hoyt, E. P. (1985). *The Bloody Road to Panmunjom.* New York: Stein & Day.

Isaacson, W. & Thomas, E. (1986). The wise men. New York: Simon & Schuster.

Jackson, R. (1973). *Air War Over Korea.* New York: Charles Scribner & Sons.

Johnson, J. E. (1985). *The Story of Air Fighting.* New York: Hutchinson.

Joy, C. T. (1955). *How Communists Negotiate.* New York: Macmillan.

Karig, W., Cagle, M. W., & Manson, F. A. (1952). *Battle Report: The War in Korea.* New York: Holt Rhinehart.

Kaufman, B. I. (1986). *The Korean War: Challenges in Crisis, Credibility, and Command.* New York: Alfred Knopf.

Kinkhead, E. (1960). *Why they collaborated.* Boston: Longman.

Knox, D. (1988). *The Korean War.* Orlando, Fla.: Harcourt, Brace, Jovanavich.

Lacey, M. J. (1989). *The Truman Presidency.* New York: Cambridge University Press.

Langley, M. (1979). *Inchon Landing: MacArthur's Last Triumph.* New York: Times Books.

Leary, W. M. (1984). *Perilous Mission: Civil Air Transport and CIA Covert Operations in Asia.* The University of Alabama Press.

Leckie, R. (1962). *Conflict: The History of the Korean War.* New York: Putnam

Linklater, E. (1954). *Our Men in Korea.* London: Her Majesty's Stationary Office.

Lowe, P. (1986). *The Origins of the Korean War.* Boston: Longman.

MacArthur, D. A. (1965). *Reminiscences.* New York: Heinemann.

Marshall, S. L. A. (1956). *Pork Chop Hill: The American Fighting Man in Action.* New York: Jove Books.

Marshall, S. L. A. (1953). *The River and the Gauntlet.* New York: Morrow.

McDonald, C. A. (1986). *Korea: The War Before Vietnam.* New York: The Free Press.

McGuire, F. R. (1956). *Canada's Army in Korea.* Ottawa: Historical Section, General Staff, Army Headquarters.

Melady, J. (1983). *Korea: Canada's Forgotten War.* Toronto: Macmillan of Canada.

Miller, J., Carroll, O. J., & Tackley, M. E. (1982). *Korea: 1951-1953.* Washington, D. C.: Department of the Army.

Montross, L & Canzona, N. (No date). *U. S. Marine Corps operations in Korea.*(Volume II). Washington, D.C. Historical Branch, U. S. M. C. HQ. U.S.G.P.O.

O'Balance, E. (1969). *Korea: 1950-1953.* London: Faber.

Orbis, P.(1962) *Strategic Surprise in the Korean War.* James Dougherty.

Packwood, N. E. Jr. (1952). "Leatherheads in Korea." Quantico, Va.: *Marine Corps Gazette.*

Paschall, R. (1995). *Witness to War: Korea.* New York: Berkeley Publishing Group.

Rees, D. (1964). *The limited war.* Hamish Hamilton.

Rees, D. (Ed.) (1984). *The Korean War: History and Tactics.* Orbis.

Ridgeway, M. (1986). *The Korean War.* New York: De Capo Press.

Russ, M. (1957). *The Last Parallel.* New York: Signet.

Scalapino, R. A. & Lee, C. S. (1972). *Communism in Korea: The Movement.* Berkeley, CA: University of California.

Stanton, S. (1992). *U. S. Army Uniforms of the Korean War.* Harrisburg, P. A.: Stackpole Books.

Stokesbury, J. L. (1988). *A Short History of the Korean War.* New York: William Morrow.

Stueck, W. (1995). *The Korean War: An International History.* Princeton, N.J.: Princeton University Press.

Taylor, M. (1972). *Swords and Plowshares.* New York: Norton.

Thompson, R. W. *Cry Korea.* London: Macdonald.

Tomedi, R. (1993). *No Bugles, No Drums.* New York: John Wiley & Sons Inc.

U. S. Naval Proceedings (1958). *Errors in the Korean War.* Washington, D. C.

Westover, J. G. (1955). *Combat Support in Korea.* Washington, D. C. Combat Forces Press.

Wheaton, J. K. (2010). *The Forgotten War: A Brief History of the Korean War.* Hustonville, Ky: Golgotha Press.

White, W. A. (1953). *Back Down the Ridge.* New York: Harcourt, Brace, & Company.

White, W. L. 1957). *The Captives of Korea.* New York: Charles Scribner.

Whiting, A. S. (1960). *China Crosses the Yalu.* New York: The Macmillan Company.

Whitney, C. (1956). *MacArthur: His Rendezvous with History.* New York: Knopf.

Whitson, W. W. (1973). *The Chinese High Command.* New York: Macmillan.

Young, K. (1968). *Negotiating with the Chinese Communists: The United States Experience 1953-1967.* New York: McGraw-Hill.

About the Author

JAMES N. BUTCHER WAS BORN IN Bergoo, West Virginia in 1933. His father was killed in a coal mining accident when he was eight years old and his mother died when he was eleven. After their deaths, he, his sister, and two brothers independently raised themselves in rather difficult circumstances. At age seventeen he enlisted in the U. S. Army and served for three years; a year and a half with the 82nd Airborne and eleven months in Korea with Fox Company of the 17th Infantry Regiment of the 7th Division. During his tour of duty in Korea, he became a sergeant first class, served as a platoon sergeant and fought in the Battle of Jane Russell Hill (Triangle Ridge) in October 1952 and in the first Battle of Pork Chop Hill in April 1953.

After his discharge from military service he attended Guilford College in North Carolina and graduated with a BA in psychology in 1960; he received an MA degree in experimental psychology in 1962 and a Ph.D. in clinical psychology in 1964 from the University of North Carolina at Chapel Hill. He served as a professor of psychology and as Director of the Clinical Psychology Program in the Department of Psychology at the University of Minnesota. He was awarded an honorary doctorate (*Doctor Honoris Causa*) from the Free University of Brussels in 1990 and received an honorary doctorate from the University of Florence in Italy in 2005 for his cross-cultural research. He is currently Professor Emeritus in the Department of Psychology at the University of Minnesota and has published fifty-eight books and more than two hundred fifty articles in personality assessment, abnormal psychology, and crisis-intervention.

He and his wife currently reside in Washington, D.C.